传承中文
Modern Chinese for Heritage Beginners

Modern Chinese for Heritage Beginners aims to serve as a stepping-stone for Chinese heritage language learners' future Chinese learning, inspiring them to reflect on their identities, learn Chinese American history, and embrace their cultural heritage.

The book starts with talking about individuals and families and then expands to the Chinese and Asian American communities in the U.S. and eventually to the entire American society, all from the unique perspective of Chinese American students. Taking a macro approach that builds learners' literacy skills on their initial abilities in speaking and listening, each lesson starts with listening and speaking activities and then moves to reading and writing. The content complexity and language difficulty are balanced to present rich content that matches students' critical thinking abilities in a language appropriate for their literacy level. Lively and humorous language makes the book a joy to read. Each lesson has a conversation and an essay to expose students to informal and formal registers. Moreover, authentic tasks are designed to facilitate students' language output, following the three modes of communication promoted by the American Council on Teaching Foreign Languages: interpersonal, interpretive, and presentational.

This theme-based Chinese textbook is written for high school and college-level Chinese heritage language learners.

Yan Liu is Assistant Professor of the Practice in the Department of Asian and Middle Eastern Studies at Duke University. Her recent research focuses on Chinese language pedagogies and interdisciplinary curriculum development. Currently, she serves as a board member of CLTA (2022–2025) and co-chairs two CLTA SIG groups: Content-based Chinese Language Courses at Advanced Levels and Chinese Heritage Language Learning.

Jingjing Ji is Associate Professor of Instruction in the Department of Asian Languages and Cultures at Northwestern University. Before joining Northwestern, she worked at Washington and Lee University and the University of Virginia. She also worked at intensive summer programs such as Middlebury College summer school. Her publications on Chinese heritage language education have appeared in various peer-reviewed academic journals.

Grace Wu is Senior Lecturer in Foreign Languages in the Department of East Asian Languages and Civilizations at the University of Pennsylvania. She has been in charge of the heritage track of Chinese courses at Penn since 1994. She published a series of Chinese Biographies with Cheng and Tsui and is Chair of the ACTFL Heritage Language SIG (2022–2024).

Min-Min Liang is Lecturer in Chinese at Massachusetts Institute of Technology. She has developed three Chinese learning websites: *Teaching Chinese Writing*, *Chinese Contemporary Writers*, and *Puzzles for Reading and Writing*, and co-authored a Chinese textbook titled *Modern Readers with Performance-based Tasks* and an online reader, *iChineseReader*. She is Vice Chair of the ACTFL Heritage Languages SIG (2022–2024).

传承中文

Modern Chinese for Heritage Beginners

Stories about Us

**Yan Liu, Jingjing Ji, Grace Wu
and Min-Min Liang**

Routledge
Taylor & Francis Group

LONDON AND NEW YORK

Designed cover image: AleksandarNakic via Getty Images

First published 2023
by Routledge
4 Park Square, Milton Park, Abingdon, Oxon OX14 4RN

and by Routledge
605 Third Avenue, New York, NY 10158

Routledge is an imprint of the Taylor & Francis Group, an informa business

British Library Cataloguing-in-Publication Data
A catalogue record for this book is available from the British Library

ISBN: 978-1-032-39978-2 (hbk)
ISBN: 978-1-032-39977-5 (pbk)
ISBN: 978-1-003-35222-8 (ebk)

DOI: 10.4324/9781003352228

Typeset in Times New Roman
by Apex CoVantage, LLC

Access the Support Material: www.routledge.com/9781032399775

Contents

前言

　　针对华裔中文学习的研究发现,华裔学生在中文学习背景、学习动机、学习兴趣、学习策略等各方面都有别于非华裔学生,因而华裔中文课所需教材以及教学方式都应针对华裔学生的特点而进行设计。

　　华裔从小或多或少都不同程度地接触过方言或普通话,对中文语音、词汇、语法都有些许知识。虽然该学生群体的中文水平差异化极大,但基本呈现出"听说好于读写,听力最强"的语言特点。因此,如何利用他们的听说能力及已有的中文知识来全面发展他们的语言能力是华裔中文教学中的首要任务。同时,由于华裔学生大多是通过家庭中的日常交流习得中文的,他们的中文表达较为口语化,阅读能力有限,写作也常常呈现"我手写我口"的特点。因此,如何提高学生的读写水平也是华裔中文教学的重点之一。此外,如何增强华裔学生学习中文的兴趣,让课堂成为他们自由交流和探索身份认同的"安全空间",去谈论与他们生活密切相关并能引发他们思考和共鸣的话题也尤为重要。

　　基于这些考虑,编者们编写了这本专为华裔学生设计的主题式中文教材:《传承中文》。这本教材以华美乃至亚美文化为主轴,适合高中及大学的华裔中文初学者。本书可作为华裔初级班一学年的教材,也可作为华裔和非华裔混班差异化教学的补充材料。

教材特色

　　此书累积了四位作者多年教学心得,然而内容的灵感则多来自好学、好奇的学生,是一个教学相长的成果。与其说是为华裔学生写一本书,不如说是一本综合了华裔学生生活和学习经验的回忆录。个中的喜怒哀乐都是他们关心的问题,也希望此书为他们的未来做好铺垫。本书的特色如下:

1. 该教材的主题始于个人和家庭,继而扩展到华裔和亚裔社群,乃至整个美国社会。同时,主题的讨论不再以中国人的视角为起点,而是以华裔学生的角度为切入点。此外,课文中还自然融入了中国的传统文化以及华裔美国人的历史。教师可以通过教材中的讨论问题以及交流性和展示性的教学任务来引导学生去学习和探究中国文化以及华裔美国人特有的文化和历史。
2. 本书前篇包括拼音篇和汉字篇,可为不识字或不会写字的学生在主题学习之前打好读写的基础,而且汉字活动设计丰富有趣。

3. 每课包含一篇对话和一篇短文。对话与短文的结合为学生提供了不同语体的语料,有助于学生了解口语与书面语的不同。对话部分的语言幽默,内容活泼,情景真实; 短文部分的语言比较正式,内容值得研究和思考。短文部分与对话部分的主题相关,但在内容上和语言上进行了拓展,也是为了增强学生篇章阅读的能力而设计的。短文后配有英语翻译,以避免汉字成为初级学生了解主题知识的绊脚石。同时,了解内容后再学汉字也会让学生们更有学习汉字的动力。

4. 教材的活动设计以学生已有的听说技能为基础,通过听说来带动读写。具体来讲,编者们在每一课都设计了阅读前的听说活动。这些活动除了有暖身的功能以外,还能鼓励学生在阅读前调动已有的背景知识和语言知识,从而帮助学生更好地阅读和理解文本。同时,每篇对话的汉字文本还配有相应的拼音。因此,即使学生最初认读汉字的能力不高,他们还是能够在预习的时候通过拼音了解文本的内容,并对讨论问题进行准备。

5. 除了传统的词汇和语法的练习外,本书还按照美国外语教学委员会(ACTFL) 所提倡的三个沟通模式: 理解性 (Interpretive)、交流性 (Interpersonal) 和展示性 (Presentational) 设计了教学任务,从而将理论落实在实践上,让学生的听、说、读、写四个技能得以齐头并进,共同发展。

6. 每课的教学目标是根据"布鲁姆认知范畴的分类法" (Bloom's Taxonomy) 设定的,因此学习目标涉及不同层次的学习范畴,由浅入深,层层推进,使学习者能够在语言学习、内容学习、思辨能力及跨文化交际能力等诸多方面得到提高。

7. 最后,该教材还提供配套的教学资源网站(含视听材料等) 供老师们参考使用。

教材结构

这本教材共五个单元: 我和家庭、家庭语言、教育、移民故事、社区和社会。每个单元有两课,共十课。每课有对话和短文。本书分为两大部分: 基础篇以及单元篇。

1. 基础篇: 拼音篇和汉字篇

   1) 拼音篇: 介绍了声母、韵母、拼音规则,并设计了相关练习。
   2) 汉字篇: 该部分收录165个字,汉字主要来自第一课以及第二课,加黑斜体字为补充汉字。根据许慎六书介绍了汉字的基本分类,也介绍了汉字的笔顺、结构以及基本部首。建议学生在开学前两周反复练习偏旁、部首、笔画等。所选汉字多为第一单元出现的汉字,我们根据这些汉字由浅入深编排了词组、短句、对话、篇章,希望通过反复操练让学生掌握165个汉字。有了这些汉字基础再进入第一单元将会事半功倍。

2. 单元篇: 五个单元,每一个单元各有两课,全书一共10课。

这本教材课文内容不但依据华裔学生特殊的文化背景和语言特长设计,更特别以华美文化和历史为主。此外,在介绍华裔移民故事中也加入了关怀理解其他族裔的活动,进而让学生反思身为华裔美国人如何为美国社会做出自己的贡献。

每一课的主要内容编排如下:

1. 每一课分为对话和短文,主题相同,前后呼应。老师可以根据学生程度做适度调整。程度比较低的班级可以只选择对话的部分教授。老师在讲解对话之前,可以先让学生听录音并且回答对错题。程度较高的班级可以加入短文进行深度讨论。

2. 对话和短文各有生词表,生词表中有加黑斜体字词是高频字词,也是我们希望学生能够熟记和书写的汉字。我们对汉字的处理以先认后写、多认少写为主。

3. 对话和短文部分分别有句型和语法,对于华裔学生的语法偏误也有针对性的解释,课后也有对应的语法句型练习供学生反复练习。

4. 本书的每一课都有部首练习和汉字组词组句练习,以巩固学生对汉字结构和汉字构词的知识。

5. 每篇对话和短文都有阅读前的讨论题和阅读后的理解题,使学生和同学、老师能借着讨论让课堂气氛更加活泼。讨论题目由浅入深。在北美长大的青少年十分善于表达自己的见解,我们不可因为学生语言水平不足而低估了他们的思辨能力。

6. 本书每一课都有根据 ACTFL 三种交流模式 (interpersonal, interpretive, and presentational) 而设计的访谈、对话、调查等综合性语言练习任务。

致谢

　　此书付梓，将我们四位作者多年的华裔中文教学理念、原则及方法以铅字呈现在各位读者面前，感慨万千。从最初产生编写这样一本教材的想法，到后来教材初具雏形，再到不断打磨完善，并最终出版，要感谢诸多人士的帮助及支持。

　　首先，我们要衷心感谢旧金山州立大学的萧旸教授。2021年4月，我们有幸邀请到萧教授作我们在美国中文教师协会的圆桌讨论上的主持人。彼次针对华裔中文写作教学的脑力激荡，收获颇丰。萧教授更是对一个小时的讨论做了画龙点睛、提纲挈领的总结。会上五位老师所提华裔中文教学的要点、原则、方法、教材编写理念等引起了参会老师们的深深共鸣。老师们普遍反映：目前华裔中文教材内容过时、针对性不强，急需一本真正从华裔视角出发、专为华裔学生设计的中文教材。会后，此书作者之一，宾夕法尼亚大学的 Grace Wu 老师提出了未来华裔中文课程应以亚美文化为主轴的期许。萧教授及另外三位作者深以为然。由此，五位对华裔中文教学充满热忱、教学理念一致的老师一拍即合，当即决定一起合作，为华裔学生编写一本贴近他们生活的、反映他们思考的、从他们视角出发的、以华美乃至亚美文化为主轴的中文教材。萧教授参与了我们的首次会议，对教材编写理念、结构、主题等方面都提出了重要的思路。这为我们后续教材的编写奠定了良好的基础。但非常遗憾的是，萧教授因身体抱恙，后续未能与我们同行。

　　在此，我们也要衷心感谢Routledge出版社。我们也要感谢两位匿名评审老师，对我们的教材提出了专业意见，让我们的教材更加完善。我们也非常感谢我们的华裔学生们，特别想要感谢 Christina Wu（吴溪）、Kelly Mei（梅洁莹）、Andrew Pai（白光宇）、James Pai（白光中）、Madeline Henzer（孟琳）、Leshui Wang（王乐水）、Bethany Qu（屈禾子）。在我们撰写课文的过程中，是他们给予了我们诸多的写作灵感，让我们的写作得以更加鲜活。课文里的对话和短文很多皆来自于他们的真实故事和亲身经历。我们也要感谢Laura Gao（高宇洋），在时间十分紧迫的情况下，为我们的教材绘制出非常生动、精彩的图片说明。也要感谢李世江老师、麻省理工学院周康老师为我们提供帮助。

　　最后，我们要向我们的家人致谢。很多时候因为诸多教材编写事宜，我们不得不牺牲陪伴家人的时间。是他们一如既往的支持与理解让我们的教材能够如期完成并出版。因此，我们将此书献给我们的家人以及我们同为华裔的孩子们。

Preface 前言

Many studies on Chinese heritage language learning have shown that Chinese heritage language learners (CHLLs) differ significantly from non-CHLLs in their learning background, motivation, and strategies. Therefore, the textbooks and pedagogies for CHLLs should be tailored to this group of learners' needs.

CHLLs have been exposed to either Chinese Mandarin or regional varieties to varying degrees since childhood. So they have developed some knowledge of Chinese pronunciation, vocabulary, and grammar. Despite the significant heterogeneity within the group, their Chinese tends to present a distinctive feature – listening and speaking skills are more developed than reading and writing skills, with listening being the strongest. Therefore, using their existing listening and speaking abilities and prior knowledge to fully develop their language competence is a primary task in Chinese heritage language instruction. Additionally, as most CHLLs acquire Chinese through daily communication at home, they are usually good at conversational Chinese but have limited literacy skills. Consequently, facilitating the development of CHLLs' reading and writing is also an important task in Chinese heritage language instruction. Furthermore, it is particularly crucial to enhance CHLLs' interest in learning Chinese and make the classroom a "safe space" for them to communicate freely, explore their identities, and discuss fascinating, relevant, and resonating topics.

Considering all the aforementioned aspects, the authors have written this Chinese thematic textbook specifically designed for CHLLs – *Story About Us*. This textbook focuses on Chinese-American and Asian-American culture and is suitable for Chinese heritage language beginners in high schools and universities. It can be used as a primary textbook for first-year Chinese in the heritage language track for an entire academic year. It can also be supplementary materials for differentiated instruction in a mixed class with heritage and non-heritage students.

Unique Features of the Textbook

This textbook is a fruit grown from decades of teaching experiences of all the authors. Their curious and hard-working Chinese heritage students provided an endless source of inspiration for writing the stories in the textbook. It reflects a long teaching and learning process, so in some ways, it is a memoir that integrates students' life and experiences. The joys and sorrows reflected in this book are of all their concerns. We hope that this textbook, as a stepping-stone for students' future Chinese language learning, will inspire them to reflect on their identities and learn Chinese American heritages.

The unique features of this textbook are as follows:

1. The theme of the textbook starts with individuals and families and then expands to the Chinese and Asian American communities in the U.S. and eventually to the entire American society. Meanwhile, the discussion of the topics starts from the perspective of Chinese American students instead of Chinese people, thereby making this textbook distinct from other textbooks. Moreover, the texts incorporate both Chinese traditional culture and the history of Chinese Americans. The discussion questions and interpersonal and presentational tasks are designed for enhancing and furthering students' content and language learning.

2. There is an introductory chapter of the Pinyin and Chinese character writing systems. This chapter, equipped with various types of interesting exercises, offers a smooth transition for students without much literacy skills to start Lesson 1.

3. Each lesson contains one dialogue and one text. The dialogues, written in spoken language, are based on real-life experiences. The content is humorous, which can engage students instantly. Compared with the dialogues, the short texts are written in a more formal register, and their content is related to the theme of the dialogue, which promotes a deeper understanding across cultures. This design allows students to get exposed to different genres of writing in Chinese. Each text is accompanied by an English translation so that beginner-level students can understand the content even though they may not be able to recognize every Chinese character. Characters should not become obstacles to reading. At the same time, learning Chinese characters after understanding the content will also give students more motivation to learn Chinese characters.

4. The activities in each lesson are designed with students' strengths in mind. This design adopts a macro-approach that utilizes students' existing speaking and listening skills to improve their reading and writing skills. In each lesson, there are listening comprehension exercises and pre-reading questions. In addition to warming up, these activities also encourage students to mobilize their funds of knowledge, thereby helping students read and understand the text better. At the same time, each dialogue in Chinese characters also comes with a Pinyin text, which enables students to comprehend the content and get prepared for the discussion questions even if they cannot recognize all the characters.

5. Aside from vocabulary and grammar exercises, the textbook also includes tasks in the three modes of communication promoted by American Council on the Teaching Foreign Languages (ACTFL): interpersonal mode, interpretive mode, and presentational mode. Through these tasks, students can improve their listening, speaking, reading, and writing skills all at the same time.

6. The learning objectives of each lesson are based on Bloom's Taxonomy, guiding students to progress in many aspects, such as language learning, content learning, critical thinking ability, and cross-cultural communication skills.
7. This textbook also has a companion website that provides supporting teaching resources, including extra reading materials, media resources, and lesson assessment, etc.

Textbook Structure

This textbook starts with two introduction chapters, followed by five units. Each unit has two lessons, ten lessons in total. Each lesson consists of two texts of different genres: a dialogue and a short text.

The Chapter of Pinyin: This part introduces the initial, consonants, finals, Pinyin rules, and provides relevant exercises at the end.

The Chapter of Chinese Characters: 165 characters are included in this part. Characters primarily come from Lesson 1 and Lesson 2. Characters in italics and bold are supplementary. Students are expected to reproduce 75 out of these characters.

According to Xu Shen's *Liushu*, this chapter introduces the basic classification of Chinese characters, the stroke order, character structures, and basic radicals. Students are advised to practice radicals and strokes and basic characters repeatedly in the first two weeks of the semester. Most of the selected Chinese characters will appear in Unit 1 (Lesson 1 and Lesson 2). We use these Chinese characters to build up phrases, sentences, dialogues, and short paragraphs. With these exercises, we hope that students will be well-prepared for Unit 1.

The main contents of each lesson are arranged as follows:

1. Each lesson is divided into a dialogue and a text, with the same theme and echoing one another. Teachers can make appropriate adjustments according to students' level. Teachers can only choose the dialogues for instruction. Also, for the dialogue, the teacher can ask the students to listen to the audio files and answer the true or false questions. For more advanced students, teachers can add the text for more in-depth discussion.
2. Both dialogues and texts have a vocabulary list. The characters or words in italics and bold are of high frequency, which are also the ones that we hope students can memorize and write. We emphasize that recognizing Chinese characters is more important than writing the characters.
3. There are sentence patterns and grammar in the dialogue and the text respectively, and there are also targeted explanations for common grammatical errors made by students. Each lesson contains corresponding grammatical exercises for students to practice.
4. Every lesson in this book provides radical exercises and word and sentence building exercises to reinforce students' character knowledge and word formation.
5. Each dialogue and text have pre-reading and post-reading questions. We hope that these questions would facilitate a lively learning atmosphere.

Students growing up in North America are often good at expressing their opinions. We should not underestimate their critical thinking ability because of their insufficient language proficiency.

6. Every lesson in this book has comprehensive tasks, such as interview, dialogue, and research, which are designed according to ACTFL's three communication modes (Interpersonal, Interpretative, and Presentation).

Acknowledgment

This textbook was born out of our years of teaching experience in Chinese heritage language education. However, the publication would have been impossible without the help and support from our friends, family, and colleagues. We are genuinely grateful throughout the entire process, from coming up with the initial idea of writing the book to starting working on it, continuously revising, and finally publishing it.

Our sincere and deepest gratitude goes first to Professor Yang Xiao-Desai from San Francisco State University. In April 2021, we were honored to have Professor Xiao as the moderator of our roundtable discussion about Chinese heritage language writing instruction at the Chinese Language Teachers Association (CLTA) annual conference. The one-hour discussion was very productive and well-received. The Chinese heritage language teaching philosophies, pedagogies, and principles for a textbook compilation that we shared at the meeting deeply resonated with the participants. A consensus was that the textbooks currently available for Chinese heritage language learners (CHLLs) are outdated, and the contents may not be relevant to our current student population. Therefore, there is an imperative need for a Chinese textbook specifically designed for CHLLs. After the meeting, Grace Wu from the University of Pennsylvania, one of the authors of this book, proposed that the Chinese heritage language curriculum in the future should focus more on Asian American culture, which was echoed by Professor Xiao and the other three authors. As a result, the five educators, who are enthusiastic about Chinese heritage language education and share the same teaching philosophy, immediately decided to collaborate on writing a Chinese textbook for CHLLs. We agreed that the book should be closely relevant to their lives, reflect their thinking, represent their perspectives, and focus on Chinese American or Asian American culture. Professor Xiao attended our first textbook meeting and proposed inspiring ideas on the book structure, themes, and compiling principles. Unfortunately, Professor Xiao was not able to continue working with us afterwards due to illness.

We would also like to thank the publisher Routledge sincerely. It is a great honor for us to work together with Routledge on this project. Special thanks are due to the two anonymous reviewers for their valuable suggestions. We are also very grateful to our Chinese heritage students, especially Christina Wu (吴溪), Kelly Mei (梅洁莹), Andrew Pai (白光宇), James Pai (白光中), Madeline Henzer (孟琳), Leshui

Wang (王乐水), Bethany Qu (屈禾子). Many of the dialogues and texts in this textbook came from their personal experiences. Thanks to all of you! Your stories make our book what it is! We would also like to thank Laura Gao (高宇洋), who provided vivid illustrations for our book on short notice. Our sincere thanks are also due to Professor Kang Zhou from MIT and Mr. Shijiang Li for their great help.

Lastly, our thanks go to our beloved families for their continued support and understanding. So many times we have had to sacrifice the time spent with them to work on the project. Our book is dedicated to them and our children, who are also Chinese Americans.

Abbreviations and Symbols

n.	noun
adj.	adjective
adv.	adverb
v.	verb
v.o.	verb object
prep.	preposition
conj.	conjunction
mw.	measure word
pron.	pronoun
ph.	phrase
idm.	idiom
/	separates alternate forms

词汇、句型部分的参考文献

Cheung, H. S., Liu, S. & Shih, L. (1994). *A Practical Chinese Grammar*. Hong Kong: The Chinese University Press.

Chinese Grammar Wiki. *AllSet Learning*. https://resources.allsetlearning.com/chinese/grammar

DeFrancis, J. (1996). *ABC Chinese-English Dictionary*. Honolulu: University of Hawai'i Press.

Kleeman, J. & Yu, H. (2010). *Oxford Chinese Dictionary*. Oxford: Oxford University Press and Foreign Language Teaching and Research Press.

Background of Main Characters

Name	Relationship	Background
Lin Wei	Joy's father	from Beijing
Wang Hong	Joy's mother	from Shanghai
Lin Yue'ai /Joy	me	Chinese American (born and grew up in America)
Lin Li / Alex	Joy's older brother	Chinese American (born and grew up in America)
Tina	Alex's girlfriend	from Malaysia
Xia Xiaojing	Joy's roommate	from Beijing
Eric	Joy's classmate	bi-racial (His father is from America, and his mother is from Singapore.)
Melinda	Joy's classmate	born and grew up in Chinatown (Her father is from Guangdong, and her mother is from Sichuan.)

Introduction

拼音篇 (Pīnyīnpiān) Chapter of Pinyin

声母 *(shēngmǔ) Initials*

b (o)	p	m	f
d (e)	t	n	l
g (e)	k	h	
j (i)	q	x	
z (i)	c	s	
zh (i)	ch	sh	r

韵母 (yùnmǔ) Finals

a	ai, ao, an, ang
o	ou, ong
e	ei, en, eng, er
i	ia, iao, ian, iang, ie, iu (iou), in, ing, iong
u	ua, uo, uai, ui (uei), un (uen), uan, uang, ueng
ü	üe, üan, ün

Pinyin Spelling Rules

1. Tone marks: when there is a single vowel, put the tone mark on it. When there are two or three vowels, follow the order of "a, o, e, i, u, ü". For example, the tone mark should be put above "a" in "tiao". When "i" and "u" are together, the tone mark is put above whichever comes last. For example, "diū" and "huǐ".
2. When the syllable starts without any initials, write Pinyin according to the following rules.

    *   When the syllable starts with "a, o, e", write Pinyin as it is. For instance, ài (爱 love). When it follows the other Pinyin, insert an apostrophe between the two syllables. For example, zhēn'ài (真爱, true love).

DOI: 10.4324/9781003352228-1

- When the syllable is one of "i, in, ing", add "y" and write the Pinyin as "yi, yin, ying". For other syllables starting with "i", replace "i" with "y". For example, "ian" becomes "yan".
- When the syllable is one of "ü, üe, üan, ün", add "y" and drop the umlaut, resulting in "yu, yue, yuan, yun".
- When the syllable is "u", add "w" and write the Pinyin as "wu". For other syllables starting with "u", replace "u" with "w". For example, "uan" becomes "wan".
- For retroflections, add "r" at the end of the Pinyin. For instance, 饭馆儿 (fànguǎnr).

3. When "ü" follows "j, q, x", write "ü" as "u", resulting in "ju, qu, xu".
4. When the finals "iou, uei, uen" work with the initials, drop the middle vowels and write them as "iu, ui, un". For example, "旧(jiù, old), 水(shuǐ, water), 困(kùn, sleepy)". When they do not have initials, follow the rules listed previously in #2. For example, "有(yǒu, have/has), 为(wèi, for), 问 (wèn, ask)".
5. The first letter of the Pinyin should be capitalized in proper nouns or at the beginning of a sentence. For example, "美国(Měiguó) America", "我是美国人。(Wǒ shì Měiguó rén.)".
6. When two third tones appear together in a group, the first third tone changes to a second tone. For example, 你好(nǐhǎo, hi) is pronounced as "níhǎo". When a third tone appears before a first, second, or fourth tone, it falls and does not rise, being pronounced as a half third tone.
7. Tone change of "不(bù)": When "不" appears before a fourth tone, it is pronounced as a second tone. For example, 不去(búqù, not going). It remains a fourth tone when it stands alone or appears before a first, second, or third tone. For example, 不吃(bùchī, not eating), 不难(bùnán, not difficult), 不好(bùhǎo).
8. Tone change of "一(yī)": When "一" appears before first, second, or third tone, it is pronounced as a fourth tone. For example, 一天(yìtiān, one day), 一年(yìnián, one year), 一起(yìqǐ, together). When "一" appears before a fourth tone, it is pronounced as a second tone. For example, 一个(yígè, one). "一" is pronounced as a first tone when it stands alone.

拼音练习 *(pīnyīnliànxí) Pinyin Practice*

1. Multiple choice: Please listen to the audio recordings and select the matching Pinyin.

1) A. hǎo	B. tǎo	C. dǎo	D. kǎo
2) A. zú	B. jú	C. cú	D. zhú
3) A. tiě	B. tiǎn	C. tě	D. tǐng
4) A. huò	B. kuò	C. gòu	D. guò
5) A. gǔn	B. guǎn	C. guǎng	D. gěng

2.   Multiple choice: Please select a Pinyin that is correctly written.

1) A. yian	B. yiang	C. yin	D. yüan
2) A. qü	B. xüe	C. zhü	D. jun
3) A. wa	B. wuan	C. wuo	D. wueng
4) A. diou	B. xiu	C. tuen	D. wuai
5) A. yue	B. wüe	C. yn	D. yie

3.   Please write down the Pinyin that you hear.

1)	2)	3)	4)	5)
6)	7)	8)	9)	10)

汉字篇 (hànzìpiān) Chapter of Characters

The Chapter of Chinese Characters: 165 characters are included in this section. These characters primarily come from Lesson 1 and Lesson 2. Characters in italics and bold are supplementary. All the 75 characters that students are expected to reproduce are listed at the end of this chapter. The rest of the characters are for recognition only.

1. The Chinese Writing System: An Overview

Unlike alphabetic languages, in the Chinese writing system, each character represents both an inherent meaning and an associated pronunciation. The best known exposition of Chinese character composition is the *Shuowen Jiezi* 说文解字, complied by *Xu Shen* 许慎 (58–147 AD). The classification identified the following six categories based on structure and representation of meaning. This chapter presents an overview and basic character practice.

The Traditional Classification of Characters

1) Pictographs 象形 xiàngxíng
Pictographs originated as pictures of objects.

Character	Pinyin	Meaning
日	rì	sun
月	yuè	moon
山	shān	mountain
水	shuǐ	water
目	mù	eye
口	kǒu	mouth
人	rén	person

Character	Pinyin	Meaning
中	zhōng	middle
父	fù	father
母	mǔ	mother

2) Ideographs 指事 zhǐshì

Ideographs represent abstract meanings; the character is an indicative sign or indirect symbol.

Character	Pinyin	Meaning
上	shàng	upper part
下	xià	go down
本	běn	root

3) Complex ideograms 会意 huìyì

Two single characters are combined to form a new character and new meaning.

	Character	Pinyin	Meaning
女 "women" + 子 "child"	好	hǎo	good
木 "wood" + 木 "wood"	林	lín	forest
手 "hand" + 目 "eye"	看	kàn	look
人 "person" + 土 "earth"	坐	zuò	sit
田 "field" + 力 "strength"	男	nán	man
羊 "sheep" + 大 "big"	美	měi	beautiful

4) Semantic-phonetic compounds 形声 xíngshēng

Semantic-phonetic compounds are the most common type of Chinese characters. One part indicates the pronunciation and the other parts indicate the meaning.

Character	Pinyin	Meaning
妈	mā	mom
吗	ma	question particle
奶	nǎi	milk, granny
样	yàng	sample
梅	méi	plum
枝	zhī	branch
湖	hú	lake

Character	Pinyin	Meaning
洋	yáng	ocean
河	hé	river
眼	yǎn	eye
睛	jīng	eye
睡	shuì	sleep

5) Derivative cognates 转注 zhuǎnzhù

Derivative cognates are characters that are used to represent a meaning that is derived from the original meaning of another character.

Character	Pinyin	Meaning
考	kǎo	test
老	lǎo	old

6) Phonetic loan characters 假借 jiǎjiè

Phonetic loan characters are characters that are "borrowed" to write another character that has the same or nearly the same pronunciation.

Character	Pinyin	Meaning
我	wǒ	I
自	zì	oneself
其	qí	his, her, its

2. 汉字笔画和笔顺 *(hànzì bǐhuà hé bǐshùn) Character Strokes and Stroke Order*

1) 笔画 (bǐhuà) Strokes

The Chinese strokes are usually termed as 永字八法 (yǒngzìbāfǎ, eight principles of *Yong*) as the character "永" contains the eight common strokes.

2) 笔顺 (bǐshùn) Stroke Order

a. top to bottom	三 (sān, three)
b. left to right	火 (huǒ, fire)
c. horizontal first, vertical second	十 (shí, ten)
d. center first in vertically symmetrical characters	小 (xiǎo, small)
e. enclosures first but the bottom horizontal stroke comes last	月 (yuè, moon), 日 (rì, sun)
f. bottom enclosures come last	进 (jìn, enter)

Figure 1 Eight principles of Yong

3. 汉字结构 (hànzì jiégòu) Chinese Character Structure

1) 独体结构 (dútǐ jiégòu) Single-component structure

一 yī (one)、人 rén (person)、口 kǒu (mouth)、日 rì (sun)、目 mù (eye)、田 tián (farmland)、马 mǎ (horse)、生 shēng (life, student)、面 miàn (side, noodle)、几 jǐ (how many)

2) 左右结构 (zuǒyòu jiégòu) Left-right structure

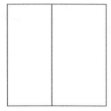

她 tā (she)、好 hǎo (good)、妈 mā (mother)、你 nǐ (you)、很 hěn (very)、的 de (of)、跟 gēn (with; follow)、刚 gāng (just)、忙 máng (busy)、饭 fàn (meal)、师 shī (teacher)、难 nán (difficult)、明 míng (bright)、昨 zuó (yesterday)

语 yǔ (language)、没 méi (not)

都 dōu / dū (all/capital)、凯 kǎi (triumphal)、部 bù (unit; section)

3) 上下结构 (shàngxià jiégòu) Top-bottom structure

多 duō (many)、男 nán (male)、第 dì (prefix indicating ordinal number)、爸 bà (father)、英 yīng (Britain; brave)、字 zì (character)、学 xué (learn)、老 lǎo (old)、去 qù (go)、只 zhī (measure word for animals); zhǐ (only)、天 tiān (sky)、家 jiā (family)

想 xiǎng (want; think)

前 qián (before; front)、宿 sù (dorm)、筷 kuài (chopsticks)

4) 品字型结构 (pǐnzìxíng jiégòu) The structure of Pin

品 pǐn (quality)、森 sēn (forest)

5) 上中下结构 (shàngzhōngxià jiégòu) Top-middle-bottom structure

常 cháng (often)、意 yì (meaning)

6) 左中右结构 (zuǒzhōngyòu jiégòu) Left-middle-right structure

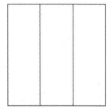

谢 xiè (thank)、树 shù (tree)、啊 a (modal particle ending sentence, showing affirmation, approval, or consent)

7) 全包围结构 (quánbāowéi jiégòu) Full enclosure structure

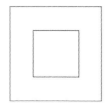

回 huí (return)、国 guó (country)、因 yīn (reason)、囚 qiú (prisoner)

8) 半包围结构 (bànbāowéi jiégòu) Half enclosure structure

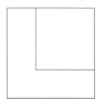

这 zhè (this)、进 jìn (enter)、过 guò (cross)

问 wèn (ask)、同 tóng (same)、风 fēng (wind)

句 jù (sentence)、可 kě (but)

区 qū (district)、医 yī (doctor)

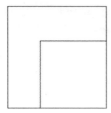

庭 tíng (courtyard)、应 yīng (should)、店 diàn (store)、友 yǒu (friend)

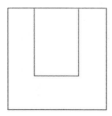

凶 xiōng (fierce)、击 jī (strike)

9) **镶嵌结构 (xiāngqiàn jiégòu) Overlaid structure**

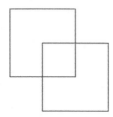

坐 zuò (sit)、里 lǐ (inside)、来 lái (come)

4. 部首 (bùshǒu) Radicals

1) **人 (亻) rén person:**
   你 nǐ (you)、什 shén (what)、们 men (plural marker for pronouns)、但 dàn (but)、候 hòu (wait; climate)、像 (xiàng resemble)、做 zuò (do、make)

2) **女 nǚ female:**
   她 tā (she)、妈 mā (mother)、好 hǎo (good)、姓 xìng (surname)、奶 nǎi (milk)

3) **言 (讠) yán speech:**
   说 shuō (speak)、语 (yǔ language)、话 huà (talk)、课 kè (class, lesson)、谁 shuí (who)

4) **辶 chuò go:**
   进 jìn (enter)、过 guò (cross)、这 zhè (this)、还 hái (still)、递 dì (hand over)

5) **口 kǒu mouth:**
   吃 chī (eat)、吗 ma (question particle for "yes-no" questions)、啊 a (modal particle ending sentence, showing affirmation, approval, or consent)、呀 ya (particle equivalent to 啊 after a vowel, expressing surprise or doubt)、叫

jiào (shout)、问 wèn (ask)、呢 ne (particle indicating that a previously asked question is to be applied to the preceding word)、句 jù (sentence)、哦 ò oh (interjection indicating that one has just learned something)、哈 hā (laughter)、叹 tàn (sigh)、名 míng (name)

6) 日 rì sun:
早 zǎo (early)、晚 wǎn (late)、时 shí (time)

7) 心 (忄) xīn heart:
您 nín (courteous form of you)、怎 zěn (how)、意 yì (meaning)、思 sī (think, thought)、想 xiǎng (think, want)、忙 máng (busy)

8) 木 mù tree:
样 yàng (pattern, shape)、极 jí (extremely)、林 lín (woods)

9) 糸 (纟) mì silk:
累 lèi (tired)、给 gěi (give)、维 wéi (dimension)、经 jīng (warp)

10) 水 (氵) shuǐ water:
河 hé (river)、海 hǎi (sea)、没 méi (not)

11) 手 (扌) shǒu hand:
把 bǎ (hold, handle)、打 dǎ (hit)

12) 刀 (刂) dāo knife:
刚 gāng (just)、到 dào (arrive)

13) 艹 cǎo grass:
草 cǎo (grass)、菜 cài (dish)、英 yīng (Britain, brave)

14) 犭 quǎn dog:
狗 gǒu (dog)、猫 māo (cat)

15) 土 tǔ earth, soil:
地 dì (ground)、坐 zuò (sit)

16) 广 yǎn shelter:
庭 tíng (courtyard)、店 diàn (store)

17) 阝 (邑) yì city:
都 dū (capital)

18) 囗 wéi enclosure:
国 guó (country)、囚 qiú (prisoner)、因 yīn (reason)

19) 足 (⻊) zú foot:
跟 gēn (with)、跑 pǎo (run)

20) 寸 cùn inch:
对 duì (right)

21) 走 zǒu walk:
起 qǐ (get up)

22) 夕 xī dusk:
多 duō (many)、外 wài (outside)、岁 suì (age)

23) 月 yuè moon:
朋 péng (friend)、有 yǒu (have; has)

24) 父 fù father:
爸 bà (father)、爷 yé (paternal grandfather)

25) 竹 (⺮) zhú bamboo:
筷 kuài (chopsticks)、笑 xiào (smile)、第 dì (prefix, indicating ordinal number)

Figure 2 Person radical

rén person
你 nǐ、
什 shén、
们 men、
但 dàn、
候 hòu、
像 xiàng、
做 zuò

Figure 3 Woman radical and its transformation

nǚ female
她 tā、
妈 mā、
好 hǎo、
姓 xìng、
奶 nǎi

Figure 4 Speech radical

yán speech
说 shuō、
语 yǔ、
话 huà、
课 kè、
谁 shuí

Figure 5 Go radical

chuò go
进 jìn、
过 guò、
这 zhè、
还 hái、
递 dì

Figure 6 Mouth radical

kǒu mouth
吃 chī、
吗 ma、
啊 a、
呀 ya、
叫 jiào、
问 wèn、
呢 ne、
句 jù、
哦 ò、
哈 hā、
叹 tàn、
名 míng

Figure 7 Sun radical

rì sun
早 zǎo、
晚 wǎn、
时 shí

Figure 8 Heart radical

xīn heart
您 nín、
怎 zěn、
意 yì、思 sī、
想 xiǎng、
忙 máng

Figure 9 Tree radical

mù tree
样 yàng、
极 jí、林 lín

Figure 10 Silk radical

mì silk
累 lèi、
给 gěi、
维 wéi、
经 jīng

Figure 11 Water radical

shuǐ water
河 hé、
海 hǎi、
没 méi

Figure 12 Hand radical

shǒu hand
把 bǎ、打 dǎ

Figure 13 Knife radical

dāo knife
刚 gāng、
到 dào

Figure 14 Grass radical

cǎo grass
草 cǎo、
菜 cài、
英 yīng

Figure 15 Dog radical

quǎn dog
狗 gǒu、
猫 māo

Figure 16 Soil radical

tǔ earth, soil
地 dì、
坐 zuò

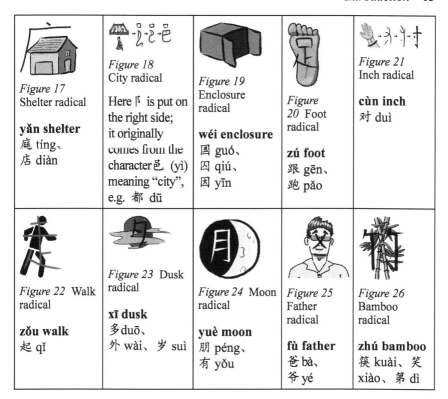

Figure 17 Shelter radical **yǎn shelter** 庭 tíng、 店 diàn	*Figure 18* City radical Here 阝 is put on the right side; it originally comes from the character 邑 (yì) meaning "city", e.g. 都 dū	*Figure 19* Enclosure radical **wéi enclosure** 国 guó、 囚 qiú、 因 yīn	*Figure 20* Foot radical **zú foot** 跟 gēn、 跑 pǎo	*Figure 21* Inch radical **cùn inch** 对 duì
Figure 22 Walk radical **zǒu walk** 起 qǐ	*Figure 23* Dusk radical **xī dusk** 多 duō、 外 wài、岁 suì	*Figure 24* Moon radical **yuè moon** 朋 péng、 有 yǒu	*Figure 25* Father radical **fù father** 爸 bà、 爷 yé	*Figure 26* Bamboo radical **zhú bamboo** 筷 kuài、笑 xiào、第 dì

汉字练习 *(hànzì liànxí) Character Exercise*

Exercise 1: Look at the following character and (1) identify the radicals and (2) write down the meanings of the radicals. Please refer to the list of common radicals on pages 10-13.

1. 忙 máng   busy   _____
2. 进 jìn   enter   _____
3. 晚 wǎn   late, evening   _____
4. 课 kè   class, lesson   _____
5. 经 jīng   warp, regular   _____
6. 叹 tàn   sigh   _____
7. 快 kuài   fast   _____
8. 姓 xìng   last name   _____
9. 庭 tíng   hall, courtyard _____
10. 和 hé   and, with   _____
11. 狗 gǒu   dog   _____
12. 地 dì   the earth, land _____
13. 给 gěi   give   _____
14. 语 yǔ   language, talk _____

15. 思 sī   think, thought   _____
16. 没 méi   not have   _____
17. 说 shuō   speak   _____
18. 很 hěn   very   _____
19. 跟 gēn   with   _____
20. 但 dàn   but   _____

Exercise 2: Word and Sentence Building

Most of the following Chinese characters will appear in Lesson 1 and Lesson 2. Please use these Chinese characters to build up phrases, sentences, dialogues, and short paragraphs. With these Chinese characters, you will be well prepared through repeated drills before starting Lesson 1.

The exercises in this section are for you to recognize words and sentences. Read them out loud and see whether you understand the meaning of these words and sentences.

主题 1 (Zhǔtí, theme): 家人

字:

月、日、今、明、昨、天、哥、爸、妈、奶、什、么、说、英、中、美、
国、文、好、久、不、看、见、问、好、时、候、非、常、对、见、到、
过、意、思、朋、友、是、会、像、发、音、经、从、起、来、没、极、
和、了、因、为、所、以、跟、家、就、小、呢、吗、可、很、一、二、
三、四、五、六、七、八、九、十

词组:

今天、明天、昨天、哥哥、爸妈、什么、奶奶、说英文、说中
文、好久不见、问好、 时候、非常、中国、美国、对、见到、意思、朋
友、会、月、日、像、发音、经常、好看、从来没、看过、好极了、因为、所
以、跟、家、起来、就、小时

句子:

1. 我爸爸妈妈是从中国来的。你呢?
2. 她的爸爸妈妈是中国人吗?
3. 好久不见了,你看起来很好,我爸爸妈妈也跟你问好。
4. 你们是什么时候来美国的?
5. 因为她父母是中国人,所以她会说中文。
6. 我和爸妈都会说英文。
7. 她对父母非常好。
8. 还有一个小时就可以见到哥哥了。
9. 今天是一月一日,昨天是十二月三十一日,明天是一月二日。
10. 我们今天去看你哥哥,好吗?
11. 父母和爸妈的意思一样。
12. 爸爸和奶奶非常像。
13. 我父母的英文发音好极了。

14. 小时候我经常跟哥哥去奶奶家。
15. 哥哥的女朋友很好看,可是妈妈从来没看过。

主题 2 (Zhǔtí, theme): 学中文

字:

有、成、语、句、子、但、而、且、刚、也、写、又、口、已、样、出、下、课、难、觉、得、才、笑、学、以、前、自、己、太、哪、儿、晚、里、这、那、个、在、多、怎

词组:

什么、有意思、成语、句子、不但……而且、因为、所以、刚来到、也、写中文、又、口音、已经、跟 …… 一样、出国、英文、下课、很难、觉得、刚才、发音、学英文、以前、自己、太难了、哪儿

句子:

1. 你们的中文说得好极了,在哪儿学的?
2. 她去过中国,所以中文说得很好。
3. 这个成语很有意思!
4. 这个句子是什么意思?
5. 我以前不会说中文。
6. 我的朋友不但会说英文,而且也会说日文。
7. 刚来到中国的时候,我不会说中文,也不会写中文。
8. 我的朋友又学中文又学日文,都说得很好。
9. 这里的口音跟那里的口音不一样。
10. 好多中国人会出国学英文。
11. 我来晚了,已经下课了。
12. 我觉得学中文很有意思,但是很难。
13. 因为我想出国,所以我学英文。
14. 刚才学过这个字的发音,太难了,我怎么说都说得不对。
15. 她觉得自己的发音很好。

主题 3 (Zhǔtí, theme): 朋友

字:

像、谁、姓、名、字、还、生、把、这、叫、男、女、快、面、想、外、林

词组:

怎么 、以为、好像、不好意思、谁、名字、什么时候、还是、姓名、才、生日、出国、把、但是、外国、这么、叫、男友、女友、快到了,一起、跟 …… 见面、就、这么、想不起来、说话、朋友

句子:

1. 你们是怎么来的?
2. 你的中文这么好,我以为你是中国人。
3. 她好像不是中国人。我想不起来她是哪里人了。

  4. 因为你说她好,但是她不好意思,所以就不说话了。
  5. 那个男的是谁?他是中国人吗?
  6. 那个女的叫什么名字?是你的什么人?
  7. 你什么时候去中国,今年十二月还是明年一月?
  8. 你叫什么名字?从哪儿来的?
  9. 我的男友 / 女友是中国人。
 10. 请把你的姓名写一下。
 12. 我明天才跟我的朋友见面,我跟她很久没见面了。
 13. 为什么你以为我是外国人?
 14. 我的朋友的生日快到了。
 15. 小林快出国了,我们今天都会一起去看他。

主题 4 (Zhǔtí, theme): 狗

字:

狗、挺、坐、进、吃、饭、上、哈、它、吧

词组:

狗叫、常常、晚上、时候、看见、家庭、经过、说话、想我、坐、它、外
国、进口、吃饭、外面、看到、从来不、可是、出来、上课、太太、哈
哈、又……、又……、跟……一起

句子:

  1. 我的狗常常在晚上的时候叫。
  2. 我看见狗了,你看见了吗?
  3. 美国很多家庭都有狗。
  4. 刚才经过你家的时候,你家的狗在叫。
  5. 我家的狗在外面看到人的时候从来不叫。
  6. 我觉得她的狗很好看。
  7. 哈哈! 她的狗好像在说话。
  9. 我不在家的时候,我的狗会很想我。
 10. 你的狗叫什么名字?为什么叫这个名字?
 11. 你的狗坐在那儿,我叫它,可是它不来,还是你叫它吧。
 12. 林太太的狗是从外国进口的。
 13. 我的狗吃饭吃得又多又快。
 14. 我到家的时候,我的狗会出来看我。
 15. 明天我的狗跟我一起去上课。

Exercise 3: 对话练习 (duìhuà liànxí) Dialogue Practice

Please complete the following conversations based on the provided
information.

  1. 美美: 你今天怎么样? 好不好?
     文文: _____。
     美美: 为什么呢?
     文文: 因为_____, 所以_____。

2. 美音: 文文中文的发音好极了, 为什么?
   林思: 他去过_____, 还_____三年的中文, 所以_____。
   美音: 哦, 他会写_____吗?
   林思: _____, 而且写_____。

3. 林朋: 你上个月去了中国, 是跟谁去的?
   英英: 我是_____的。
   林朋: 你觉得中国怎么样?
   英英: 我觉得_____。
   林朋: 你以前去过吗?
   英英: _____。

4. 小音: 你从哪儿来的?
   小为: _____。
   小音: 所以你的英文才这么好!
   小为: 你英文不会, 我可以_____。

5. 美美: 你学过成语吗?
   文文: _____。我觉得_____。
   美美: 学成语难不难?
   文文: 我觉得_____, 而且_____。

6. 妈妈: 小美, 我们今天去看你哥哥, 好吗?
   小美: 好呀。我_____了。
   妈妈: 是呀。你们有一个月没见面了。看哥哥以前, 你想做什么?
   小美: 我_____。

7. 美美: 爸, 妈, 我想_____。
   爸爸: 好啊。那你要好好学英文。
   妈妈: 是的! 你的发音不太好。
   美美: 好。我会_____。

8. 小文: 英英, 你家有狗吗?
   英英: 有啊! 美国_____。
   小文: 它_____?
   英英: 有啊。它叫林林。

9. 奶奶: 小美, 你哥哥_____?
   小美: 有啊, 是美国人, 可是_____, 跟中国人一样。
   奶奶: 太好了! 他为什么来中国?
   小美: 他_____。

10. 英英: 林朋, 你父母_____口音吗?
    林朋: 有啊。我觉得他们的发音_____。
    英英: 他们没有上发音课吗?
    林朋: 没有, 他们_____。

Exercise 4: 阅读练习 (yuèdú liànxí) Reading Practice

I. The following sentences are statements about nine individuals. Please read the sentences and then answer the questions.

1. 他去年去美国了。   2. 我已经在中国一年了。   3. 奶奶不会说英文。
4. 小美会说日文。   5. 今天三月十六日。   6. 小文是我的男朋友。
7. 小林今天生日。   8. 常老师去过外国。   9. 我跟小林是好朋友。

1) 第一个人去哪里了? 他是什么时候去的?
2) 第二个人在中国多久了?
3) 第三个, 谁不会说英文?
4) 第四个, 小美会说什么?
5) 第六个, 小文是谁?
6) 第九个, 我的好朋友是谁?
7) 第五个, 今天是几月几日? 明天呢? 昨天呢?
8) 第七个, 小林的生日是什么时候?
9) 第八个, 常老师去过哪儿?

II. Read the following texts and answer the questions based on the texts.

小美, 是女的, 十六岁, 今天很忙, 课很多, 还没吃饭。
中中, 是女的, 二十五岁, 是小学老师, 昨天第一天上课, 很忙, 今天好
多了。
林朋, 是男的, 十九岁, 是常老师中文课的学生, 他是大学生。
小文, 是男的, 十八岁, 是中国人, 刚来美国上大学, 可是英文非常好。
音音, 是女的, 十五岁, 是中学生, 今天的课很难, 很累。

Answer the questions according to the text in the previous section:

1) 小美今天怎么样? 小美吃饭了吗? 她多大?
2) 中中是谁? 忙不忙? 为什么?
3) 音音为什么很累? 是大学生吗?
4) 林朋的老师姓什么? 是什么课的老师?
5) 谁是学生? 谁是老师?
6) 小文是哪国人? 会说什么话?

III. Rearrange the following sentences to a logical order:

1.

    1) 他们是英国人、美国人和日本人
    2) 所以他们常常在上课的时候说中文
    3) 小美有三个好朋友
    4) 因为大家都上中文课

2.

    1) 所以英文好极了
    2) 奶奶已经六十五岁了
    3) 爸爸妈妈都想奶奶来美国看我们
    4) 因为以前是英文老师

3.

    1) 有的是中国人, 有的是日本人, 有的是英国人
    2) 我家的对面有一个大学

3) 也有很多外国学生
4) 不大也不小

4.

1) 天天很忙, 只好在外面吃饭
2) 中国饭很好吃
3) 可是有的时候很想吃美国饭
4) 我常常吃中国饭
5) 我来中国已经三个月了

5.

1) 我不会说中文
2) 可是现在我的中文说得好极了
3) 刚来中国的时候
4) 我是一个来中国学中文的美国人
5) 也不会写中文

6.

1) 而且我的中文发音很好笑
2) 所以他们跟我和哥哥说中文
3) 因为我觉得中文很难
4) 我的父母想让我们学中文
5) 哥哥会跟父母说中文
6) 可是我不跟他们说中文

7.

1) 可是我还是觉得它很好
2) 它经常在早上和晚上叫
3) 它的名字是笑笑
4) 我有一只狗
5) 我的朋友说好狗不会经常叫

8.

1) 可是她不但会跟我们学英文
2) 奶奶不会说英文
3) 我们很想她
4) 而且会给我们做好吃的饭
5) 我们已经很久没去看奶奶了
6) 小时候我常常跟哥哥去奶奶家

9.

1) 我以为她是中国人
2) 因为她觉得学中文很有意思
3) 但是哥哥说她是从日本来的
4) 她的中文说得非常好
5) 所以来中国学了很多年的中文了
6) 我哥哥有一个女朋友

IV. Follow the clues and solve the puzzle.

小音、小美、小文三个人明天出国, 他们去不一样的国家, 他们去哪儿?
Clues:
1)　小音去的国家, 很多人不会说英文
2)　小文不去英国

Circle the correct country under each person.

小音	小美	小文
美国	美国	美国
日本	日本	日本
英国	英国	英国

V. Read the following paragraph and come up with the questions that you can ask based on it.

　　林小美是一个中国学生, 今年十八岁, 在美国上大学。她觉得美国的大学很难, 但是也很有意思。她有很多朋友, 有的是美国人, 有的不是美国人。她们常常一起吃饭、上课、说话。她的朋友都对她很好。小美的家里还有爸爸、妈妈、哥哥。他们都在中国。小美自己在美国上学。有的时候, 她非常想她的家人, 也想吃中国饭。还有一个月, 大学就没有课了, 她就可以看到家人, 吃到中国菜了。
　　For example: 林小美是哪里人?

VI. List of 75 characters that students are expected to reproduce.

一 一	二 二	三 三	四 四	五 五	六 六
yī, one	èr, two	sān, three	sì, four	wǔ, five	liù, six
七 七	八 八	九 九	十 十	山 山	月 月
qī, seven	bā, eight	jiǔ, nine	shí, ten	shān, mountain	yuè, month
日 日	水 水	目 目	口 口	人 人	中 中
rì, date	shuǐ, water	mù, eye	kǒu, mouth	rén, person	zhōng, middle

父 父	母 母	女 女	子 子	木 木	手 手
fù, father	mǔ, mother	nǚ, female	zǐ, child	mù, wood	shǒu, hand
土 土	田 田	力 力	羊 羊	大 大	小 小

tǔ, earth	tián, farm	lì, strength	yáng, sheep	dà, big	xiǎo, small
上 上	下 下	好 好	林 林	男 男	看 看
shàng, up	xià, down	hǎo, good	lín, woods	nán, male	kàn, look

美 美	爸 爸	妈 妈	吗 吗	奶 奶	样 样
měi, beautiful	bà, father	mā, mother	ma, question	nǎi, milk	yàng, type
我 我	你 你	他 他	的 的	姓 姓	名 名
wǒ, I	nǐ, you	tā, he	de, particle	xìng, surname	míng, name
叫 叫	是 是	可 可	朋 朋	友 友	多 多
jiào, call	shì, be	kě, can	péng, companion	yǒu, friend	duō, many

没 没	有 有	都 都	很 很	忙 忙	常 常
méi, not	yǒu, have	dōu, all	hěn, very	máng, busy	cháng, often
想 想	进 进	过 过	说 说	问 问	来 来
xiǎng, think	jìn, enter	guò, pass	shuō, speak	wèn, ask	lái, come
去 去	早 早	国 国	家 家	因 因	为 为
qù, go	zǎo, early	guó, country	jiā, home	yīn, because	wèi, for

坐 坐	这 这	那 那			
zuò, sit	zhè, this	nà, that			

Unit One

我和家庭

Lesson One 我的名字

Learning Objectives

In this lesson, you will learn to do the following:

1. Describe your names.
2. Explain the origin and meaning of your names.
3. Compare naming cultures and taboos.
4. Discuss naming trends in the past and present.
5. Demonstrate your knowledge of naming cultures.

I. Warm-up: Pre-reading Discussion

1. 你有中文名字吗? 你的中文名字叫什么? 怎么写?
   Do you have a Chinese name? What is your Chinese name? How do you write it?
2. 你的家人叫你中文名字还是英文名字?
   Does your family call you by your Chinese name or English name?
3. 要是你没有中文名字, 你想取一个中文名字吗? 会取什么名字?
   If you do not have a Chinese name, would you like to get one? What would it be?

II. Interpretive Task: Listening Comprehension

Please listen to the lesson dialogue and choose True (T) or False (F) for each of the following audio recordings of the statements.

1. (F)   2. (F)   3. (T)   4. (F)   5. (T)

Main Text

Part I 对话: *我的名字*

Joy 是大学一年级的学生, 她刚搬进学校宿舍的第一天晚上跟爸爸妈妈视频聊天。

DOI: 10.4324/9781003352228-3

妈妈： Joy, 大学第一天过得怎么样？你见到室友了吗？

Joy： 好忙呀！我今天认识了好多新朋友。我的室友人很好，她是从北京来的留学生，英文说得好极了。

爸爸： 从北京来的留学生，她叫什么名字？

Joy： 她叫夏小京。对了，她问我有没有中文名字？怎么写的？我就说不出来了。我的中文名字是什么？

妈妈： 你的中文名字叫林约爱，"约"是"纽约"的"约"，"爱"是"谈恋爱"的"爱"。

爸爸： 因为爸爸妈妈是在纽约谈恋爱的，所以我们给你起了这个名字啊！

Joy： 什么？我的名字是这样来的？那哥哥呢？哥哥的中文名字也有故事吗？

妈妈： 哥哥的中文名字叫林立。中国有一句成语叫"三十而立"，意思是男人三十岁以前结婚生子，有自己的事业和家庭。哥哥出生的时候，爸爸三十岁，所以给哥哥起了林立这个名字。

爸爸： 你知道我们家的拉布拉多犬 (Labrador Retriever) Link 也有中文名字哦？

Joy： 什么？ Link 也有中文名字？

妈妈： 是啊！ Link 的中文名字叫林克。"克"是"克制"的"克"，因为狗狗得学会好好地"克制"自己啊！

Wǒ de míngzi

Joy shì dàxué yī niánjí de xuéshēng, tā gānggāng bān jìn xuéxiào sùshè de dìyītiān wǎnshàng gēn bàba māma shìpín liáotiān.

Māma: Joy, dàxué dìyītiān guò de zěnmeyàng? Nǐ jiàndào shìyǒu le ma?

Joy: Hǎo máng ya! Wǒ jīntiān rènshi le hǎoduō xīn péngyou, wǒ de shìyǒu rén hěnhǎo, tā shì cóng Běijīng lái de liúxuéshēng, Yīngwén shuō de hǎo jí le.

Bàba: Cóng Běijīng lái de liúxuéshēng, tā jiào shénme míngzi?

Joy: Tā jiào Xià Xiǎojīng. Duìle, tā wèn wǒ yǒuméiyǒu Zhōngwén míngzi? Zěnmexiě de? Wǒ jiù shuō bu chūlái le. Wǒ de Zhōngwén míngzi shì shénme?

Māma: Nǐ de Zhōngwén míngzi jiào Lín Yuē'ài, "yuē" shì "Niǔyuē" de "yuē", "ài" shì "tán liàn'ài" de "ài".

Bàba: Yīnwèi bàba māma shì zài Niǔyuē tán liàn'ài de, suǒyǐ wǒmen gěi nǐ qǐle zhège míngzi a!

Joy: Shénme? Wǒ de míngzi shì zhèyàng lái de? Nà gēge ne? Gēge de Zhōngwén míngzi yěyǒu gùshi ma?

Māma: Gēge de Zhōngwén míngzi jiào Lín Lì. Zhōngguó yǒu yījù chéngyǔ jiào "sānshí érlì", yìsi shì nánrén sānshí suì yǐqián jiéhūn shēngzǐ, yǒu zìjǐ de shìyè hé jiātíng. Gēge chūshēng de shíhòu, bàba gānghǎo sānshí suì, suǒyǐ gěi gēge qǐle Lín Lì zhège míngzi.

Bàba: Nǐ zhīdào wǒmen jiā de Lābùlāduō quǎn (Labrador Retriever) Link yěyǒu Zhōngwén míngzi o?

Joy: Shénme? Link yěyǒu Zhōngwén míngzi?

Māma: Shì a! Link de Zhōngwén míngzi jiào Lín Kè, "kè" shì "kèzhì" de "kè", yīnwèi gǒugou děi xuéhuì hǎohǎo de "kèzhì" zìjǐ a.

生词 Vocabulary

Students are required to recognize and pronounce all the vocabulary listed. For the characters/words in italics and bold, students are also expected to know how to write.

1.	**名字**	名字	míngzi	n.	name
2.	**大学**	大學	dàxué	n.	university
3.	年级	年級	niánjí	n.	grade
4.	刚	剛	gāng	adv.	just
5.	搬	搬	bān	v.	move
6.	**学校**	學校	xuéxiào	n.	school
7.	宿舍	宿舍	sùshè	n.	dormitory
8.	视频聊天	視頻聊天	shìpín liáotiān	v.	video chat/FaceTime
9.	室友	室友	shìyǒu	n.	roommate
10.	**忙**	忙	máng	adj.	busy
11.	**认识**	認識	rènshi	v.	meet (a person); recognize
12.	新	新	xīn	adj.	new
13.	留学生	留學生	liúxuéshēng	n.	oversea student
14.	谈恋爱	談戀愛	tán liàn'ài	v.o.	be in a relationship
15.	起 (名字)	起 (名字)	qǐ	v.	to give (a name), interchangeable with 取 qǔ
16.	故事	故事	gùshì	n.	story
17.	句	句	jù	mw.	measure word for sentences
18.	**三十**而立	三十而立	sānshí érlì	idm.	age when a man should stand on his own feet
19.	**岁**	歲	suì	n.	years old; year (of age)
20.	**以前**	以前	yǐqián	adv.	before
21.	结婚	結婚	jiéhūn	v.o.	marry; get married

22.	事业	事業	shìyè	n.	career; undertaking
23.	**家庭**	家庭	jiātíng	n.	family
24.	**出生**	出生	chūshēng	v.	be born
25.	**知道**	知道	zhīdào	v.	know; become aware of
26.	克制	克制	kèzhì	v.	restrain; control; self-control

Proper Names

1.	北京	北京	Běijīng	Beijing
2.	夏小京	夏小京	Xià Xiǎojīng	a person's name; 夏(天) is summer
3.	纽约	紐約	Niǔyuē	New York
4.	拉布拉多犬	拉布拉多犬	Lābùlāduō quǎn	Labrador Retriever

Sentence Patterns / Grammar

1. 从+ place + 来/去/回huí: come/go/return from a place
Unlike English, the word order in Chinese is different. 从 goes first and then the verb at the end. A frequent mistake is omitting the verb. For example, "I am from the U.S." should be "我从美国来的". 来cannot be omitted.

她是从北京来的留学生。
She is an international student from Beijing.

Examples:

1) 他是从纽约来的。
   He is from New York.
2) 她今天从北京去纽约。
   She went to New York from Beijing today.

2. Adj.极了: very much adj.; extremely adj.

很好 means "very good" and 好极了 means "extremely good".

她是从北京来的留学生,英文说得好极了。
She is an international student from Beijing, and she speaks English extremely well.

Examples:

1) 今天刚开学, 我忙极了。
   School just started today. I was extremely busy.
2) 今天的天气好极了, 你应该 (yīnggāi) 出去走走。
   Today's weather is extremely good; you should go out and take a walk.

3. 有没有: a choice-type question produces the effect of the English word "if"

她问我有没有中文名字。
She asked me if I had a Chinese name.

Examples:

1) 朋友问我纽约有没有好的中国餐馆 (cānguǎn)。
   My friend asked me if there are any good Chinese restaurants in New York.
2) 我问室友学校附近 (fùjin) 有没有超市 (chāoshì)。
   I asked my roommate if there was a supermarket near the school.

4. 因为 …… 所以: because ... therefore ...

"因为 …… 所以 (yīnwèi . . . suǒyǐ . . .)" is used in both written and spoken Chinese. This sentence pattern can make the logic clearer and more persuasive.

起 (取) 名字: give a name; pick a name
因为爸爸妈妈是在纽约谈恋爱的, 所以我们给你起了这个名字。
Because Mom and Dad fell in love in New York, we gave you this name.

Examples:

1) 因为你是在夏天出生的, 所以我们给你起了这个名字。
   Because you were born in summer, we gave you this name.
2) 因为我 *dōng tiān chū shēng*, 所以父母给我起了这个名字。
   My parents gave me this name because I *born in winter*.

5. 你的中文名字叫林约爱, "约" 是 "纽约" 的 "约", "爱" 是 "谈恋爱" 的 "爱"。
Your Chinese name is Lin Yue'ai, "yue" is the "yue" of "Niu Yue", and "love" is the "love" of "falling in love".

Examples:

1) 我的中文名字叫夏小京, "小" 是 "大小" 的 "小", "京" 是 "北京" 的 "京"。
   My Chinese name is Xia Xiaojing. "Xiao" is the small of the "big and small", and "jing" is the "jing" of Beijing.
2) 我的中文名字叫 *zou you rui*, " *you* " 是 " *you you* " 的 " *you* ", " *rui* " 是 " *rui zhi* " 的 " *rui* "。

6. 得 (děi): verb. have to, need to; Structure: (subject/time/location) + 得 + verb
学会: to master something by . . . (V + resultative complements)

狗狗得学会控制自己。
The doggie has to learn how to control itself.

Examples:

1) 我得学会写自己的中文名字。
   I have to learn to write my own Chinese name.
2) 生病的时候, 你得休息。
   When you are ill, you should rest.

学会, "会" here is a resultative complement that indicates the results of actions. Resultative complements are placed after verbs of action. These words can also be used as verbs or stative verbs in sentences. For instance, "会" itself could be used as a verb, e.g., 我会 (know how to do a skill) 写我的名字。Or it could mean "will", e.g., 我明天会去纽约。

3) 我爸爸还没学会用智能手机 (shǒujī)。
   My father hasn't learned how to use a smartphone yet.
4) 我妈妈学会开车了。
   My mother learned how to drive.

III. Vocabulary and Grammar Exercise

1. Radical Recognition

Please identify the radicals of the following characters. Write down the radical and its meaning.

Examples: 好 → (女) *woman*

扌 1) 搬 → (shǒu) hand
忄 2) 忙 → (xīn) heart
讠 3) 谈 → (yán) speech
女 4) 婚 → (nǚ) woman
宀 5) 家 → (mián) roof
日 6) 晚 → (rì) sun
讠 7) 认 → (yán) speech
心 8) 恋 → (xīn) heart
宀 9) 宿 → (mián) roof
讠 10) 识 → (yán) speech

2. Word-building Exercises

For each of the characters in the next example, write three more words that include that character.

1) 文: 中文 yīng wén, wén huà, wén lǐ   英文, 文化, 文理
2) 学: 大学 xué xiào, xué xí, kē xué   学校, 学习, 科学
3) 友: 朋友 shì yǒu, yǒu ài, yǒu yì   室友, 友爱, 友谊

爱好, 热爱, 亲爱

4) 爱: 恋爱 ài hào rè ài qīn ài
5) 家: 家庭 jiā rén bān jiā jiā lǐ

家人, 搬家, 家里

3. Matching Exercise: Please match Pinyin and characters

1)	宿舍	a. míngzi
2)	意思	b. dàxué
3)	名字	c. sùshè
4)	事业	d. jiéhūn
5)	年级	e. shìyè
6)	成语	f. jiātíng
7)	学校	g. yìsi
8)	大学	h. chéngyǔ
9)	结婚	i. xuéxiào
10)	家庭	j. niánjí

4. Fill in the blanks with the appropriate words

结婚生子	岁	事业	北京	起名字	极	成语	年级	室友	家庭

1) 夏小京是我的 室友 ，她也是大学一 年级 的学生。她的家在 北京 ，英文说得好 极 了。

2) 我哥哥出生的时候，我爸爸三十 岁 ，所以爸爸妈妈给我的哥哥 起名字 叫林立，中国有一句 成语 叫"三十而立"。意思是男人三十岁以前 结婚生子 ，有自己的 家庭 和 事业 。

5. Complete the following sentences with the given correlatives and words

1) 因为 ...... 所以

很多新朋友。

a. 因为大一的学生都住在学校的宿舍， 所以我认识了 (认识)。

b. 因为我爸爸妈妈都不是在美国出生的， 所以我有一个 (名字)。

中文名字。

2) Adj. 极了

Examples:

聪明极了 cōngming jíle extremely smart	热闹极了 rènao jíle extremely lively
漂亮极了 piàoliang jíle extremely pretty	好喝极了 hǎohē jíle extremely tasty
可爱极了 kě'ài jíle extremely cute	舒服极了 shūfu jíle extremely comfortable
兴奋极了 xīngfèn jíle extremely excited	感动极了 gǎndòng jíle extremely touched

a. 我们家的小狗拉布拉多犬 (Labrador Retriever)   刚出生不久, 真是 *rè nao* 。 *jí le*

b. 昨天晚上校的篮球比赛你去了吗? 真是 *xīng fèn jí le* 。

c. 我的室友考了12门AP 5 分, 真是 *cōng míng jí le* 。

d. 学校附近 (fùjìn) 新开的珍珠奶茶店你去了吗? 真是 *hǎo hē jí le* 。

e. Your sentence *wǒ de jiě jiě zhēn* 。 *shì piào liang jí le*

IV. Post-reading Discussion

1. 你知道你的中文名字是怎么来的吗? 有什么意思? 英文名字呢?
   How did you get your Chinese name? What is the meaning of it? How about your English name?

2. 你是先有中文名字还是英文名字的? 为什么?
   Did you first get your Chinese name or English name? Why?

3. 你听说过很有意思的中文名字或者英文名字吗? 请举例 (jǔlì)。
   Have you heard of any interesting Chinese or English names? Please provide some examples.

4. 夏小京还没有英文名字, 请帮她起一个英文名字。为什么你想给她起这个英文名字?
   Xia Xiaojing does not have an English name. Please pick one for her and explain why.

5. 如果你有孩子, 你会给他们起什么中英文名字? 为什么?
   If you have children, what Chinese and English names will you give them and why?

V. Interpersonal Tasks

1. 角色扮演 (juésè bànyǎn) Role-play

大学开学第一天在宿舍, 你见到了你的室友。他/她是一个中国留学生, 他/她的中文名字和英文名字都很有意思。请你跟他们认识一下, 问问他们的名字的故事, 也请介绍(jièshào) 你自己。

On the first day of college, you met your roommate in the dorm. He/She is an international student from China. Both their Chinese and English names are interesting. Please get to know them, ask the story of their names, and introduce yourself.

2. 采访 (cǎifǎng) Interview

请采访一下你的家人或中国朋友, 问问 (1) 中国的取名文化(wénhuà); (2) 家人的中文名字的故事; (3) 他们那个年代 (niándài) 中国人喜欢给孩子起什么名字? 现在呢? (4) 中国人起名字有什么禁忌 (jìnjì)。

Please interview your family or a Chinese friend and ask about (1) Chinese naming culture; (2) the story of their Chinese names; (3) what did Chinese people like to name their children in their time? What about now? and (4) any taboos in Chinese naming culture?

Part II *短文：起名字*

I. Warm-up: Pre-reading Discussion

1. 你喜欢你的名字吗 (英文名、中文名)? 为什么?
   Do you like your name? Why?
2. 你听过哪些中国的姓? 你听过两个汉字的姓吗? 有哪些?
   What Chinese last names have you heard? Have you heard any last name
   that has two characters?
3. 你知道起英文名字有哪些禁忌 (jìnjì)?
   Do you know any taboos about English names?

II. Interpretive Task: Listening Comprehension

Please listen to the text and choose True (T) or False (F) for each of the following
audio recordings of the statements.

1.(T)   2.(F)   3.(T)   4.(F)   5.(T)

　　我很喜欢我的中文名字"林约爱"。我喜欢它，因为它很特别。中国父母
常常在每个名字上花很多心思，每一个名字都有一定的意义。
　　华裔家庭希望子女继承传统文化，为子女起中、英文名字。在学校用英
文名字，在家里和长辈交流时多用中文名字。起个完美的名字并不容易。名
字不是一个简单的符号，它有很多信息。有的父母根据孩子英文名字的发音
给他们起中文名字，比如，David中文名叫大维，Kevin中文名叫凯文。我的哥
哥的中文名字叫林立，英文名字叫Alex，可是我的奶奶不喜欢哥哥的英文名
字，她说Alex听起来像"爱你克死"。
　　我的爸爸叫林伟，妈妈叫王红。爸爸说六十年代在中国出生的男性很多
叫建国、建军、伟、强，而且单名在当时比较常见。根据2019年全国姓名报
告，全中国有差不多三十万人叫张伟呢!

Naming in Chinese

I like my Chinese name, Lin Yue'ai, very much. I like it because it is very special.
Chinese parents often put a lot of effort into picking a name. Each name has certain
meanings.

Parents of Chinese Americans want their children to inherit and pass down
tradition and culture, so they will give their children a Chinese name and an
English name, then their children can use their English names at school but
use their Chinese names while talking to the elders at home. Picking a perfect
name for a child is not an easy task because a name is not simply a symbol. It
contains a lot of information. Some parents give their children Chinese names
based on their children's English names. For example, David's Chinese name
will be "Dawei". Kevin's Chinese name will be "Kaiwen". My older brother's
Chinese name is "Lin Li", and his English name is Alex. However, my grandmother does not like his English name because she said that it sounds like "Ai
Ni Ke Si".

My father's name is Lin Wei, and my mother's name is Wang Hong. Dad said that in the sixties, many boys born in China were named "Jianguo, Jianjun, Wei, or Qiang", and single-character names were very common at the time. According to the 2019 national name report, there are almost 300,000 people in China named Zhang Wei!

生词 Vocabulary

Students are required to recognize and pronounce all the vocabulary listed. For the characters/words in italics and bold, students are also expected to know how to write.

1.	喜欢	喜歡	xǐhuān	v.	like
2.	特别	特別	tèbié	adj./adv.	special; particularly
3.	花心思	花心思	huā xīnsi	v.o.	put thought/effort into
4.	每	每	měi	pron.	every; each
5.	一定的	一定的	yīdìng de	adj.	certain; particular
6.	意义	意義	yìyì	n.	meaning
7.	**华裔**	華裔	huáyì	n.	ethnic Chinese
8.	希望	希望	xīwàng	v.	hope; wish
9.	**子女**	子女	zǐnǚ	n.	children
10.	继承	繼承	jìchéng	v.	inherit
11.	传统	傳統	chuántǒng	adj./n.	traditional; tradition
12.	**文化**	文化	wénhuà	n.	culture
13.	长辈	長輩	zhǎngbèi	n.	elders
14.	交流	交流	jiāoliú	v.	communicate
15.	完美	完美	wánměi	adj.	perfect
16.	**容易**	容易	róngyì	adj.	easy
17.	简单	簡單	jiǎndān	adj.	simple
18.	符号	符號	fúhào	n.	symbol
19.	信息	信息	xìnxī	n.	information
20.	根据	根據	gēnjù	prep.	according to
21.	发音	發音	fāyīn	v.o./n.	pronounce; pronunciation
22.	**比如**	比如	bǐrú	adv.	for example

23.	听起来	聽起來	tīngqǐlái	v.	sound; 听(聽): listen to; obey; comply
24.	年代	年代	niándài	n.	age; years; time; decades
25.	**男**性	男性	nánxìng	n.	male
26.	单名	單名	dānmíng	n.	one-character name
27.	当时	當時	dāngshí	adv.	at that time
28.	比较	比較	bǐjiào	adv./v.	relatively; compare
29.	**常见**	常見	chángjiàn	adj.	common
30.	报告	報告	bàogào	n.	report
31.	全	全	quán	adv.	all
32.	差不多	差不多	chàbùduō	adv.	about; roughly
33.	万	萬	wàn	num.	ten thousand

Proper Names

1.	爱你克死	愛你克死	Àinǐkèsǐ	transliteration of Alex in Chinese; 死 sǐ means "die"
2.	建国	建國	Jiànguó	boy's name, literary meaning of "building country"
3.	建军	建軍	Jiànjūn	boy's name, literary meaning of "building army"
4.	伟	偉	Wěi	a common character used in boys' names, meaning "tall and big" or "great"

Sentence Patterns / Grammar

1. 在 ⋯⋯ 上花心思: put thought or effort into ... It is often used as "somebody在something上花心思".

中国父母常常在每个名字上花很多心思。
Chinese parents often put a lot of thought into each name.

Examples:

1) 我父母希望我在学习上花心思。
   My parents hope that I can put effort into study.
2) 老师想知道这个留学生有没有在中文学习上花心思。

The teacher wants to know whether the international student has put any effort into Chinese learning.

2. 并 + 不/没 + (verb) emphasizing a negation (usually negate the previous statement or assumption)

起个完美的名字并不容易。
It's not easy to have a perfect name.

Examples:

1) A: 你是中国人吗?
    Are you Chinese?
   B: 我并不是中国人, 我是华裔美国人。
    I'm NOT Chinese. I'm Chinese American.
2) A: 我听说他现在还常常跟朋友视频聊天, 是不是?
    I heard that he still often video-chats with friends. Is that so?
   B: 并没有, 他现在花很多心思在家庭上。
    Not really. Now he puts a lot of effort into family.

3. 根据 ⋯⋯ base on; according to; it can be used at the beginning of a sentence like "According to" (see example #2 later) or it can be used as "somebody + 根据 + something + verb + noun" (see example #1 later).

有的父母根据孩子英文名字的发音给他们起中文名字。
Some parents give their children Chinese names based on their children's English names.
根据2019年全国姓名报告, 全中国有差不多三十万人叫张伟呢!
According to the 2019 national name report, there are almost 300,000 people in China named Zhang Wei!

Examples:

1) 有的人会根据出生地给孩子起名字。
    Some will name their children based on their birth places.
2) 根据中国的传统, 人名都是姓在前, 名在后。
    According to Chinese tradition, people's family name comes first and their first name comes last.

4. verb起来

 "起来" can be used literally, like the usage of "up" in English; for example, 站(zhàn)起来 means "stand up".

 "起来" can be also used figuratively, often as a direction complement, to indicate a spontaneous action (like 哭kū, cry; 笑xiào, laugh; 唱chàng, sing; 跳tiào, dance; 聊liáo, chat) or a state (like 冷lěng, cold; 热rè hot, 好) has started and is ongoing. For example, 哭起来 (start crying); 天气热起来了(It's getting hot); 爸爸的身体好起来了 (Dad's health is getting better).

When "起来" is used with perception verbs such as 看、听、闻 (wén, smell)、摸 (mō, touch), etc., it expresses that the subject seems adjective when the action of the verb is performed.

Alex听起来像"爱你克死"。
Alex sounds like "Àinǐkèsǐ".

Examples:

1) 妈妈在电话里听起来很不高兴。
   Mom sounds very unhappy over the phone.
2) 老师看起来很累。
   The teacher looks very tired.

III. Vocabulary and Grammar Exercise

1. 你觉得大学生应该 (yīnggāi) 在下面哪些事情上多花心思? 哪些事情上少花心思或者不花心思? 为什么?

What do you think college students should put more effort into? What things do you think they should put less or little effort into? Why?

> (1) 学习　(2) 恋爱　(3) 运动　(4) 打扮 (dǎbàn, dress up)　(5) 直播(zhíbō, live streaming)　(6) 赚钱 (zhuànqián, earn money)　(7) 其他(qítā, other)事情, 比如?

2. 请用"并"造句完成对话. Please complete the dialogue with a sentence using "并".

1) 朋友:大学生活(shēnghuó, life)怎么样? 轻松(qīngsōng, relaxed and easy)吗?
   我: _____bing bù shì_____。我每天都有很多功课要做。
2) 老师:你是从美国来的, 是吗?
   留学生: _bing bù shì_ ,我是从加拿大来的。　并不是

3. 选择填空 Fill in the blanks. qǐ lái

> 听起来　　看起来　　站起来　　冷起来　　笑起来

1) 看到老师走了进来, 学生们马上 _zhàn_ 。站起来
2) 这个名字 _tīng_ 不像是中国人的名字。　听起来
3) 听完他的话, 大家 _xiào_ 。笑起来
4) 这个面包 _kàn_ 很好吃。看起来
5) 十月以后, 天气就 _lěng_ 。冷起来

4. 小作文 Short essay:

华裔父母常常希望子女怎么样? 请选用下面五个词和所有句型写一篇最少150字小作文。

What do parents of Chinese Americans often want from their children? Please write a short essay of no less than 150 characters with **all** the sentence patterns provided and **five** of the following words:

生词 (words): 继承 传统 文化 长辈 报告 交流 完美 常见 差不多
句型 (patterns): 根据 ……; 在 …… 上花心思; 因为 …… 所以 ……; 比如

IV. Post-reading Discussion

1. 六十年代流行 (liúxíng) 什么英文名字? 现在呢?
   In the sixties, what were the popular English names? How about now?
2. 你觉得孩子的名字对他的未来 (wèilái) 有影响吗? 为什么?
   Do you think the name of a child will influence his/her future? Why?
3. 你知道哪些起中文名字的禁忌 (jìnjì)?
   Do you know any taboos about Chinese names?
4. 夏小京的堂兄弟姐妹叫"夏小风、夏小雨、夏小雪、夏小晴", 他们的名字都有什么字? 你知道为什么吗?
   Xia Xiaojing's cousins from her father's side are called "Xia Xiaofeng, Xia Xiaoyu, Xia Xiaoxue, Xia Xiaoqing". Anything in common in their names? Do you know why?

V. Presentational Task

Make an e-book about your Chinese name and share it with your classmates. In your book, please include the following:

1. Meanings of each character in your name.
2. How to write your name.
3. The reason why your parents gave you this name.
4. Any nickname and why.
5. Any fun stories about your name.

Lesson Two 我是华裔美国人

Learning Objectives

In this lesson, you will learn to do the following:

1. Describe Chinese immigrants' habits.
2. Explain procedures for international travels at the airport.
3. Narrate a story of stereotyping.
4. Understand special traditions, customs, habits, and values in different cultures.
5. Discuss one's nationality and their identity development.

I. Warm-up: Pre-reading Discussion

1. 你这学期你选了几门课? 哪几门课?
   How many courses are you taking this semester? What courses?
2. 你喜欢看些什么电视节目 (diànshìjiémù)? 网络 (wǎngluò) 视频? 为什么?
   What TV programs or online videos do you like to watch and why?
3. 你可以给同学推荐 (tuījiàn) 一个比较西方和亚洲文化不同的视频吗? 这个视频在讨论什么?
   Can you recommend a video comparing Western cultures and Asian cultures to your classmates? What is this video talking about?

II. Interpretive Task: Listening Comprehension

Please listen to the lesson dialogue and choose True (T) or False (F) for each of the following audio recordings of the statements.

1.(对) 2.(对) 3.(错) 4.(错) 5.(对)

Main Text

Part I 对话： **我是华裔美国人**

Joy 这学期选了一门中文课, 同学都是华裔。今天, Joy来得很早, 碰到了同学Eric。

DOI: 10.4324/9781003352228-4

Joy: Eric, 你也来得这么早? 你在看什么? 怎么笑得那么开心?

Eric: 我在看油管 (YouTube) 视频, 讲亚洲父母的特点, 很好笑。

Joy: 是吗? 他们讲了什么?

Eric: 他们讲了亚洲妈妈喜欢用筷子打鸡蛋, 我妈妈就是这样! 虽然她移民来美国已经快二十五年了, 但是还保留了很多中国人的生活习惯。

Joy: 哈哈, 我妈妈也是! 她说不管移民来美国多久了, 她都是中国人。我妈妈常常跟我说: "虽然你是在美国出生长大的, 但是你也是中国人。你是中国北京人!" 因为中国人觉得爸爸是哪儿人, 孩子就是哪儿人。我爸爸是从北京来的。

Eric: 哦, 我是混血儿, 我妈妈是新加坡人, 我爸爸是美国人。其实我小时候不清楚自己是哪儿人。

Joy: 我小时候也跟你一样, 后来才想清楚我是中国人, 也是美国人, 我就是华裔美国人啊。

Wǒ shì huáyì Měiguórén

Joy zhè xuéqī xuǎnle yī mén Zhōngwén kè, tóngxué dōu shì huáyì. Jīntiān, Joy láide hěn zǎo, pèngdào le tóngxué Eric.

Joy: Eric, nǐ yě láide zhème zǎo? Nǐ zài kàn shénme? Zěnme xiào de nàme kāixīn?

Eric: Wǒ zài kàn Yóuguǎn (YouTube) shìpín, jiǎng yàzhōu fùmǔ de tèdiǎn, hěn hǎoxiào.

Joy: Shì ma? Tāmen jiǎngle shénme?

Eric: Tāmen jiǎngle yàzhōu māma xǐhuān yòng kuàizi dǎ jīdàn, wǒ māma jiùshì zhèyàng! Suīrán tā yímín lái Měiguó yǐjīng kuài èrshíwǔ niánle, dànshì hái bǎoliúle hěnduō Zhōngguó rén de shēnghuó xíguàn.

Joy: Hāha, wǒ māma yěshì! Tā shuō bùguǎn yímín lái Měiguó duōjiǔle, tā dōu shì Zhōngguórén. Wǒ māma chángcháng gēn wǒ shuō: "Suīrán nǐ shì zài Měiguó chūshēng zhǎngdà de, dànshì nǐ yěshì Zhōngguó rén. Nǐ shì Zhōngguó Běijīng rén!" Yīnwèi Zhōngguó rén juéde bàba shì nǎ'er rén, háizi jiùshì nǎ'er rén. Wǒ bàba shì cóng Běijīng lái de.

Eric: Ò, wǒ shì hùnxuè'ér, wǒ māma shì Xīnjiāpō rén, wǒ bàba shì Měiguó rén. Qíshí wǒ xiǎoshíhou bù qīngchǔ zìjǐ shì nǎ'er rén.

Joy: Wǒ xiǎoshíhòu yě gēn nǐ yīyàng, hòulái cái xiǎng qīngchǔ wǒ shì Zhōngguó rén, yěshì Měiguó rén, wǒ jiùshì huáyì Měiguó rén a.

生词 Vocabulary

Students are required to recognize and pronounce all the vocabulary listed. For the characters/words in italics and bold, students are also expected to know how to write.

1.	**学期**	學期	xuéqī	n.	term; semester
2.	**选**	選	xuǎn	v.	choose; pick; select
3.	**同学**	同學	tóngxué	n.	classmate
4.	碰	碰	pèng	v.	touch; bump into

5.	**开心**	開心	kāixīn	adj.	happy
6.	**讲**	講	jiǎng	v.	speak; be particular about
7.	特点	特點	tèdiǎn	n.	characteristic; trait; feature
8.	好笑	好笑	hǎoxiào	adj.	laughable; funny
9.	亚洲	亞洲	yàzhōu	n.	Asia
10.	筷子	筷子	kuàizi	n.	chopsticks
11.	**打**	打	dǎ	v.	hit; break; fight; dial
12.	鸡蛋	雞蛋	jīdàn	n.	egg
13.	虽然	雖然	suīrán	conj.	although
14.	**移民**	移民	yímín	v./n.	immigrate; immigrant
15.	保留	保留	bǎoliú	v.	keep; retain
16.	**生活**	生活	shēnghuó	n.	life
17.	**习惯**	習慣	xíguàn	n./v.	habit; be used to
18.	**不管**	不管	bùguǎn	conj.	no matter; regardless of
19.	**长大**	長大	zhǎngdà	v.	grow up
20.	混血儿	混血兒	hùnxuè'ér	n.	multiracial children
21.	其实	其實	qíshí	adv.	actually; in fact
22.	小时候	小時候	xiǎoshíhou	n.	in one's childhood
23.	清楚	清楚	qīngchǔ	adj./v.	clear; distinct; understand thoroughly; be clear about
24.	**后来**	後來	hòulái	adv.	later

Proper Names

1.		油管	油管	Yóuguǎn	YouTube
2.		新加坡	新加坡	Xīnjiāpō	Singapore

Sentence Patterns / Grammar

1. 虽然 ⋯⋯ 但是/可是 ⋯⋯ although ... yet ...

This pattern usually appears as a pair. You cannot just use 虽然 by itself.

虽然她移民来美国已经快二十五年了,但是还保留了很多中国人的生活习惯。
Although she has immigrated to the United States for almost 25 years, she still retains many Chinese habits.

Examples:

1) 虽然这个学期我很忙, 但是我还想选中文课。
   Although I am busy this semester, I still want to take Chinese.
2) 虽然我们是同学, 但是我不清楚他的中文名字是什么。
   Although we are classmates, I don't know what his Chinese name is.

2. Question pronouns as indefinite references (whoever, whatever, whenever, etc.)

A question pronoun repeated in two separate but related clauses of the same sentence forms the equivalent of the "question pronoun + -ever" expression in English. 就 jiù (then) frequently appears in the second clause.

中国人觉得爸爸是 哪儿人, 孩子就是哪儿人。
Chinese people think that wherever the father is from, the child is from.

Examples:

1) 你想吃什么, 我就吃什么。
   I'll eat whatever you want.
2) 谁的生活习惯跟我的一样, 我就选谁做室友。
   I will choose whoever has the same habits as me as my roommate.

3. 是 …… 的

To describe or inquire about the time, the place, the manner, or the initiator of an action that we know already happened, we need to use the 是 …… 的 structure. The use of 是, however, is optional.

我爸爸是从北京来的。
My father is from Beijing.

Examples:

1) 我是在美国出生长大的。
   I was born and raised in America.
2) 她的名字是她爸爸给她起的。
   It was her father who gave her the name.

4. A 跟 (gēn) B 一样 (yíyàng) + verb/adj. the same as . . .

我小时候也跟你一样 (不清楚自己是哪儿人)。
I was just like you when I was a kid (not very clear about where I was from).

Examples:

1) 她跟她的室友一样不会用筷子。
   Like her roommate, she can't use chopsticks.
2) 他们的视频跟冯氏兄弟的一样好笑。
   Their videos are as funny as the Fung Brothers'.

5. 才 cái + verb, only then; not until

The adverb 才 indicates that the occurrence of an action or situation is later than the speaker may have expected. 才 never takes the particle 了, whether or not it pertains to an action or situation in the past.

后来才想清楚我是中国人, 也是美国人, 我就是华裔美国人啊。
Not until later did I figure out that I am both Chinese and American. I am Chinese American.

Examples:

1) 已经开学一个月了, 我的室友现在才搬进宿舍。
It's been a month since school started. My roommate did not move into the dorm until now.

2) 中国有一句成语叫"三十而立", 但是我哥哥40岁才结婚生子。
There is a Chinese idiom called "a man should stand on his own feet at 30 years old", but my older brother did not marry and have children until he was 40.

III. Vocabulary and Grammar Exercise

1. Radical Recognition

Please identify the radicals of the following characters. Write down the radical and its meaning.

Examples: 好 → (女) woman

辶 1) 选 → (chuò) go   日 2) 早 → (rì) sun
扌 3) 打 → (shǒu) hand   囗 4) 国 → (wéi) enclosure
忄 5) 筷 → (xīn) heart   忄 6) 惯 → (xīn) heart
讠 7) 讲 → (yán) speech   8) 点 → (   ) _____ ?
氵 9) 清 → (shuǐ) water   10) 美 → (   ) _____ ?

2. Word-building Exercises

For each of the characters in the next example, write three more words that include that character.

1) 同: 同学 bù tóng tóng yì tóng shì   不同 同意 同事
2) 心: 开心 xīn lǐ dān xīn fàng xīn   心里 担心 放心
3) 点: 特点 yì diǎn diǎn píng wǔ diǎn   一点 点评 五点
4) 子: 筷子 hái zi mào zi píng zi
5) 生: 生活 chū shēng shēng mìng shēng cí

孩子 帽子 瓶子 出生 生命 生词

3. Matching Exercise: Please match Pinyin and characters

1. 选
2. 学期
3. 特点
4. 好笑
5. 移民
6. 保留
7. 生活
8. 习惯
9. 出生
10. 清楚

a. qīngchǔ
b. yímín
c. shēnghuó
d. tèdiǎn
e. xuǎn
f. hǎoxiào
g. xíguàn
h. bǎoliú
i. xuéqī
j. chūshēng

4. Fill in the blanks with the appropriate words

| 混血儿 | 特点 | 习惯 | 筷子 | 清楚 | 保留 | 跟 | 长大 | 移民 |

1) 冯氏兄弟 (Fung Brothers) 的油管视频讲了亚洲父母的 *tè diǎn* ，比如，用 *kuài zi* 打鸡蛋。他们讲了很多亚洲妈妈虽然 *yí mín* 来美国二十几年了，但是还 *bǎo liú* 了很多中国人的生活 *xí guàn* 。

2) Eric妈妈是中国人，爸爸是美国人，所以他是一个 *hùn xuè er* 。小时候他不 *qīng chǔ* 自己是哪儿人。Joy小时候 *gēn* Eric一样，不知道自己是哪儿人。Joy妈妈觉得虽然 Joy是在美国出生 *zhǎng dà* 的，但是她是中国人。

5. Complete the following sentences with the given correlatives and words

1) 虽然 …… 但是

   a. 虽然我已经是大学四年级的学生了，但是我还不 ___习惯___ (习惯)。

   b. 虽然大学第一天我认识了很多朋友，但是___清楚___(清楚)。

2) Question pronouns as indefinite references (whoever, whatever, whenever, etc.)

   a. 选课
   Eric: Joy, 你这个学期想选什么课?
   Joy: 哪门课容易，我就 ___选了___ 。

   b. 视频聊天
   爸爸: Joy, 你今天几点跟我们视频聊天?
   Joy: 您跟妈妈___选吧___，我就什么时候跟你们视频。

3) 是 …… 的
   Joy是华裔美国人，她 __出生长大__ 在美国 (出生长大)。她的中文名字叫林约爱。这个名字 __爸妈起了__ (起)，因为他们 __在NY谈恋爱__ (谈恋爱)，所以给她起了这个名字。

4) A跟B一样

Example:

我姐姐是在美国出生的, 我也是在美国出生的。

→我跟我姐姐一样是在美国出生的。

    a. 大一的学生住在学校的宿舍, 大二的学生也住在学校的宿舍。

    →_____ 。

    b. 请你选一个人 (比如室友、兄弟姐妹), 比一比, 你们一样还是不一样?

一样	不一样
e.g., 我跟我的室友一样喜欢看冯氏兄弟的油管视频。	e.g., 我的生活习惯跟我室友的不一样。我喜欢早起,她喜欢晚起。

5) 才

	学了第一课以后才知道:
我一直不知道中国的起名文化,	a. 名字里可能会有地名。
	b.
	c.

IV. Post-reading Discussion

1. 你的父母跟Joy的妈妈一样, 保留了很多中国人的生活习惯吗? 请举例。
    Like Joy's mother, do your parents keep a lot of Chinese habits? Please give examples.
2. 你的父母跟Joy的妈妈有一样的想法吗?
    Do your parents have the same idea as Joy's mother?

    a.   不管移民来美国多久, 我都是中国人。
    No matter how long I immigrated to America, I am Chinese.

    b.   虽然你是在美国出生长大的, 但是你也是中国人!
    Although you were born and raised in America, you are also Chinese!

    c.   爸爸是哪儿人, 孩子就是哪儿人。
    Where the father is from, the child is from.

    d.   Your answer _____

3. 你跟Joy或者Eric有一样的经历吗? 你小时候就很清楚自己是哪儿人吗? 现在呢?
    Do you have the same experience as Joy or Eric? Did you know exactly where you came from when you were a kid? And now?
4. 你的文化中, 有没有什么特别的生活习惯, 请举例。
    Is there any unique custom in your culture? Please give examples.

V. Interpersonal Tasks

1. 小组讨论 (xiǎozǔ tǎolùn) Group Discussion

请你和你的组员讨论一些亚洲家庭的生活习惯，你的爸爸妈妈、家人或中国朋友会做以下哪些事？他们为什么这么做？

Please discuss some habits of Asian families with your team members. Which of the following things will your parents, family members, or Chinese friends do? Why are they doing this?

a.   用筷子打鸡蛋
     Whip eggs with chopsticks.
b.   进屋子脱鞋 (tuōxié)
     Take off shoes in the house.
c.   不用洗碗机 (xǐwǎnjī)
     Never use the dishwasher.
d.   家里有钢琴 (gāngqín)
     There is a piano at home.
e.   喜欢喝 (hē) 热水
     Like drinking hot water.
f.   炉台包锡箔纸 (lútái bāo xǐbó zhǐ)
     Protect the gas range with aluminum foil.
g.   孩子学习乐器 (yuèqì)
     Children learn musical instruments.
h.   晚上洗澡 (xǐzǎo)
     Take shower at night.
i.   收集 (shōují) 超市 (chāoshì) 的塑料袋 (sùliàodài)，再次使用
     Collect plastic bags from supermarkets and reuse them.

除了以上，请再讨论其他答案。Please discuss other answers besides those in the list in the previous section.

2. 采访 (cǎifǎng) Interview

请采访一个来自其他文化的朋友，问问他们有什么特别的传统、方言口音、习俗和生活习惯或价值观念，并在班上做一个3分钟的简介。

Please interview a friend of another culture and ask about their special traditions, regional varieties of their language, accents, customs, habits, or values. And give a three-minute introduction in class.

Part II 短文：在机场

I. Warm-up: Pre-reading Discussion

1.   有人问过你是哪儿人吗？你是怎么回答的？
     Has anyone asked where you are from? How did you answer this question?

2. 在机场安检的时候, 安检人员会检查 (jiǎnchá) 什么?
   At the airport security, what will the security personnel check?
3. 你觉得谁可以算是 "美国人"?
   Who do you think can be regarded as "American"?

II. Interpretive Task: Listening Comprehension

Please listen to the text and choose True (T) or False (F) for each of the following audio recordings of the statements.

1. (错)　2. (错)　3. (对)　4. (错)　5. (对)

　　有一年, 我拉着行李箱在芝加哥机场排队过安检。到我的时候, 我赶紧把护照和机票递给安检人员。"早上好。" 我用英语跟他打招呼。安检人员用外语回复了我。我以为他说的是日语, 所以告诉他我不是日本人。

　　"我说的是韩语。你是韩国人吗?" 安检人员问。

　　"不是!"

　　"那你是哪儿人? " 他又问。

　　这不是我第一次碰到这样的问题, 我有点儿生气, 但是为了快点儿过安检, 我给了他他想要的答案: "我是中国人。"

　　"你好。" 他又用中文跟我打招呼。

　　"你好。" 我叹了口气。

　　太奇怪了! 我给他看的是美国护照, 跟他说的是英语, 坐的是美国国内航班, 为什么他不用英语跟我打招呼? 为什么他以为我是韩国人? 亚洲人看起来都一样吗? 在他看来, 谁可以算是 "美国人" ?

At the Airport

One year, I queued through the security check at the Chicago airport with my suitcase. When it was my turn, I quickly handed my passport and ticket to the security staff. "Good morning," I greeted him in English. The security officer replied to me in a foreign language. I thought he spoke Japanese, so I told him I was not Japanese.

"I speak Korean. Are you Korean?" the security officer asked.

"No!"

"Then where are you from?" he asked again.

This is not the first time I have encountered such a question. I was a little angry, but in order to get through the security check quickly, I gave him the answer he wanted: "I am Chinese."

"Hello." He greeted me again in Chinese.

"Hello." I sighed.

That's weird! I showed him an American passport, spoke English to him, and took a domestic flight in the United States. Why didn't he greet me in English? Why did he think I'm Korean? Do Asians all look the same? In his opinion, who can be regarded as an "American"?

生词 Vocabulary

Students are required to recognize and pronounce all the vocabulary listed. For the characters/words in italics and bold, students are also expected to know how to write.

1.	拉	拉	lā	v.	pull
2.	**行李**箱	行李箱	xínglixiāng	n.	luggage; baggage
3.	机场	機場	jīchǎng	n.	airport
4.	排队	排隊	páiduì	v.o.	stand in line
5.	安检	安檢	ānjiǎn	n./v.	security check
6.	赶紧	趕緊	gǎnjǐn	adv.	hurriedly
7.	护照	護照	hùzhào	n.	passport
8.	机票	機票	jīpiào	n.	plane ticket
9.	人员	人員	rényuán	n.	personnel
10.	打招呼	打招呼	dǎ zhāohu	v.o.	say hello
11.	回复	回覆	huífù	v.	reply
12.	**以为**	以為	yǐwéi	v.	think; believe; consider erroneously
13.	**告诉**	告訴	gàosu	v.	tell; inform
14.	**问题**	問題	wèntí	n.	question; problem
15.	有点儿	有點兒	yǒudiǎnr	adv.	a little; somewhat; a bit
16.	**生气**	生氣	shēngqì	v.o.	get angry
17.	想要	想要	xiǎngyào	v.	intend; want
18.	答案	答案	dá'àn	n.	answer
19.	奇怪	奇怪	qíguài	adj.	strange

20.	国内	國內	guónèi	n./adj.	interior of country; domestic
21.	航班	航班	hángbān	n.	flight
22.	算	算	suàn	v.	calculate; consider; count as

Proper Names

1.	芝加哥	芝加哥	Zhījiāgē	Chicago
2.	**日本**	日本	Rìběn	Japan
3.	韩国	韓國	Hánguó	Korea
4.	**英**/日/韩+**语**	英/日/韓+語	Yīng/Rì/Hán + yǔ	English/ Japanese/Korean language

Sentence Patterns / Grammar

1. V1着 ······ + V2   Doing V1 and V2 at the same time.

This pattern is used for describing how to carry out the main action. V2 is the focused action in this pattern, and V1 is more about describing how you carry out the focused action, such as doing something sitting down, standing, lying down, and so on.

我拉着行李箱在芝加哥机场排队过安检。
I am in line for the security check with my luggage at the Chicago airport.
Examples:

1) 他们坐 (zuò) 着聊天。
   They are chatting while sitting down.
2) 我喜欢躺 (tǎng) 着看书。
   I like to read while lying down.
3) 我_____手机 (shǒujī)_____。
   I am waiting in line while checking my cell phone (kàn shǒujī).

Describe the following pictures with V1着 ······ + V2

a. The teacher

Figure 27 Teaching

b. The students

Figure 28 Reading

c. This person

Figure 29 Singing in shower

c. This person

Figure 30 Running

2. 把(bǎ) + O + V + complement do an action to the object

Negation form 没/别/不要/不想/不会 ⋯⋯ + 把 (bǎ) + O + V + complement
This pattern is unique to the Chinese language, and there is no equivalent counterpart in English. The primary purpose is to focus on one particular object/matter and to emphasize the effects of an action on its object. 把sentence cannot end the sentence with a single verb. The verb has to be followed by nouns, phrases, or complements. The object after 把 has to be a definite thing that is known to both speaker and listener. For the negation, 没/别/不要/不想/不会 ⋯⋯ has to go before 把, **NOT before the verb.**

我赶紧把护照和机票递给 (dìgěi) 安检人员。
I quickly gave my passport and tickets to the security check personnel.

Examples:

1) 我把功课 (gōngkè) 写完 (wán) 了。
   I finished writing my homework.
2) 我把这个汉字写在手上了。
   I wrote this character on my hand.

3. 为 (wèi)了 + purpose . . . In order to . . .

This pattern is usually used to express a purpose of doing something and often is placed at the beginning of the sentence.

为了快点儿过安检, 我给了他他想要的答案。
In order to pass the security check quickly, I gave him the answer that he wanted.

Example:

1) 为了去中国工作 (gōngzuò), 我现在 (xiànzài) 每天都好好学习 (xí) 中文。
   In order to go to China to work, I now study Chinese hard every day.
2) 为了上中国的好大学, 中国高中生每天都努力 (nǔlì) 学习。
   In order to get into good colleges in China, Chinese high schoolers study hard every day.

4. someone V 的 Noun

In Chinese language, the relative clause structure in English grammar, such as which, what, that, where and who, is expressed with 的 in Chinese. Words and phrases that go before 的 are considered as modifiers, and the noun right after 的 is the object that being modified. This structure is frequently used in the Chinese language. "someone V 的 Noun" can be used as both a subject and an object in a sentence. See examples:

我给了他他想要的答案。
I gave him the answer that he wanted.

Example:

1) 在说话 (shuōhuà) 的人是我的妈妈。
   The person who is speaking now is my mother.
2) 我的妈妈是那个在说话 (shuōhuà) 的人。
   My mother is the person who is speaking now.
3) Transcribe the following into Pinyin or characters.

   a. The person who wears red top (yīfu).
   b. The place I like to go the most.
   c. The drink that I dislike to drink the most.
   d. The languages that I know how to speak.

5. 在 someone 看来 as far as someone is concerned; in someone's view

There are many ways to express the idea of "someone's view". In later lessons, we will encounter another way to express the same idea. While the English translation could be the same, this pattern is more about expressing an opinion of things, and these things are not necessarily personal to the speaker's experience.

在他看来, 谁可以算是"美国人"?
In his view, who can be considered to be "American"?

Example:

1) 在我看来, 华裔美国人也应该 (yīnggāi) 有中文名字。
   In my view, Chinese Americans should also have Chinese names.
2) 在我妈妈看来, 跟容易生气的人谈恋爱不好。
   As far as my mother is concerned, being in a relationship with someone who gets angry easily is not a good idea.

6. 以为 "think something mistakenly"

Different from English, Chinese has a specific verb for the concept of "I mistakenly thought".

人家问我要不要"cash back", 我还以为人家要给我钱 (qián) 呢!
When I paid in the supermarket, people asked me if I wanted to "cash back". I thought they were going to give me money!

Examples:

1) 她是你妈妈? 我以为她是你姐姐呢!
   Is she your mother? I thought she was your sister!
2) 你喜欢吃米饭? 我以为你喜欢吃面条呢!
   Do you like rice? I thought you liked noodles!

III. Vocabulary and Grammar Exercise

1. Make at least five sentences with the characters provided. You can use the same character repeatedly as long as you use 15 different characters in total.

我	告	很	日	学
以	常	认	想	是
问	人	生	欢	为
识	话	他	家	本
气	喜	题	说	诉

Example: 我喜欢他。

1)
2)
3)
4)
5)

2. 填空 Fill in the blanks with the provided words.

> 长大 答案 生气 清楚 算 告诉 以为 站着 问题 奇怪

我的室友_____我一个故事。有一天,她_____排队的时候,有一个人问她是哪里人? 她就回复"美国人。" 可是问_____的人还是问她 "你是哪里人?" 她就说 "我家在芝加哥。" 那个人_____我的室友没听_____, 又 (yòu) 问了一次。我的室友就_____地说: "我就是美国芝加哥人,你想要什么_____?" 我也常碰到这样_____的事。我想在美国出生_____的人,如果不是美国人,那_____是哪里人呀?

3. Use "把(bǎ) + O + V+ complement" structure to describe following tasks in full sentences in Pinyin or characters:

Example:

I finished writing <u>my homework</u>.
Wǒ bǎ <u>gōngkè</u> xiě wán le.   我把<u>功课</u>写完了。

1) I finished eating <u>all the dishes</u> (cài) that my mom made.
2) I finished doing <u>my laundry</u> (yīfu).
3) Don't eat <u>my food</u>!
4) I finished cooking <u>dinner</u>.
5) Give the teacher <u>your homework</u>.

4. 小作文 Short essay:

Rewrite the text 在机场 into a coherent narrative paragraph of no less than 150 characters. Please include all the provided patterns in your paragraph.

为了……;　　　　在someone看来;　　　虽然…… 但是……;

因为……, 所以;　　不管…… 都……

IV. Post-reading Discussion

1. 当有人问你是哪儿人的时候, 你有什么感觉 (gǎnjué)? 还有哪些问题会让 (ràng) 你有一样的感觉 (gǎnjué)?
    How do you feel when someone asks where you are from? What other questions will make you feel the same way?
2. 你觉得为什么有人会问你是哪儿人?
    Why do you think someone will ask where you are from?
3. 如果你是作者, 过安检的时候, 你会怎么回答安检人员的问题?
    If you were the author, how would you answer the security inspector's question when going through the security check?
4. 你觉得, 在课文里的安检人员看来, 谁可以算是美国人? 你同意 (tóngyì) 他/她的看法吗?为什么?
    In your opinion, who can be regarded as an American by the security officer in the text? Do you agree with him/her? Why?

V. Interpersonal Tasks

1. 角色扮演 (juésè bànyǎn) Role-play

两人一组, 一位是机场的安检人员, 一位是华裔美国人。把短文里的故事表 演出来。
Please work in pairs, one as the security officer at the airport and the other as the Chinese American, and act out the story in the lesson text.

2. 采访 (cǎifǎng) Interview

请采访一下你的家人, 问问他们 (1) 谁可以算是美国人? 为什么?(2) 如果有人 问他们是从哪儿来的, 他们会怎么回答? 为什么? (3) 目前华裔/亚裔(yàyì)美 国人在美国面临 (miànlín) 哪些挑战 (tiǎozhàn) ? (4) 如果要用一个词 (cí, word) 来形容 (xíngróng) 他们对自己双重身份 (shuāngchóngshēnfèn) 的感觉 (gǎnjué), 他们会用哪一个词 (cí, word)? 为什么?
Please interview your family and ask them (1) Who can be considered an American? Why? (2) If someone asked where they came from, how would they respond? Why? (3) What challenges do Chinese/Asian Americans currently face in the United States? (4) If they were to use one word to describe their feelings about their dual identities, which word would they use? Why?

VI. Presentational Task

写一篇350字左右的文章或者准备一个3-5分钟的口头报告, 分享 (fēnxiǎng) 一下你对家人的采访结果 (jiéguǒ) 以及自己的反思 (fǎnsī)。

Write an essay of about 350 characters or prepare a three- to five-minute oral report to share the results of your interviews with your family and your own reflections.

Unit Two
家庭语言

Lesson Three 我家的方言

Learning Objectives

In this lesson, you will learn to do the following:

1. Describe the languages and regional varieties spoken in your family.
2. Explain the reasons for the maintenance of the regional varieties of a language.
3. Narrate a personal travel experience.
4. Discuss the different roles of Mandarin and other varieties in China.
5. Differentiate "regional varieties of a language" and "accent".

I. Warm-up: Pre-reading Discussion

1. 你会说哪几种语言？你的家人呢？
   What languages do you speak? What about your family members?
2. 你的家人会说什么方言？你听得懂吗？你会说吗？
   What varieties of Chinese does your family speak? Can you understand it?
   Can you speak?
3. 你跟你的家人用什么语言交流？
   In what languages do you communicate with your family?

II. Interpretive Task: Listening Comprehension

Please listen to the lesson dialogue and choose True (T) or False (F) for each of the following audio recordings of the statements.

1. (错) 2. (错) 3. (对) 4. (错) 5. (对)

Main Text

Part I 对话： *我家的方言*

Joy： 爸爸，你的普通话跟妈妈的有点不一样，为什么？还有，妈妈跟小姨说的上海话，我也听不懂。

DOI: 10.4324/9781003352228-6

爸爸: 哦, 我是北京人, 北京话跟普通话非常像呀! 妈妈是上海人, 所以她说
　　　　普通话的口音不太一样。
Joy: 上海人说普通话跟北京人有什么不同?
爸爸: 上海话是个方言, 中国的方言多得不得了, 也很不同, 两个说不同方言
　　　　的人常常互相听不懂, 所以得用普通话交流呀, 也因为这样, 每个地方
　　　　的人说的普通话会有那个地方的口音。上海话里没有翘舌音, 所以
　　　　"zh、ch、sh、r 跟z、c、s" 不分。
Joy: 怪不得! 上次妈妈送朋友出门时, 我在里面听到妈妈大声地跟朋友
　　　　说: "你要死掉了!" 后来听到她的朋友说: "谢谢。" 我觉得奇怪极
　　　　了! 妈妈进来时, 看着糊里糊涂的我, 她只说了一个词 "Key"。
爸爸: 哈哈! 妈妈说的是 "你钥匙掉了。"
Joy: 哦, 原来是这样!

Wǒ jiā de fāngyán

Joy: Bàba, nǐ de pǔtōnghuà gēn māma de yǒudiǎn bù yīyàng, wèishéme? Hái yǒu, māma gēn xiǎoyí shuō de Shànghǎi huà, wǒ yě tīng bù dǒng.

Bàba: Ò, wǒ shì Běijīngrén, Běijīnghuà gēn pǔtōnghuà fēicháng xiàng ya. Māma shì Shànghǎi rén, suǒyǐ tā shuō pǔtōnghuà de kǒuyīn bù tài yīyàng.

Joy: Shànghǎirén shuō pǔtōnghuà gēn Běijīngrén yǒu shénme bùtóng?

Bàba: Shànghǎi huà shìge fāngyán, Zhōngguó de fāngyán duō de bùdéliǎo, yě hěn bùtóng, liǎng gè shuō bùtóng fāngyán de rén chángcháng hùxiāng tīng bù dǒng, suǒyǐ děi yòng pǔtōnghuà jiāoliú ya, yě yīnwèi zhèyàng, měi gè dìfāng de rén shuō de pǔtōnghuà huì yǒu nàgè dìfāng de kǒuyīn. Shànghǎi huà lǐ méiyǒu qiàoshéyīn, suǒyǐ "zh, ch, sh, r" gēn "z, c, s" bù fēn.

Joy: Guàibùdé! Shàngcì māma sòng péngyou chūmén shí, wǒ zài lǐmiàn tīng dào māma dàshēng de gēn péngyou shuō "nǐ yào sǐdiào le!" Hòulái tīngdào tā de péngyou shuō "xièxiè." Wǒ juédé qíguài jíle! Māma jìnlái shí, kànzhe húlihútú de wǒ, tā zhǐ shuōle yīgè cí "Key".

Bàba: Hāha! Māma shuō de shì "nǐ yàoshi diàole".

Joy: Ò, yuánlái shì zhèyàng!

生词 Vocabulary

Students are required to recognize and pronounce all the vocabulary listed. For the characters/words in italics and bold, students are also expected to know how to write.

1.	**语言**	語言	yǔyán	n.	language
2.	**普通话**	普通話	pǔtōnghuà	n.	Putonghua; Mandarin
3.	小姨	小姨	xiǎoyí	n.	mother's youngest sister

4.	上海话	上海話	Shànghǎi huà	n.	Shanghai dialect
5.	听到	聽到	tīngdào	v.	hear
6.	**懂**	懂	dǒng	v.	understand; know
7.	**非常**	非常	fēicháng	adv.	very
8.	口音	口音	kǒuyīn	n.	accent
9.	方言	方言	fāngyán	n.	regional varieties of Chinese
10.	互相	互相	hùxiāng	adv.	each other; mutually; mutual
11.	地方	地方	dìfāng	n.	local; locality
12.	怪不得	怪不得	guàibùdé	adv.	no wonder; so that's why; that explains why
13.	翘舌音	翹舌音	qiàoshéyīn	n.	retroflex; zh, chi, shi Some people say 卷舌音 juǎnshéyīn
14.	掉	掉	diào	adv./v.	drop; fall; V+掉; indicates that the position moves or disappears
15.	死掉	死掉	sǐ diào	v.	die; kick the bucket
16.	糊里糊涂	糊里糊塗	húlihútú	adj.	The mind is in a vague state; muddle-headed
17.	词	詞	cí	n.	word
18.	钥匙	鑰匙	yàoshi	n.	key
19.	**原来**	原來	yuánlái	adj./adv.	original; originally; 原来是这样 = I see

Proper Names

1.	上海人	上海人	Shànghǎi rén	Shanghainese; Shanghai people

Sentence Patterns / Grammar

1. 有(一)点 + adj. : a bit adj. (imply something negative)

In spoken Chinese, the "一" in 有一点 (yǒuyīdiǎn) is often dropped, leaving 有点 (yǒudiǎn). In northern China, that's usually pronounced 有点儿 (yǒudiǎnr).

爸爸的普通话和妈妈的有一点不一样。
My father's Mandarin is a little different from my mother's.

Examples:

1) 我对这里的服务 (fúwù) 有一点不满意 (mǎnyì)。
   I'm a little dissatisfied with the service here.
2) 住学校宿舍有点不方便 (fāngbiàn), 寒假 (hánjià) 得 (děi) 搬出去。
   It's a little inconvenient to live in the school dormitory. You have to move out during the winter break.

2. Verb 得/不 + Verb (potential complement): can/cannot verb. This pattern indicates whether or not an action is possible.

我一句都听不懂。
I cannot understand even one sentence.

听得懂; 听不懂 can/cannot understand
睡 (shuì) 得着 (zháo); 睡不着 can/cannot fall asleep
听得到; 听不到 can/cannot hear
拿得动; 拿不动 can/cannot hold

Examples:

1) 上海话我听不太懂。
   I cannot quite understand Shanghainese.
2) 外面太吵了, 我睡不着。
   It's so noisy outside that I cannot fall asleep.

3. 互相 + verb (the verb should be at least two syllables): verb back and forth action

Usually 互相 (hùxiāng) is used with two-syllable words, and for one-syllable words, some other information will be added after the verb to make it sound more natural, such as 互相看了一眼 (glanced at each other).

两个说不同方言的人常常互相听不懂。
Two people who speak different dialects often can't understand each other.

Examples:

1) 朋友应该 (yīnggāi) 互相帮助 (bāngzhù)。
   Friends should help each other.
2) 夫妻 (fūqī) 应该 (yīnggāi) 在生活上互相扶持 (fúchí)。
   A married couple should support each other in life.

4. A跟B不同 (tóng)：not as same as

上海人说普通话跟北京人有什么不同?
What's the difference between Shanghainese speaking Mandarin and Beijingers?

Examples:

1) 美国现在的经济 (jīngjì) 跟疫情 (yìqíng) 以前不同了。
   The American economy is different from before the pandemic.

2) 我的室友和我的生活习惯有很大的不同。
   My roommate and I have very different living habits.

5. **adj/stative verb 得+不得了: extremely adj.** It is usually used to imply that the situation is serious or may lead to terrible consequences. But it may also be used in a positive sense, e.g., 高兴得不得了。

中国的方言多得不得了！
There are so many dialects in China!

Examples:

1) 听说儿子又和同学打架 (dǎjià) 了，爸爸气得不得了！
   When the father heard that his son was fighting with his classmates again, he was furious!
2) 最近功课好多，忙得不得了。
   Recently, I have a lot of homework and am extremely busy.
3) 她的好朋友没跟她打招呼，_____(生气)。
4) 路上车太多 _____ (堵 dǔ, be traffic-jammed)。

6. **adj + 地 + verb**

The word "de" is usually placed after adjectives in order to turn them into adverbs. It is most like the suffix "–ly" in English. The adjective usually has more than one syllable. If it is a one-syllable adjective, it needs to be repeated, such as 慢慢地. Also, "一 measure word 一 measure word" phrase is often used with 地, such as 一天一天地长大.

我在里面听到妈妈大声地跟朋友说："你要死掉了。"
I was inside the room and heard my mother say loudly to her friends, "You are going to die."

Examples:

1) 他慢慢地吃妈妈做的早饭。
   He ate the breakfast his mother made slowly.
2) 他认真 (rènzhēn) 地学习。
   He is studying hard.

7. **后来： later on, used in the past event**

后来听到她的朋友说："谢谢。"
Then I heard her friend say, "Thank you."

Examples:

1) 后来他们谁也不理 (lǐ) 谁了。
   Later, they didn't talk to each other.
2) 后来，"排华法案 (Pái huá fǎ'àn)" 在1943年废除 (fèichú) 了。
   Later, the "Chinese Exclusion Act" was repealed in 1943.

III. Vocabulary and Grammar Exercise

1. Radical Recognition

Please identify the radicals of the following characters. Write down the radical and its meaning.

Examples: 好 → (女) <u>woman</u>

氵 1) 海 → (shuǐ) <u>water</u>　　　　口 2) 听 → (kǒu) <u>mouth</u>

女 3) 姨 → (nǚ) <u>woman</u>　　　　讠 4) 话 → (yán) <u>speech</u>

讠 5) 语 → (yán) <u>speech</u>　　　　忄 6) 懂 → (xīn) <u>heart</u>

厂 7) 原 → (chǎng) <u>cliff</u>　　　　日 8) 普 → (rì) <u>sun</u>

讠 9) 词 → (yán) <u>speech</u>　　　　忄 10) 怪 → (xīn) <u>heart</u>

日 11) 音 → (rì) <u>sun</u>　　　　月 12) 钥 → (yuè) <u>moon</u>

口 13) 奇 → (kǒu) <u>mouth</u>　　　　辶 14) 通 → (chuò) <u>go</u>

氵 15) 流 → (shuǐ) <u>water</u>

2. Word-building Exercises

For each of the characters in the next example, please write three more words that include that character.

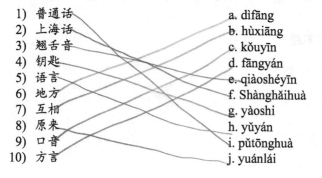

1) 姨: 小姨 <u>yí mā　yí fū　yí pó</u>　　姨妈 姨夫 姨婆
2) 话: 上海话 <u>shuō huà tīng huà jiǎ huà</u>　说话 听话 假话
3) 语: 语言 <u>hàn yǔ yīng yǔ yǔ fǎ</u>　汉语 英语 语法
4) 流: 交流 <u>liú xíng liú dòng liú chéng</u>　流行 流动 流程
5) 言: 方言 <u>yán lùn yán shuō fā yán</u>　言论 言说 发言

3. Matching Exercise: Please match Pinyin and characters

1) 普通话　　　　　　a. dìfāng
2) 上海话　　　　　　b. hùxiāng
3) 翘舌音　　　　　　c. kǒuyīn
4) 钥匙　　　　　　　d. fāngyán
5) 语言　　　　　　　e. qiàoshéyīn
6) 地方　　　　　　　f. Shànghǎihuà
7) 互相　　　　　　　g. yàoshi
8) 原来　　　　　　　h. yǔyán
9) 口音　　　　　　　i. pǔtōnghuà
10) 方言　　　　　　　j. yuánlái

4. Fill in the blanks with appropriate words

> 互相　方言　听不懂　听得懂　翘舌音　北京话　语言　上海话　普通话　口音

1) 中国是一个多<u>方言</u>的国家，两个不同地方的人常常因为<u>听不懂</u>不能<u>互相</u>交流。

2) <u>北京话</u>和<u>上海语</u>都是中国的方言，<u>普通话</u>是中国人用得最多的语言，我们在美国学中文，学的就是普通话。

3) 北京话和上海话好像 (hǎoxiàng, seems) 是不同的<u>语言</u>，北京话有很多<u>翘舌音</u>，但是上海话没有。有些说方言的人说普通话有<u>口音</u>，但是可以<u>听得懂</u>。

5. Complete the following sentences with the given correlatives and words

1) 有(一)点 + adj. imply something negative

Examples:

有(一)点儿不一样 = a little different
有(一)点儿累 (lèi) = a little tired
有(一)点儿难 (nán) = a little difficult
有(一)点儿乱 (luàn) = a little messy
有(一)点儿冷 (lěng) = a little cold

有一点儿乱
有一点儿难
有一点儿冷

a. 我的宿舍 *yǒu yī diǎn er luàn*。
b. 上大学的中文课 *yǒu yī diǎn er nán*。
c. 纽约的冬天 (dōngtiān, winter) *yǒu yī diǎn er lěng*。
d. Your sentence: *wǒ jīn tiān yǒu yī diǎn er lèi*。

2) adj/stative verb 得 + 不得了

我今天有一点儿累

Examples:

后悔 (hòuhuǐ, regret) + 得不得了
爱 + 得不得了
喜欢 + 得不得了
羡慕 (xiànmù) + 得不得了
担心 + 得不得了
佩服 (pèifú, admire) + 得不得了

爱得不得了

a. 我们全家对刚出生的小狗拉布拉多犬(Labrador Retriever) _____。
b. 昨天室友Covid-19 检测结果 (jiǎncè jiéguǒ, test result) 是阳性 (yángxìng, positive), _____。
c. 我期中考试中文考了100分, _____。
d. Your sentence _____。

IV. Post-reading Discussion

1. 除了中国,还有很多地方(比如: 印尼Yìnní、新加坡)也说华语。你知道还有哪些地方说华语吗? 他们说的华语跟中国的普通话有什么不同? 请举例。
   Besides China, there are many places (such as Indonesia and Singapore) where Chinese is spoken. Do you know where else Chinese is spoken? What's the difference between their Chinese and Mandarin spoken in China? Please give an example.

2. 中国的方言多得不得了,别的国家呢? 请问一下其他国家的同学。
   In terms of language, there are so many regional varieties in China. What about other countries? Please ask students from other countries.

3. 跟你的家人或中国朋友学用方言说一个词或者一句话,请上课的时候教你的同学。
   Please learn from your family or Chinese friends to say a word or a sentence in their regional variety of Chinese and teach your classmates in class.

4. 请跟你的同学分享一个说普通话的好玩儿的经历。
   Please share with your classmates a fun experience of speaking Mandarin.

V. Interpersonal Tasks

1. 两两对话 (liǎngliǎng duìhuà) Pair-work

两个人一起,请说说你家的语言使用 (shǐyòng) 情况 (qíngkuàng)。
比如, 你们的家人都会说方言吗? 会说什么方言? 他们什么时候说方言? 什么时候说普通话? 他们说的普通话有口音吗? 你跟他们用什么语言交流? 你说话有口音吗? 你们对口音有什么看法? 你们自己的问题。
For example, do all your families speak regional varieties of Chinese? What varieties can they speak? When do they speak varieties of Chinese? When do they speak Mandarin? Do they speak Mandarin with an accent? In what languages do you communicate with them? Do you speak with an accent? What is your opinion of speaking Mandarin with an accent? Ask additional questions of your choice.

2. 采访 (cǎifǎng) Interview

请采访一个中国留学生,问问他/她 (1)听得懂什么方言? 会说什么方言? (2) 小时候是怎么学习普通话的? (3) 说的方言有什么特点? (4) 说普通话有口音吗? 他/她的家人呢? (5) 跟家人用方言还是普通话交流? (6) 对口音有什么看法? (7) 你自己的问题。
Please interview a Chinese international student and discuss the following: (1) What regional varieties of Chinese can they understand? What regional varieties of Chinese can they speak? (2) How did they learn Mandarin when they were a child? (3) What are the characteristics of the regional varieties of Chinese that they speak? (4) Does their Mandarin have an accent? What about their family? (5) Do they communicate with their family in regional varieties or Mandarin? (6) What do they think of speaking Mandarin with an accent? (7) Ask additional questions of your choice.

Part II 短文: 我的家庭语言

I. Warm-up: Pre-reading Discussion

1. 你去过中国吗? 记得什么吗? 如果你没去过, 你想去中国什么地方? 为什么?

   Have you been to China? What do you remember about it? If you have not been there, where in China would you like to go? Why?

2. 你想在什么季节去中国? 为什么?

   In what season would you like to go to China? Why?

3. 你觉得到了中国以后, 什么事会让你不习惯? 为什么?

   What challenges would you encounter after you arrive in China? Why?

II. Interpretive Task: Listening Comprehension

Please listen to the text and choose True (T) or False (F) for each of the following audio recordings of the statements.

1. (错) 2. (错) 3. (错) 4. (错) 5. (对)

　　我爸爸是北京人, 妈妈是上海人, 所以在家我们说普通话。可是从小到大, 我跟哥哥在一起时都说英文, 我们觉得用英文更清楚、更方便。我记得小时候, 有一年冬天跟着妈妈去上海过春节, 刚开始很不习惯。一方面, 当时外公家没有暖气, 冷得不得了。另一方面, 妈妈一家人在一起的时候都说上海话。有的时候, 还指着我说话, 可是我一句都听不懂。虽然他们跟我说话的时候, 说的是普通话, 可是我还是有很多听不懂的地方, 每次都得问妈妈。后来, 我发现在街上说上海话的人很多, 但是也会听到各种口音的普通话。

　　在上海, 我吃了好多好吃的东西, 妈妈的一家人也很照顾我, 很关心我吃得好不好, 玩得高兴不高兴, 所以那次去上海我还是很开心的。回来以后, 我一直忘不了上海话。中文老师教我们说标准的普通话, 可是其实在中国, 大家的普通话都有口音。虽然现在上海话我还是听不太懂, 不过我对上海话的感觉已经不太一样了, 觉得很亲切, 因为这也是我的家庭语言。

My dad is from Beijing, and my mom is from Shanghai, so we speak Mandarin at home, but my older brother and I have been speaking English to each other since we were little because we think that it is clearer and more convenient to speak English to each other. I remember when I was a child, I went to Shanghai with my mom for the Chinese New Year one winter. I was not comfortable when I first got there. On the one hand, there was no heating at my grandpa's house, and it was terribly cold all the time. On the other hand, my mom spoke Shanghainese with her family when we were all together, and sometimes, they would point at me and speak Shanghainese, but I did not understand a word. Although they spoke to me in Mandarin, I still could not understand a lot, and I had to ask Mom all the time. Later on, I realized that people spoke Shanghainese on the street everywhere, but at the same time, I could also hear Mandarin with various accents.

In Shanghai, I ate a lot of delicious food. Mom's family really took good care of me. They often asked whether I ate well and was having fun or not, so despite the discomfort, I actually had a good time there. After I came back, the sound of Shanghainese has been on my mind all the time. At school, my Chinese teacher teaches us standard pronunciation of Mandarin, but in fact, I know that everyone speaks Mandarin with different accents in China. My feelings toward Shanghainese have changed over time even though I still don't quite understand it. I find the sound of this language dear to my heart because it is also my home language.

生词 Vocabulary

Students are required to recognize and pronounce all the vocabulary listed. For the characters/words in italics and bold, students are also expected to know how to write.

1.	*方便*	方便	fāngbiàn	adj./v.	convenient; make something convenient
2.	*记得*	記得	jìdé	v.	remember
3.	冬天	冬天	dōngtiān	n.	winter
4.	*春节*	春節	chūnjié	n.	Spring Festival
5.	*开始*	開始	kāishǐ	v./n.	begin; beginning
6.	*外公*	外公	wàigōng	n.	maternal grandfather
7.	暖气	暖氣	nuǎnqì	n.	heating
8.	指	指	zhǐ	v.	point
9.	*各*	各	gè	pron.	each
10.	*种*	種	zhǒng	mw.	type; kind
11.	照顾	照顧	zhàogù	v.	take care of
12.	关心	關心	guānxīn	v.	care for
13.	教	教	jiāo	v.	teach
14.	标准	標准	biāozhǔn	n./adj.	standard
15.	感觉	感覺	gǎnjué	v./n.	feel; feeling
16.	亲切	親切	qīnqiè	adj.	dear; kind
17.	方面	方面	fāngmiàn	n.	aspect

Sentence Patterns / Grammar

1. 更 + adj.

"even more ... ", a way of adding "-er" to an adjective but can also be used with "比" (i.e., A 比 B + 更 + Adj.). In both cases, "更" adding the meaning of "even more".

我们觉得用英文更清楚、更方便。

We find it even clearer and more convenient to use English.

Examples:

1) 老师的普通话比妈妈的更标准。

    The teacher's Mandarin is even more standard than my mom's. (It is implied that my mom's Mandarin is already quite standard, but the teacher's is even more standard.)

2) 上海冬天没有暖气, 所以有时候比北京更冷。

    There is no heating in the winter in Shanghai. So it is even colder than Beijing sometimes.

3) 我喜欢在网上买书, 因为＿＿＿＿＿＿＿。

2. 一方面 ……; 另一方面 ……

Similar to "on the one hand, on the other hand", often used to talk about various aspects of a situation. The two aspects in the sentence can be similar in tone or in direct opposition to each other. Sometimes, "又" "也" or "还" is used after "另一方面" for emphasis.

刚开始很不习惯。一方面, 当时外公家没有暖气, 冷得不得了。另一方面, 妈妈一家人在一起的时候都说上海话。

I was not used to it at first. On the one hand, there was no heating at my grandpa's house, and it was terribly cold. On the other hand, my mother's family spoke Shanghainese when they were together.

Examples:

1) 我觉得学习方言很重要 (zhòngyào)。一方面, 方言体现 (tǐxiàn) 不同地方的文化; 另一方面, 方言也体现了语言的多样性。

    I think it's important to learn regional varieties of a language. On the one hand, these varieties reflect the cultures of different places. On the other hand, the varieties also reflect the diversity of languages.

2) 很多学生一方面想回学校上课, 另一方面又担心感染 (gǎnrǎn) 上新冠病毒 (xīnguān bìngdú)。

    Many students want to go back to school on the one hand and worry about catching Covid-19 on the other.

3. **一 + measure word + (noun) + 都 / 也+ 不 / 没 + verb: "not even one". It is often used as "Subject + 一 + measure word + (noun) + 都 / 也 + 不 / 没 + verb". This structure indicates that someone did not do something at all.**

我一句都听不懂。

I cannot understand even one sentence.

Examples:

1) 今天的早饭看起来不好吃, 所以我一口都没吃。

    The breakfast today didn't look good, so I didn't eat a bite.

2) 我上海话一句都不会说。or 我一句上海话都不会说。
   I can't speak a word of Shanghainese.

4. Verb + 得 + adj.: how well an action is done.

"得 + adj" is a degree complement here to provide additional information of degree for the verbs.

妈妈的家人很关心我吃得好不好, 玩得高兴不高兴。
My mother's family was very concerned about whether I ate well and whether I had fun or not.

Examples:

1) 这个美国留学生的普通话说得很好。
   This American student speaks Mandarin very well.
2) 同学们的中文学得很快。Or 同学们学中文学得很快。
   Students learn Chinese quickly.

   **同学们学中文很快。   (X)
   同学们学中文得很快。   (X)

5. Topic + comment: This is a unique structure in the Chinese language and is not found in European languages. The topic of the sentence is usually a person or a thing, and it is what is being talked about. It acts more like the subject matter of a conversation rather than the subject of a sentence. Once the topic is raised and established, the rest of the sentence or a dialogue functions as a comment or comments on this topic. It is generally placed at the beginning of a dialogue/sentence. The comment can range from one predicate or one sentence to a series of sentences. In other words, a topic operates on a discoursal level and is beyond the grammatical confines of a sentence.

上海话我还是听不懂。Topic, subject-predicate sentence.
Shanghainese, I still cannot understand.

Examples:

1) A: 她的普通话很标准。
      Her Mandarin is very standard.
   B: 是很标准。
      Yes, indeed, it is.
2) 外公家冬天不冷, 空间 (kōngjiān) 很大, 我们都喜欢去。
   My grandpa's house is not cold in winter. It has a lot of space, and we all like to go.

III. Vocabulary and Grammar Exercise

1. Complete the following sentences with the given patterns.

1) "更 + adj"

　　a. 姚明 (Yáo Míng) 太太的身高是1.9米, 姚明的身高是2.26米, 所以姚明_____。

　　b. 昨天气温90华氏度 (huáshìdù Fahrenheit), 今天气温96华氏度。所以, 今天_____。

2) 一方面 …… 另一方面 ……

　　a. 我觉得大学生活和高中生活不太一样。_____。

　　b. 很多华裔小时候都不是很清楚自己是哪国人。_____。

3) 一 + measure word + noun + 都 / 也不

　　a. 杰克是一个美国来的留学生。来中国以前, 杰克_____(说),
　　　 _____(写), _____(认识)。

　　b. 圣诞节 (Shèngdànjié, Christmas) 那天, 学校里_____, 因为大家都在家里跟家人过节。

4) Verb 得 / 不+Verb

　　a. 如果一个上海人和一个北京人只说方言, 他们没办法交流, 因为北京_____上海人说的话。但是如果他们都会说普通话, 那么他们就可以互相_____了。

　　b. 睡觉前不要喝咖啡 (hēkāfēi, drink coffee), 要不然你会_____。

5) Verb + 得 + adj.

　　a. 外公的普通话_____(清楚), 我一句都听不懂。

　　b. 妈妈告诉我, 吃饭如果_____(快), 肚子会疼 (téng, painful)。

6) Topic + comment

　　a. 老师: 中文难学吗?
　　　 学生: 对我来说, 听和说_____, 可是读和写_____,　特别是汉字_____。

　　b. 妈妈: 你的宿舍怎么样?
　　　 Joy: 我的宿舍洗衣服很方便, 去上课_____, 住的人_____, 可是做饭_____。

3. 选择填空 Fill in the blanks with the appropriate words.

清楚	口音	听不懂	标准	感觉	关心	更	另一方面	其实

　　在美国的华裔家庭里, 有些父母喜欢说方言, 可是他们的孩子喜欢说英文, 因为一方面, 他们 *tīng bù dǒng* 方言, *lìng yì fāng miàn* 他们觉得用英文很 *qīng chǔ*, 也 *gèng* 方便。这些孩子对方言的 *gǎn jué* 不太好, 他们觉得方言太难学, 而且学了也没什么用。还有一些父母很 *guān xīn* 孩子的中文学习, 所以他们在家里一直跟孩子说普通话。可是因为他们都是从中国不同的地方来的, 所以他们的普通话都有 *kǒu yīn*。这些父母觉得, 虽然他们的普通话不是很 *biāo zhǔn*, 但 *qí shí* 很多中国人说的普通话都不一样, 并不会影响大家的交流。

1)听不懂　2)另一方面　3)清楚　4)更　5)感觉
6)关心　7)口音　8)标准　9)其实

4. 小作文 Short essay :

请写一篇150字左右的作文, 说说你家的语言。请用至少5个所给生词和所有的句型。Please write an essay of about 150 characters and talk about the languages spoken in your family. Please use at least five given words and all sentence patterns.

生词 (words): 清楚、习惯、种、口音、其实、感觉、亲切、标准、关心
句型 (patterns): 更; Verb得 / 不+Verb; 一 + measure word + noun + 都 / 也不;
Verb+得+adj; Topic + comment; 一方面 ······ 另一方面 ······

IV. Post-reading Discussion

1. 西班牙 (Xībānyá) 语有很多口音, 但是在中国要学标准的普通话, 你有什么看法?
   Spanish has various accents, but it is expected to learn "standard Mandarin" in China. What do you think about it?
2. 中国有各种口音的普通话。美国的英语也有各种口音吗? 请举例。
   Chinese speak Mandarin with all kinds of accents in China. How about the U.S.? Do people speak English with different accents? Please give an example.
3. 你的父母常跟你说他们老家的事吗? 有哪些?
   Have your parents talked to you about their hometowns in China? Like what?
4. 什么口音会让你有亲切的感觉? 为什么?
   What accent will touch your heart? Why?

V. Presentational Task

按照 (ànzhào) 我们的课文, 做一个口头介绍 (jièshào) 你的一个旅游 (lǚyóu) 经历 (jīnglì)。旅游的地方可以是任何 (rènhé) 地方。
Model our text. Do an oral presentation on your travel experience. It could be any place of your choice.

Lesson Four 普通话和方言

Learning Objectives

In this lesson, you will learn to do the following:

1. Identify major regional varieties of Chinese and their characteristics.
2. Explain the origin of Chinese Pinyin system.
3. Compare the language policies of different countries.
4. Discuss the importance of one's mother tongue.
5. Compose a short biography of a historical figure.

I. Warm-up: Pre-reading Discussion

1. 说普通话难吗? 你觉得什么最难? 发音还是声调? 为什么?
   Is it difficult to speak Mandarin? What do you find the hardest? Pronunciation or tone? Why?
2. 请在网上看一段中国方言的视频。你注意到了什么?跟普通话有什么不一样?你觉得语音识别系统(yǔyīn shíbié xìtǒng)可以分辨出(fēnbiànchū)方言吗?为什么?
   Please watch a video clip of a regional variety of Chinese. What did you notice? What are the differences between standard Mandarin and other varieties? Do you think the speech recognition system is able to distinguish the language varieties? Why?
3. 你觉得政府(zhèngfǔ)应不应该(yīnggāi)推广(tuīguǎng)方言教育?为什么?
   Do you think the government should promote the education of regional varieties of a language and why?

II. Interpretive Task: Listening Comprehension

Please listen to the lesson dialogue and choose True (T) or False (F) for each of the following audio recordings of the statements.

1. (对) 2. (错) 3. (错) 4. (对) 5. (对)

DOI: 10.4324/9781003352228-7

Main Text

Part I 对话：　**普通话和方言**

Joy:	老师，昨天爸爸告诉我中国有很多方言。您知道中国现在有多少种方言吗？
老师：	照官方说法，现在有十大方言，包括官话方言，比如北京话；吴方言，比如上海话；粤方言，也就是广东话；还有客家方言等等。每种方言都很不同，特别是南方方言和北方方言，无论是发音、词汇还是语法都不一样。所以南方人和北方人常常互相听不懂。
Melinda:	是的。我爸爸说广东话，我妈妈说四川话。爸爸说，如果他和妈妈两个人都用方言说话，就会像"鸡同鸭讲"，根本听不懂。哈哈。
老师：	是啊。还会常常闹笑话呢。
Melinda:	嗯。我妈妈给我讲过一个笑话。有一次，一个四川人坐船的时候，突然说她"hai子"掉进河里了。一个东北人听到后马上跳到河里帮她找，可是找了半天都没有找到孩子。后来他才知道，不是"孩子"，而是"鞋子"掉到水里去了。四川人都把"鞋子"读成"孩子"。
Joy:	哈哈，太好笑了！老师，现在在中国，大家都说普通话了吧？
老师：	在学校，大家一般都说普通话，电视节目也大多是普通话的。但是，在日常生活中，很多地方的人还是喜欢用方言，比如四川人、上海人和广东人。
Melinda:	是的！我的爷爷奶奶、外公外婆就喜欢说方言。虽然我常常听不懂他们说的话，但是我觉得很亲切，也很有意思。
Joy:	我同意！虽然普通话很重要，但是如果没有了方言，那该多无聊啊！

Pŭtōnghuà hé fāngyán

Joy:	Lǎoshī, zuótiān bàba gàosu wǒ Zhōngguó yǒu hěnduō fāngyán. Nín zhīdào Zhōngguó xiànzài yǒu duōshǎo zhǒng fāngyán ma?
Lǎoshī:	Zhào guānfāng shuōfǎ, xiànzài yǒu shí dà fāngyán, bāokuò Guānhuà fāngyán, bǐrú Běijīng huà; Wú fāngyán, bǐrú Shànghǎi huà; Yuè fāngyán, yě jiùshì Guǎngdōng huà; hái yǒu Kèjiā fāngyán děngděng. Měi zhǒng fāngyán dōu hěn bùtóng, tèbié shì nánfāng fāngyán hé běifāng fāngyán, wúlùn shì fāyīn, cíhuì háishì yǔfǎ dōu bù yīyàng. Suǒyǐ nánfāng rén hé běifāng rén chángcháng hùxiāng tīng bù dǒng.
Melinda:	Shì de. Wǒ bàba shuō Guǎngdōng huà, wǒ māma shuō Sìchuān huà. Bàba shuō, rúguǒ tā hé māma liǎng gè rén dōu yòng fāngyán shuōhuà, jiù huì xiàng "jītóngyājiǎng", gēnběn tīng bù dǒng. Hāha.
Lǎoshī:	Shì a. Hái huì chángcháng nào xiàohuà ne.
Melinda:	En. Wǒ māma gěi wǒ jiǎngguò yīgè xiàohuà. Yǒu yīcì, yīgè Sìchuān rén zuò chuán de shíhòu, tūrán shuō tā de "hái zi" diào jìn hé lǐ le. Yīgè dōngběi rén tīng dào hòu mǎshàng tiào dào hé lǐ bāng tā zhǎo, kěshì zhǎole bàntiān dōu méiyǒu zhǎo dào háizi. Hòulái tā cái zhīdào,

bùshì "háizi", ér shì "xiézi" diàodào shuǐlǐ qù le. Sìchuān rén dōu bǎ "xiézi" dúchéng "háizi".

Joy: Hāha, tài hǎoxiàole! Lǎoshī, xiànzài zài Zhōngguó, dàjiā dōu shuō pǔtōnghuà le ba?

Lǎoshī: Zài xuéxiào, dàjiā yì bān dōu shuō pǔtōnghuà, diànshì jiémù yě dàduō shì pǔtōnghuà de. Dànshì, zài rìcháng shēnghuó zhōng, hěnduō dìfāng de rén háishì xǐhuān yòng fāngyán, bǐrú Sìchuān rén, Shànghǎi rén hé Guǎngdōng rén.

Melinda: Shì de! Wǒ de yéye nǎinai, wàigōng wàipó jiù xǐhuān shuō fāngyán. Suīrán wǒ chángcháng tīng bù dǒng tāmen shuō de huà, dànshì wǒ juéde hěn qīnqiè, yě hěn yǒuyìsi.

Joy: Wǒ tóngyì! Suīrán pǔtōnghuà hěn zhòngyào, dànshì rúguǒ méiyǒule fāngyán, nà gāi duō wúliáo a!

生词 Vocabulary

Students are required to recognize and pronounce all the vocabulary listed. For the characters/words in italics and bold, students are also expected to know how to write.

1.	照 …… (的)说法	照 …… (的)說法	zhào . . . (de) shuōfǎ	ph.	according to . . .
2.	官方	官方	guānfāng	adj.	official
3.	包括	包括	bāokuò	v.	include; comprise
4.	词汇	詞彙	cíhuì	n.	vocabulary
5.	*语法*	語法	yǔfǎ	n.	grammar
6.	鸡同鸭讲	雞同鴨講	jītóngyājiǎng	ph.	Individuals have difficulty communicating with each other, like a chicken talking to a duck.
7.	根本 (不 / 没有)	根本 (不 / 沒有)	gēnběn (bù/ méiyǒu)	adv.	not at all; absolutely not
8.	闹笑话	鬧笑話	nào xiàohua	v.o.	make a fool of oneself
9.	坐船	坐船	zuòchuán	v.o.	by ship; take a boat
10.	突然	突然	tūrán	adv.	suddenly; abruptly
11.	*跳*	跳	tiào	n./v.	jump; hop
12.	*帮*	幫	bāng	v.	help; assist
13.	*找*	找	zhǎo	v.	look for; seek

14.	**读**	**讀**	dú	v.	read
15.	一般	一般	yībān	adj./ adv.	ordinary; generally; in general
16.	电视	電視	diànshì	n.	television
17.	**节目**	節目	jiémù	n.	program; show
18.	**日常**	日常	rìcháng	adj.	daily
19.	同意	同意	tóngyì	v.	agree; approve
20.	**重要**	重要	zhòngyào	adj.	important; significant
21.	无聊	無聊	wúliáo	adj.	bored; boring; silly

Proper Names

1.	官话方言	官話方言	Guānhuà fāngyán	Guan (Mandarin) dialect (spoken primarily in northern and southwestern China)
2.	吴方言	吳方言	Wú fāngyán	Wu dialects (spoken primarily in Shanghai and surrounding areas)
3.	粤方言	粤方言	Yuè fāngyán	Yue dialect (spoken primarily in Guangdong, Guangxi, Hong Kong, and Macau)
4.	客家方言	客家方言	Kèjiā fāngyán	Hakka dialect (spoken primarily in southeastern China)
5.	广东	廣東	Guǎngdōng	Guangdong Province in south China
6.	四川	四川	Sìchuān	Sichuan Province in southwest China

Sentence Patterns / Grammar

1. 照 ⋯⋯ (的) 说法： according to someone's statement/ways of saying a thing

Besides "说法", you can also use "看法 (opinion)、做法 (ways of doing a thing)". For instance, 照我的看法, 每个人都应该 (yīnggāi) 上大学。今天我想照我妈妈的做法来做这个菜 (cài)。

照官方说法, 现在有十大方言。
According to the official statement, there are now ten regional varieties of Chinese.

Examples:

1) 照中国人的说法, 男人三十岁以前应该 (yīnggāi) 结婚生子, 有自己的家庭和事业。
   According to the Chinese, men should marry and have children before the age of 30 and have their own family and career.

2) 照我妈妈的说法, 学生不应该 (yīnggāi) 在吃、穿上花心思。
   According to my mother, students should not put a lot of thought into eating and dressing.

2. 无论 + question,　都 / 还 …… no matter . . . Please note that what follows 无论 should be a question, not a statement

南方方言和北方方言, 无论是发音、词汇还是语法都不一样。
No matter if it is pronunciation, vocabulary, or grammar, the language varieties in the southern regions and the northern regions are different.

Examples:

1) 照他的说法, 中国人无论移民来美国多久了, 还是中国人。
   According to him, no matter how long he has immigrated to the United States, he is still Chinese.

2) 周末 (zhōumò) 的时候, 无论哪个航班都有很多人。
   On weekends, no matter which flight, there are many people.

3. 根本 (不 / 没有) not at all; absolutely not

根本 cannot be followed by an affirmative statement.

如果他和妈妈两个人都用方言说话, 就会像 "鸡同鸭讲", 根本听不懂。
If he and his mother both spoke in language varieties, they would be like how "a chicken talks to a duck", and they would not understand each other at all.

Examples:

1) 我跟他打招呼, 可是他根本没看到。
   I greeted him, but he didn't see me at all.

2) 上海冬天没有暖气, 我春节的时候去根本不习惯。
   There is no heating in Shanghai in winter, so I am not used to it at all when going there during the Spring Festival.

4. V了半天: literally means doing something for half a day, but the pattern is most commonly used to indicate that the action lasted for a long time and is often followed by "也 / 都 / 还没有+resultative verb".

一个东北人听到后马上跳到河里帮她找, 可是找了半天都没有找到孩子。
After hearing that, a northeasterner immediately jumped into the river to help her but still could not find the child after searching for a long time.

Examples:

1) 今天机场的人很多，我排了半天也没安检完。

There are a lot of people at the airport today, and I haven't been through the security check after waiting for a long time in the line.

2) 这个事不简单，他说了半天都没说清楚。

This is not a simple matter. He talked for a long time without making it clear.

5. 把 …… V成 …… (mistakenly) read/see/regard/call/other verbs something as something else

四川人都把"鞋子"读成"孩子"。

Sichuan people pronounce "xiezi" as "haizi".

Examples:

1) 我把"少"看成了"小"。

I misread 少 as 小.

2) 机场安检人员把我认成韩国人。

The airport security officer misrecognized me as a Korean.

6. 那该多adj. 啊 Then how adjective it would be

如果没有了方言，那该多无聊啊！

If there were no language varieties, then how boring it would be!

Examples:

1) 要是我听得懂外公外婆说的方言，那该多好啊！

If I could understand the language spoken by my grandparents, how great that would be!

2) A. 他跟女朋友谈恋爱谈了八年，可是现在不想跟她结婚了。

He has been with his girlfriend for eight years, but now he doesn't want to marry her.

B. 那他女朋友该多生气啊！

Then how angry his girlfriend would be!

III. Vocabulary and Grammar Exercise

1. Radical Recognition

Please identify the radicals of the following characters. Write down the radical and its meaning.

Examples: 好 → （女）woman

1) 根 → () mù tree   2) 坐 → () tǔ earth

3) 跳 → () zú foot   4) 笑 → () zhú bamboo

口 5) 船 → ( ) _kǒu_ mouth   扌6) 找 → ( ) _shǒu_ hand

讠 7) 读 → ( ) _yán_ speech   心 8) 意 → ( ) _xīn_ heart

礻 9) 视 → ( ) _shì_ spirit   耳 10) 聊 → ( ) _ěr_ ear

2. Word-building Exercises

For each of the characters in the next example, write three more words that include that character.

坐车　坐下　请坐　　春节　节目　中秋节
生词　词语　词典
电话　电脑　电影
经常　常见　平常

1) 坐： 坐船 _zuò chē   zuò xià   qǐng zuò_
2) 节： 节目 _chūn jié   jié mù   zhōng qiū jié_
3) 词： 词汇 _shēng cí   cí yǔ   cí diǎn_
4) 电： 电视 _diàn huà   diàn nǎo   diàn yǐng_
5) 常： 日常 _jīng cháng   cháng jiàn   píng cháng_

3. Matching Exercise: Please match Pinyin and characters

1) 同意　　　　　a. yǔfǎ
2) 电视　　　　　b. zhòngyào
3) 节目　　　　　c. rìcháng
4) 词汇　　　　　d. guānfāng
5) 语法　　　　　e. yībān
6) 一般　　　　　f. gàosu
7) 告诉　　　　　g. cíhuì
8) 重要　　　　　h. diànshì
9) 日常　　　　　i. jiémù
10) 官方　　　　　j. tóngyì

4. Fill in the blanks with the appropriate words

> 日常　包括　根本　语法　官方　亲切　告诉　无论　节目

　　今天老师 告诉 我，照 官方 说法，中国现在有十大方言， 包括 吴方言和粤方言。南方方言和北方方言， 无论 是发音、词汇还是 语法 都不一样。如果他们都用方言交流， 根本 互相听不懂。现在电视 节目 大多是普通话的，但是在 日常 生活中，很多地方的人还是喜欢说方言，他们觉得方言更 亲切 。

5. Complete the following sentences with the given patterns

1) 照 …… 的说法

　　a. 照一些中国朋友的说法，很多人来美国是为了＿＿＿＿＿＿＿＿＿。
　　b. 照＿＿＿＿＿＿的说法，在中国人人都得学说普通话，因为＿＿＿＿＿＿。

2) 无论 + question, 都 / 还 ……

今天是感恩节(Gǎn'ēnjié, Thanksgiving)，你最想谢谢谁? 为什么?
比如, 我最想谢谢我的妈妈, 因为<u>无论多忙多累, 她都一直非常花心思照顾</u>(zhàogù, take care of) <u>我, 你呢?</u>

3) 根本 (不 / 没有)

　　a. 过18岁生日的时候, 爸爸说要送我一辆车, 可是我＿＿＿＿＿＿＿啊。
　　b. 很多人买脸书 (Liǎnshū, Facebook) 的股票 (gǔpiào, stock), 可是其实他们＿＿＿＿。

4) V了半天

　　a. 这一课太难了!　我昨天先看课文＿＿＿＿＿＿, 后来又听录音＿＿＿＿＿＿才学会。
　　b. 他是谁? 看起来很像我的大学同学, 可是我＿＿＿＿＿＿＿＿。

5) 把 …… V成 ……

　　a. 有的汉字太像了! 比如, "少" 和 "小", 我常常＿＿＿＿＿＿＿＿。
　　b. 脸书在中国有别的名字, 有的中国人把 "脸书" ＿＿＿＿＿＿＿＿。

6) 那该多adj. 啊
　　今年你过生日, 有什么愿望 (yuànwàng, wish) 吗?

愿望清单 (qīngdān, list)	
要是/如果……	那该多 …… 啊!

6. 十大方言图 (tú): 上网 (wǎng) 查 (chá) 中国的十大方言图, 然后填入下一页的方言图 Figure 31 里 (中、英文都可以) 。哪几个方言是使用最多的方言?

Regional varieties of Chinese map: look up the language varieties of Chinese on the Internet, and then fill in the map of Figure 31 on the next page (either in Chinese or English). Do you know which regional varieties are the most spoken?

IV. Post-reading Discussion

1.　你去过中国哪些地方? 你听到过那儿的方言吗? 有什么特点?
　　Where have you been in China? Have you heard of the regional varieties of Chinese there? What are the characteristics?

Figure 31 The map of Sinitic language family

2.　你或你的家人说方言吗? 你觉得推行 (tuīxíng) 普通话以后是不是应该
　　(yīnggāi) 禁止 (jìnzhǐ) 方言? 为什么? 语言文字的统一 (tǒngyī) 会使 (shǐ)
　　一个国家进步 (jìnbù) 还是更落后 (luòhòu)? 为什么?
　　Do you or your family speak regional varieties of Chinese? Do you think
　　the regional varieties should be banned after the implementation of Putong-
　　hua? Why? Will the unification of languages make a country progress or fall
　　behind? Why?
3.　你听过王照这个人吗? 普通话成为国语和他有关系 (guānxi), 请你读一下
　　下面的介绍, 并和同学老师谈谈你的想法。
　　Have you ever heard of Wang Zhao? He is a key figure in making Mandarin
　　the official language of China. Please read the following paragraph and talk
　　to your classmates and teacher about your thoughts.

　　Few of the delegates at the 1913 conference on pronunciation seem to have had
any idea of what they were up against. The negotiations were marked by frustrat-
ingly naïve arguments. "Germany is strong," it was said, "because its language contains many voiced sounds and China is weak because Mandarin lacks them." But if
linguistic knowledge was in short supply, commitment to position was not. Passions
were hot, and frustrations grew. Finally, after months of no progress, Wang Zhao,
the leader of the Mandarin faction, called for a new system of voting in which each
province would have one and only one vote, knowing full well that the numerically

superior Mandarin-speaking area would then automatically dominate. Delegates in other areas were incensed. The situation became explosive. Then, as tempers flared, Wang Rongbao, one of the leaders of the Southern faction, happened to use the colloquial Shanghai expression for "ricksha," wangbo ts'o. Wang Zhao misheard it for the Mandarin curse wángba dàn "son of a bitch [literally turtle's egg]," and flew into a rage. He bared his arms and attacked Wang Rongbao, chasing him out of the assembly hall. Wang Rangbao never returned to the meetings. Wang Zhao's suggestion to change the voting procedure was adopted, and after three months of bitter struggling, the Mandarin faction had its way. The conference adopted a resolution recommending that the sounds of Mandarin become the national standard.

The Languages of China (Princeton: Princeton University Press, 1987), pp. 7–8.

V. Interpersonal Tasks

1. 两两对话 (liǎngliǎng duìhuà) Pair-work

纳尔逊·曼德拉说：“如果用一个人听得懂的语言和他交流, 触动 (chùdòng)的是他的思维 (sīwéi)。如果用一个人的母语和他交流, 触动的是他的心灵 (xīnlíng)。”

你同意这句话吗？为什么？中文是你的母语吗？为什么？请和你的同伴讨论, 在班上报告你们的看法。

Nelson Mandela said, " If you talk to a man in a language he understands, that goes to his head. If you talk to him in his own language, that goes to his heart."

Do you agree with this? Why? Do you think Chinese is your mother tongue? Why? Please discuss with your partner and share your group's opinions with the rest of the class.

2. 采访 (cǎifǎng) Interview

请上网找一段中国方言的歌曲或视频, 采访一位你认识的中国人, 请你把问题和回答记录下来然后分享给班上同学。

Please find a song or video in a regional variety of Chinese on the Internet and interview a Chinese person you know about what you found. Please take notes and share your questions and responses with your classmates in class.

方言歌曲 (视频)：_____

	你的问题 Your questions	面谈者的回答 Interviewee's responses
1		
2		

3		
4		
5		

Part II 短文：周有光

I. Warm-up: Pre-reading Discussion

1. 你知道汉语拼音是谁发明的吗？你听过周有光这个人吗？
    Do you know who invented Hanyu Pinyin? Have you ever heard of Zhou Youguang?
2. 你觉得汉语拼音对你的中文学习有帮助吗？为什么？
    Do you think Hanyu Pinyin is helpful to your Chinese study? Why?
3. 有些人主张用汉语拼音代替汉字，你同意吗？为什么？
    Some people advocate replacing Chinese characters with Chinese Pinyin. Do you agree? Why?

II. Interpretive Task: Listening Comprehension

Please listen to the text and choose True (T) or False (F) for each of the following audio recordings of the statements.

1. (错) 2. (对) 3. (错) 4. (对) 5. (对)

你知道汉语拼音是谁发明的吗？你听过周有光这个人吗？

周有光是中国有名的语言学家，也有很多人说他是"汉语拼音之父"。他原来的名字是周耀平，1906年1月13日出生在江苏常州。1923年，他考上了上海的一所美国教会大学，他的专业是经济学，但他对语言学也很有兴趣。毕业后，他成了一位银行家。但50岁以后，他却成了一位语言文字学家。1955年，他参加了中国的文字改革。他和同事们花了三年的时间，用26个拉丁字母编写出了现在的汉语拼音。汉语拼音的出现不但大大地提高了中国人的读写能力，而且让外国人学习中文变得容易多了。另外，拼音也方便了人们在电脑或手机上打字。2017年，周有光111岁的时候在北京去世。

有些人主张用汉语拼音代替汉字，你同意吗？为什么？

Zhou Youguang

Do you know who invented Hanyu Pinyin? Have you ever heard of Zhou Youguang?

Zhou Youguang is a famous linguist in China, and many people say that he is the "Father of Hanyu Pinyin". His original name was Zhou Yaoping, and he was born on January 13, 1906, in Changzhou, Jiangsu Province. In 1923, he was admitted to an American church university in Shanghai. His major was economics, but he was also interested in linguistics. After graduation, he became a banker. But after the age of 50, he became a linguist. In 1955, he took part in the reform of Chinese characters. It took him and his colleagues three years to compile the current Hanyu

Pinyin using 26 Latin letters. The emergence of Hanyu Pinyin not only greatly improves Chinese people's literacy skills but also makes it much easier for foreigners to learn Chinese. In addition, Pinyin makes it easier for people to type on computers or mobile phones. In 2017, Zhou Youguang died in Beijing at the age of 111.

Some people advocate replacing Chinese characters with Hanyu Pinyin. Do you agree? Why?

生词 Vocabulary

Students are required to recognize and pronounce all the vocabulary listed. For the characters/words in italics and bold, students are also expected to know how to write.

1.	拼音	拼音	pīnyīn	n.	official Chinese alphabetic system
2.	*发明*	發明	fāmíng	n./v.	invention; invent
3.	***有名***	有名	yǒumíng	adj.	famous
4.	语言学家	語言學家	yǔyánxuéjiā	n.	linguist
5.	***考上***	考上	kǎoshàng	v.	pass entrance examination
6.	***教会***	教會	jiàohuì	n.	church
7.	***专业***	專業	zhuānyè	n.	major
8.	经济学	經濟學	jīngjìxué	n.	economics
9.	***兴趣***	興趣	xìngqù	n.	interest
10.	***毕业***	畢業	bìyè	v.	graduate
11.	银行家	銀行家	yínhángjiā	n.	banker
12.	却	卻	què	adv./conj.	yet; but; however
13.	文字学	文字學	wénzìxué	n.	philology
14.	参加	參加	cānjiā	v.	join; attend; take part in
15.	文字改革	文字改革	wénzì gǎigé	n.	reform of Chinese characters
16.	***同事***	同事	tóngshì	n.	colleague
17.	拉丁字母	拉丁字母	Lādīng zìmǔ	n.	Latin alphabet
18.	编写	編寫	biānxiě	v.	compile

19.	**出现**	出現	chūxiàn	v.	appear; emerge
20.	提高	提高	tígāo	v.	raise; increase; improve
21.	**能力**	能力	nénglì	n.	ability
22.	**让**	讓	ràng	v.	allow; induce someone to do something
23.	变	變	biàn	v.	change; become
24.	另外	另外	lìngwài	conj.	additionally; in addition; besides
25.	电脑	電腦	diànnǎo	n.	computer
26.	**手机**	手機	shǒujī	n.	cell phone
27.	打字	打字	dǎzì	v.o.	type
28.	去世	去世	qùshì	v.	pass away
29.	主张	主張	zhǔzhāng	v./n.	advocate; view
30.	代替	代替	dàitì	v.	take place of

Proper Names

1.	周有光	周有光	Zhōu Yǒuguāng	a person's name
2.	周耀平	周耀平	Zhōu Yàopíng	a person's name
3.	江苏	江蘇	Jiāngsū	Jiangsu province
4.	常州	常州	Chángzhōu	Name of a city in Jiangsu province; it is about 185 km west of Shanghai

Sentence Patterns / Grammar

1. 对 + something + 有兴趣 / 感 (gǎn) 兴趣 be interested in something

This pattern is used to express "someone is interested in something". When it is used with "people", it means being interested in this person as a study subject, not conveying a romantic feeling. Expressing a romantic feeling for someone should not use this term.

他对语言学也很有兴趣。
He is interested in linguistics.

Example:

1)   他对学中文很有兴趣。
     He is very interested in learning Chinese.
2)   我对做饭(zuòfàn)很有兴趣。
     I am interested in cooking.

Frequent mistake
我对她很有兴趣。   **(X)**
我对她很有意思。   **(✓)**
I am interested in her (romantically).

2. Subject / Topic 不但 ⋯⋯ 而且 ⋯⋯ Not only . . . but also . . .

The first part and the second part of the sentence should be in the same realm, either both positive or both negative, and the focus of the comment is the second part of the sentence.

> 汉语拼音不但提高了中国人的读写能力, 而且让外国人学习中文变得容易多了。
> The Pinyin system not only improves Chinese people's reading and writing abilities but also makes learning Chinese for foreigners much easier.

Example:

1)   他不但喜欢吃中国菜, 而且喜欢做中国菜。
     He not only likes to eat Chinese food but also likes to cook Chinese food.
2)   他不但不做功课, 而且不来上课。
     He not only does not do any homework but also misses classes.

3. 另外 + sentence in addition . . .

This pattern is often placed in the beginning of the sentence, and the sentence often has 也.

> 另外, 拼音也方便了人们在电脑或手机上打字。
> Besides, Pinyin also makes typing on computers and cell phones more convenient.

Example:

1)   我们要去北京看家人。另外, 我们在北京的时候也可以去看长城(Chángchéng)。
     We are going to visit the family in Beijing. Besides that, we can also go to visit the Great Wall when we are in Beijing.
2)   你把这个东西给小夏。另外, 请你也叫小林来这里一下。
     Please give this to Xiaoxia. Also, please ask Xiaolin to come here for a minute.

4. V + 过 have done something before

This usage focuses on the experience of the action in the past that has an impact on your current experience. For example, if you have been to China in the past, this experience will contribute to your current experience with China or understanding of China.

> 你听过周有光这个人吗?
> Have you heard of this person, Zhou Youguang?

Example:

1) 你去过中国吗?
    Have you been to China?
2) 我去过纽约市,所以我知道纽约很多地方。
    I have been to NYC, so I know many places in NYC.

5. 却 + V however

The sentence with 却 often indicates a surprise element to the assumption. Unlike English, 却 goes before verb, not in the beginning of the sentence.

> 他原来是银行家。50岁以后,他却成了一位语言文字学家。
> He originally was a banker. After turning 50 years old, he, however, has become a linguist.

Example:

1) 他是中国人,却不喜欢吃中国菜!
    He is Chinese, but he does not like to eat Chinese food!
2) 他会(huì)说很多亚洲语言,却不会说中文。
    He knows how to speak many Asian languages, but he does not know how to speak Chinese.

III. Vocabulary and Grammar Exercise

1. Make at least five sentences with the characters provided. You can use the same character repeatedly as long as you use 15 different characters in total.

会	手	有	事	学
这	对	兴	语	字
名	人	个	话	趣
吗	韩	你	写	打
电	说	的	同	机

Example: 你会打字吗?

1)
2)
3)
4)
5)

1) 听过　2) 却　3) 发明　4) 容易
5) 读　6) 能力　7) 另外
8) 所以　9) 兴趣　10) 打字

2. 选择填空 Fill in the blanks.

> 容易　兴趣　打字　另外　却　发明　听过　所以　能力　读

　　很多人都 听过(tīngguò) 拼音。但是怎么来的, 知道的人 却(què) 不多。如果没有拼音, 怎么学汉字呢? 拼音的 发明(fāmíng) 真是让学习汉字 容易(róngyì) 多了。不认识汉字的人, 可以先学怎么 读(dú), 然后再学怎么写, 读写的 能力(néng lì) 提高了, 想要学新(xīn, new)东西也就快了。另外(lìngwài), 因为学习汉字容易多了, 所以(suǒ yǐ) 外国人对学中文更有 兴趣(xìngqù) 了。有了拼音以后, 就可以在电脑上 打字(dǎ zì) 了。

3. 用英文总结上面的填空短文。

Use English to summarize the fill-in-the-blank passage in the previous section.

4. 小作文 Short essay:

说说你学中文的故事。请包括:

1) 是什么时候开始学中文的?
2) 是怎么学中文的?
3) 有什么好的方法吗?
4) 是先学的拼音还是汉字?
5) 发生过好玩儿的或者让你难忘的事吗?

请选用下面的五个词和所有句型写一篇最少150字的小作文。
Write a short story about learning Chinese of no less than 150 characters with all the sentence patterns provided and five of the following words.
Your essay should include the following:

1) When did you start learning Chinese?
2) How did you learn Chinese?
3) Do you have any good strategies for learning Chinese?
4) Did you learn Pinyin first or characters first?
5) Has anything fun or memorable happened to you?

Here are the provided words and patterns:

　　生词 (words): 能力、方便、让、发明、毕业、考上、参加、有名
　　句型(patterns): 对……有兴趣; 不但……而且……; 另外; 无论……都/还;
　　虽然……但是……

这里提供了可能会用到的生词。Here are some words that you might need in your essay:

背 (bèi, memorize)、次 (cì, times)、难 (nán, difficult)、笔画 (bǐhuà, strokes)、顺序(shùnxù, order of things)

IV. Post-reading Discussion

1. 你知道中国政府 (zhèngfǔ) 为什么要进行文字改革吗?
   Why does the Chinese government conduct the reform of characters?
2. 你觉得应该 (yīnggāi) 不应该取消汉字, 只用拼音? 为什么?
   Do you think that Chinese characters should be eliminated and only Pinyin should be used? Why?
3. 你觉得学中文要学手写汉字吗? 为什么?
   Do you think that learning Chinese requires learning how to handwrite Chinese characters? Why?
4. 你上过中文学校吗? 你觉得中文学校需要(xūyào)做什么改革?
   Have you studied Chinese in a Chinese school (weekend Chinese school)? What reforms do you think Chinese schools need to make?
5. 日本和韩国历史 (lìshǐ) 上都曾用过汉字, 但是日本在1946年进行 (jìnxíng) 文字改革, 现在也限制 (xiànzhì) 小学生学习太多汉字; 韩国在1970禁止 (jìnzhǐ) 小学教汉字, 改为全韩文教育 (quán Hánwén jiàoyù)。你对这两个国家的文字改革有什么看法? 社会 (shèhuì) 是不是更进步 (jìnbù)? 为什么?
   Both Japan and South Korea have used Chinese characters in history, but Japan carried out Kanji reform in 1946. The government also restricts primary school students from learning too many Chinese characters. In 1970, South Korea banned the teaching of Chinese characters in primary schools and changed it to all-Korean education. What do you think of the reform of Chinese characters in these two countries? Is society more progressive? Why?

V. Interpersonal Tasks

1. 采访 (cǎifǎng) Interview

请采访一位以中文为母语的学生和一位正在学习或学过中文的学生, 问问他们 (1) 学中文的经历; (2) 对拼音的看法: 应不应该 (yīnggāi) 学? 为什么? (3) 对汉字的看法: 应不应该学? 为什么? 怎么学? 要学手写汉字吗? 为什么?
采访以后, 请比较一下, 说一说:

(1) 他们的经历和看法, 有什么一样和不一样?
(2) 他们的经历和看法跟你的一样吗? 有什么一样和不一样?
(3) 你觉得什么可能会影响 (yǐngxiǎng) 一个人学中文的经历和他们对拼音和汉字的看法?

Please interview a student whose mother tongue is Chinese and a student who is studying or has studied Chinese and ask them about (1) their experience of learning Chinese, (2) their views on Pinyin: should students learn it? Why? And (3) views on Chinese characters: should students learn it? Why? How to learn? Should students learn handwriting Chinese characters? Why?

After the interviews, please compare their experiences of Chinese learning and their views on Pinyin and Chinese characters. What are the similarities and differences? Are their experiences and views the same as yours? What are the similarities and differences? What factors do you think will influence a person's Chinese learning experience and their views about Pinyin or Chinese characters?

VI. Presentational Tasks

1. 研究报告 (yánjiū bàogào) Research Report

请查阅相关资料, 研究一下中国的文字改革, 然后写一篇350字左右的小报告, 介绍 (jièshào) 一下中国为什么要进行文字改革? 做了哪些改革? 你对这些改革有什么看法?

Please refer to relevant materials, study the reform of Chinese characters, and then write a short report of about 350 characters, introducing why China is carrying out the reform of characters? What reforms have been made? What is your opinion on these reforms?

2. 人物传记 (rénwù zhuànjì) Biography

仿照 "周有光" 的短文第二段, 写一篇250字左右的一位历史 (lìshǐ) 名人的人物传记。

Please use the second paragraph of the text as a model and write a 250-character biography of a historical figure.

Unit Three
教育

Lesson Five 家庭教育

Learning Objectives

In this lesson, you will learn to do the following:

1. Describe a person's appearance in details.
2. Demonstrate understandings of "filial piety" in Chinese culture.
3. Discuss the pros and cons of Chinese parenting style.
4. Compare parenting styles in different cultures.
5. Analyze and discuss the stereotypes of Asian traits.

I. Warm-up: Pre-reading Discussion

1. 你这个学期忙吗? 在忙什么呢?
   Are you busy this semester? What are you busy with?
2. 你多久跟家人联系一次? 你们怎么联系? 会视频聊天吗?
   How often do you contact your family? How do you contact them? Do you video-chat?
3. 在你家, 谁最操心你的生活? 为什么你这么说?
   Who cares and worries about your life the most in your family? Why do you think so?

II. Interpretive Task: Listening Comprehension

Please listen to the lesson dialogue and choose True (T) or False (F) for each of the following audio recordings of the statements.

1. (错) 2. (错) 3. (对) 4. (对) 5. (错)

Main Text

*Part I 对话：**操心的妈妈***

妈妈: Joy, 你已经一个月没跟爸爸妈妈视频聊天了! 你在忙什么呢?

Joy: 妈, 我这个学期的课都很重, 有很多功课。除了上课以外, 我也参加了两个社团, 另外还想找实习, 真的好忙啊。

DOI: 10.4324/9781003352228-9

妈妈:	忙得连打电话的时间都没有吗? 你哥哥也这样, 已经好久没跟爸爸妈妈联系了。你们兄妹俩, 真不孝顺! 一点都不关心父母!
Joy:	啊 …… 妈妈, 哥哥的工作应该也很忙吧。
妈妈:	哎, 他应该忙着谈恋爱吧。对了, 上个月你哥哥带女朋友去看你, 怎么样? 怎么样? 他找了一个什么样的女孩? 我问了他好几次, 他就是不说。
Joy:	挺好的, 大大的眼睛, 细细的眉毛, 高高的鼻子, 鹅蛋脸, 棕色的皮肤, 跟我差不多高, 身材非常苗条。她留着黑黑的长发, 戴着一副眼镜, 看起来挺有气质的。她跟哥哥很谈得来。
妈妈:	性格怎么样? 她是哪个大学毕业的? 是学什么专业的? 现在在做什么工作? 父母是哪儿人啊?
Joy:	哎呀, 妈妈, 您怎么这么操心啊。
妈妈:	三十而立, 你哥哥快三十岁了, 还没有结婚, 我真的急死了, 当然要问清楚他找了什么样的女孩。对了, 我加了你们兄妹俩的脸书, 已经5天了, 你们俩怎么都还没接受我啊! 妈妈有了你们的脸书, 看到你们的生活, 就不用那么担心了!
Joy:	啊 …… 啊 …… 这个这个 …… 哦, 对了, 妈妈, 您跟爸爸最近怎么样?

Cāoxīn de māma

Māma:	Joy, nǐ yǐjīng yīge yuè méi gēn bàba māma shìpín liáotiān le! Nǐ zài máng shénme ne?
Joy:	Mā, wǒ zhège xuéqī de kè dōu hěn zhòng, yǒu hěnduō gōngkè. Chúle shàngkè yǐwài, wǒ yě cānjiāle liǎng ge shètuán, lìngwài hái xiǎng zhǎo shíxí, zhēn de hǎo máng a.
Māma:	Máng de lián dǎ diànhuà de shíjiān dōu méiyǒu ma? Nǐ gēge yě zhèyàng, yǐjīng hǎojiǔ méi gēn bàba māma liánxì le. Nǐmen xiōngmèi liǎ, zhēn bù xiàoshùn! Yīdiǎn dōu bù guānxīn fùmǔ!
Joy:	A . . . māma, gēge de gōngzuò yīnggāi yě hěn máng ba.
Māma:	Āi, tā yīnggāi mángzhe tán liàn'ài ba. Duìle, shàng ge yuè nǐ gēge dài nǚ péngyǒu qù kàn nǐ, zěnmeyàng? Zěnmeyàng? Tā zhǎole yīge shénme yàng de nǚhái? Wǒ wènle tā hǎojǐ cì, tā jiùshì bù shuō.
Joy:	Tǐng hǎo de, dàdà de yǎnjīng, xìxì de méimáo, gāogāo de bízi, édànliǎn, zōngsè de pífū, gēn wǒ chàbùduō gāo, shēncái fēicháng miáotiáo. Tā liúzhe hēihēi de chángfà, dàizhe yī fù yǎnjìng, kàn qǐlái tǐng yǒu qìzhì de. Tā gēn gēge hěn tándelái.
Māma:	Xìnggé zěnmeyàng? Tā shì nǎge dàxué bìyè de? Shì xué shénme zhuānyè de? Xiànzài zài zuò shénme gōngzuò? Fùmǔ shì nǎ'er rén a?
Joy:	Āiya, māma, nín zěnme zhème cāoxīn a.
Māma:	Sānshí érlì, nǐ gēge kuài sānshí suìle, hái méiyǒu jiéhūn, wǒ zhēnde jísǐle, dāngrán yào wèn qīngchǔ tā zhǎole shénmeyàng de nǚhái. Duìle, wǒ jiā le nǐmen xiōngmèi liǎ de Liǎnshū, yǐjīng wǔ tiānle, nǐmen liǎ zěnme

dōu hái méi jiēshòu wǒ a! Māma yǒule nǐmen de Liánshū, kàn dào
nǐmen de shēnghuó, jiù bùyòng nàme dānxīnle!

Joy: A . . . a . . . zhège zhège . . . ò, duìle, māma, nín gēn bàba zuìjìn
zěnmeyàng?

生词 Vocabulary

Students are required to recognize and pronounce all the vocabulary listed. For
the characters/words in italics and bold, students are also expected to know how
to write.

1.	社团	社團	shètuán	n.	organization; group; club
2.	实习	實習	shíxí	v./n.	intern; internship
3.	**联系**	聯繫	liánxì	v.	contact; connect
4.	孝顺	孝順	xiàoshùn	v./adj.	show filial obedience; filial
5.	**工作**	工作	gōngzuò	v./n.	work
6.	**应该**	應該	yīnggāi	v.	should; ought to; must
7.	带	帶	dài	v.	take along; bring; carry
8.	眼睛	眼睛	yǎnjīng	n.	eyes
9.	鼻子	鼻子	bízi	n.	nose
10.	鹅蛋	鵝蛋	édàn	n.	goose egg
11.	脸	臉	liǎn	n.	face
12.	棕色	棕色	zōngsè	n.	brown
13.	皮肤	皮膚	pífū	n.	skin
14.	身材	身材	shēncái	n.	figure
15.	苗条	苗條	miáotiáo	adj.	slim
16.	**戴**	戴	dài	v.	to wear; *Both 穿 (chuān) and 戴 (dài) are verbs, meaning to put on or wear.
17.	副	副	fù	mw.	pair
18.	气质	氣質	qìzhì	n.	temperament; personality traits; manners
19.	性格	性格	xìnggé	n	personality
20.	**操心**	操心	cāoxīn	adj/v.	concerned about; concern
21.	**担心**	擔心	dānxīn	v.	worry
22.	**最近**	最近	zuìjìn	adv.	recently; lately; in the near future

Proper Name

1.	脸书	臉書	Liǎnshū	Facebook

*穿 vs. 戴

Generally, 穿 (chuān) is used when referring to frequent or habitual actions or behaviors ; 戴 (dài) is used to refer to accessories, for example, gloves, caps, hats, necklaces, rings, earrings, glasses, etc.

穿衣服 (制服、西装、运动服 …… 等等)	chuān yīfu (zhìfú, xīzhuāng, yùndòng fú . . . děng děng)	wear clothes (uniforms, suits, sportswear . . . etc.)
穿裤子	chuān kùzi	wear pants
穿袜子	chuān wàzi	wear socks
穿鞋子 (球鞋、凉鞋、高跟鞋 …… 等等)	chuān xiézi (qiúxié, liángxié, gāogēnxié . . . děng děng)	wear shoes (sports shoes, sandals, high heels . . . etc.)
穿裙子	chuān qúnzi	wear a skirt
戴手套	dài shǒutào	wear gloves
戴围巾	dài wéijīn	wear a scarf
戴耳环	dài ěrhuán	wear earrings
戴项链	dài xiàngliàn	wear a necklace
戴帽子	dài màozi	wear a hat
戴眼镜	dài yǎnjìng	wear glasses
戴戒指	dài jièzhi	wear a ring

Sentence Patterns / Grammar

1. Subject + (已经) + Duration + 没 + Verb + 了 : have not done something for a period of time

*Note that 已经 can be omitted.

你已经一个月没跟爸爸妈妈视频聊天了。
You haven't had a video chat with Mom and Dad for a month.

Examples:

1) 我已经两星期没运动了。
I haven't exercised for two weeks.
2) 疫情期间 (yìqíng qījiān) 我和家人已经十八个月没见面了。
I haven't seen my family for 18 months during the pandemic.

2. 除了 …… 以外 …… (也/还/) …… Besides / in addition to . . .

　　除了 …… 以外 …… 都 …… except

除了上课以外, 我也参加了两个社团, 另外还想找实习。
Besides attending classes, I also joined two clubs, and I also want to find an internship.

Examples:

1) 除了钱 (qián) 和时间以外, 你还需要努力 (nǔlì)。
　　Besides money and time, you also need to work hard.
2) 世界上最穷的人是除了钱以外什么都没有的人。
　　The poorest people in the world are those who have nothing but money.

3. Subject + 一点 (儿) + 也 / 都 + 不 + Adj.

　　Subject + 一点 (儿) + (noun) + 也 / 都 + 不 + Verb Phrase

　　The phrases 一点 (儿) 也不 and 一点 (儿) 都不 can both be used to express "not at all".

你们俩一点都不关心父母!
You two don't care about your parents at all!

Examples:

1) 他做的菜一点儿也不好吃。
　　His cooking is not delicious at all.
2) 学生一点都不知道这件事。
　　Students don't know anything about it.

4. 挺adj 的

挺 (tǐng) can be used before an adjective to mean "quite", "rather", or "pretty", as in "pretty good". This pattern is quite common in spoken Chinese.

Examples:

挺好的 pretty good
挺年轻的 pretty young
挺关心的 ＿＿＿＿＿＿＿＿＿
挺无聊的 ＿＿＿＿＿＿＿＿＿
挺重要的 ＿＿＿＿＿＿＿＿＿
挺孝顺的 ＿＿＿＿＿＿＿＿＿

5. Reduplication of monosyllabic adjectives: it's mostly for adjectives that describe the physical world: colors, sizes, shapes, and other physical descriptors.

大大的眼睛 (big eyes)，细细的眉毛 (thin eyebrows)
高高的鼻子 (tall nose)，黑黑的头发 (dark hair)

Examples:

圆圆的脸 (liǎn)   红红的脸颊 (liǎnjiá)
高高的个子   胖胖的身体 (pàngpàng de shēntǐ)
长长的头发   尖尖的下巴 (jiānjiān de xiàbā)

6. A跟B谈得来 be able to talk to; get along

谈得来 refers to the kind of relationship in which two people enjoy talking with each other or get along well due to perhaps the same interest or personality.

她跟哥哥很谈得来。
She gets along well with her brother.

Examples:

1) 我喜欢和我的室友在一起, 因为我跟她很谈得来。
   I like being with my roommate because I can talk with her very well.
2) 上了大学以后, 我觉得我跟什么人都谈得来。
   After I went to college, I felt I could talk to anyone.

7. Adj+ 死了

In English, you might use the expression "you scared me to death!" In Chinese, 死了 (sǐ le) is used similarly to intensify an adjective with an unpleasant connotation.

Examples:

急 (jí) 死了; 热 (rè) 死了; 累 (lèi) 死了; 贵 (guì) 死了; 吵 (chǎo) 死了; 饿 (è) 死了

夏天穿这件皮大衣, 我快要_____。
我今天什么都没吃, 快要_____。
私立 (sīlì, private) 大学的学费真是 _____。
站着上班一整天 (zhěng tiān, whole day) 都没休息, 真是要_____。
孩子整夜 (zhěng yè, whole night) 不回家把妈妈 _____。
在飞机场附近 (fùjìn) 住真是_____, 飞机的噪音 (zàoyīn, noise) 太大。

III. Vocabulary and Grammar Exercise

1. Radical Recognition

Please identify the radicals of the following characters. Write down the radical and its meaning.

1. Examples: 好 → (女) woman

示 1) 社 → (shì) spirit

目 3) 眼 → (mù) eye

木 5) 材 → (mù) tree

扌 7) 操 → (shǒu) hand

忄 9) 性 → (xīn) heart

耳 2) 联 → (ěr) ear

艹 4) 苗 → (cǎo) grass

月 6) 脸 → (yuè) moon

扌 8) 担 → (shǒu) hand

月 10) 肤 → (yuè) moon

2. Word-building Exercises

For each of the characters in the next example, write three more words that include that character.

1) 习: 实习 xué xí xí guàn liàn xí
2) 色: 棕色 yán sè sè cǎi —
3) 眼: 眼睛 yǎn jìng yǎn guāng —
4) 气: 气质 shēng qì kōng qì tiān qì
5) 皮: 皮肤 pí xié pí dài

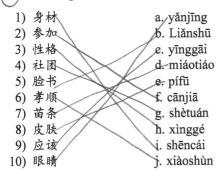

学习 习惯 练习　颜色 色彩
眼镜 眼光
生气 空气 天气
皮鞋 皮带

3. Matching Exercise: Please match Pinyin and characters

1) 身材
2) 参加
3) 性格
4) 社团
5) 脸书
6) 孝顺
7) 苗条
8) 皮肤
9) 应该
10) 眼睛

a. yǎnjīng
b. Liǎnshū
c. yīnggāi
d. miáotiáo
e. pífū
f. cānjiā
g. shètuán
h. xìnggé
i. shēncái
j. xiàoshùn

4. Fill in the blanks with the appropriate words

专业　担心　功课　毕业　脸书　视频　结婚　实习　社团　恋爱

1) 大学生在学期中常常有很多 gōng kè ，也要参加 shè tuán 和找暑假 shí xí ，常常没时间和父母 shì pín 聊天。
2) 华裔父母亲常常非常关心孩子什么时候谈 liàn ài ，什么时候要 jié hūn ，交往的男女朋友是哪一个学校 bì yè ，读什么 zhuān yè 和做什么工作的。他们觉得如果加入孩子们的 liǎn shū 看到他们的生活，就不会那么 dān xīn 。

1)功课 2)社团 3)实习 4)视频 5)恋爱
6)结婚 7)毕业 8)专业 9)脸书 10)担心

5. 请看图完成人物描述(miáoshù)

1) 美丽   5) 深色
2) 有光滑   6) 明亮
3) 比较短   7) 圆圆
4) 苗条   8) 友好

Figure 32 My roommate

我的室友XXX身高一米六八，长得非常＿＿＿＿＿① ＿＿＿＿＿，她＿＿＿②＿＿＿的皮肤，＿＿＿③＿＿＿的头发，头发有一些自然卷。她长着一张＿④＿脸，看上去很成熟。她有＿＿⑤＿＿的眉毛，＿＿⑥＿＿的眼睛和＿⑦＿的下巴。她又有礼貌又有＿＿＿⑧＿＿＿，非常受人欢迎。

IV. Post-reading Discussion

1. 不常跟父母联系是不孝顺的表现吗？你是一个孝顺的孩子吗？你觉得"孝顺"是指什么？请举例。
    Is it not filial for kids not to keep in touch with parents often? Are you a filial child? What do you think "filial piety" means? Please give an example.
2. 你觉得Joy会把她妈妈加为脸书的好友吗？她应该怎么做？
    Do you think Joy will add her mom as a friend on Facebook? What would she do?
3. 你跟你的家人在一些社交媒体 (shèjiāoméitǐ) 上是好友吗？为什么？
    Are you and your family members on some social media? Why?
4. 一般来说，对亚裔 (yàyì) 外貌 (wàimào) 有哪些刻板印象 (kèbǎnyìnxiàng)？
    Generally speaking, what are some stereotypes about Asian appearance that you know of?
5. 不同国家对美有什么不同的标准？跟中国一样吗？你们怎么看这些标准？
    What are the different beauty standards in different countries? Is it the same as China? What do you think of these standards?

V. Interpersonal Tasks

1. 说一说，画一画 (huà draw) Describe and Draw

这个活动有三步 (bù, step):

第一步: 两个人一起,先照课文里 Joy 的描述 (miáoshù, description), 把 Joy 哥哥的女朋友画出来。

第二步：你想象 (xiǎngxiàng) 中的Joy哥哥是什么样子? 请用中文描述 (miáoshù) 一下。另一个同学得照这个描述 (miáoshù) 把Joy哥哥画出来。画的时候，可以问一些问题，比如，确认 (quèrèn, confirm) 你没听错或者问问同伴 (tóngbàn, partner) 没提 (tí, mention) 到的信息。

第三步：跟全班同学分享，一起看看你们画的 Joy 哥哥和他的女朋友。

There are three steps in this activity.

Step 1: two students together, draw Joy's brother's girlfriend according to Joy's description in the lesson dialogue.

Step 2: what does Joy's brother look like in your imagination? Please describe him in Chinese. Another student has to draw Joy's brother according to the description. When drawing, please ask some questions, for example, make sure you hear the description correctly or ask for information that your partner does not mention.

Step 3: share your drawings of Joy's brother and his girlfriend with the rest of class.

2. 角色扮演 (juésè bànyǎn) Role-play

已经开学两个月了，可是你一直没跟家人联系，他们开始非常担心你是不是都还好。晚上七点你正在做功课，XXX (e.g., 爸爸/妈妈/爷爷/奶奶/外公/外婆……)给你打了视频电话，你们说了什么?

请跟一个同学一起，请用至少十个生词和五个句型进行这个对话。

生词(words)：孝顺、关心、担心、操心、气质、谈得来、性格、毕业、专业、工作、实习、社团、接受

句型 (patterns)：

Subject + (已经) + Duration + 没 + Verb + 了
除了 …… 以外 …… 也 / 还 / 都 ……
Subject + 一点 (儿) + 也 / 都 + 不 + Adj.
Subject + 一点 (儿) + (Noun) + 也 / 都 + 不 + Verb
挺adj 的
Reduplication of monosyllabic adjectives (e.g., 高高的)
A跟B谈得来
Adj. + 死了

It's been two months since school started, but you haven't contacted your family. They are very worried about whether you are all right. At seven o'clock in the evening, you were doing your homework. XXX (e.g., dad/mom/grandpa/grandma) gave you a video call. What did you say?

Please pair up with a classmate and choose at least ten words and five patterns from the list in the previous section to carry out the conversation.

Part II 短文: 望子成龙、望女成凤

I. Warm-up: Pre-reading Discussion

1. 你的父母严格吗? 请举例。
   Are your parents very strict? Please give some examples.
2. 你觉得你父母教育你的方法跟你同学的父母的方法一样还是不一样? 为什么?
   Do you find your parents' way of parenting different from your classmates' parents'? Why?
3. 你觉得虎妈的教育方法好不好? 为什么?
   Did you find the tiger mom's way of parenting good? Why?

II. Interpretive Task: Listening Comprehension

Please listen to the text and choose True (T) or False (F) for each of the following audio recordings of the statements.

1. (对)   2. (错)   3. (对)   4. (对)   5. (对)

望子成龙、望女成凤

成绩不可以低于A!
不可以在同学家过夜!
不可以玩电脑游戏!
不可以看电视!

耶鲁大学的华裔教授蔡美儿在《虎妈战歌》里介绍了她对两个女儿的"中国式教育"。她对女儿们有很多要求, 这是其中四条。虽然我的父母没有蔡美儿那么严格, 但是也有望女成凤的想法, 常常给我很大的压力。

一些压力来自于父母喜欢拿我跟"别人家的孩子"做比较, 比如:

"我听说李叔叔的女儿SAT考了1600分。她还比你小呢。"

"你看, 王阿姨的儿子大学选的专业是计算机, 一毕业就拿到了年薪10万美金的工作。你对计算机感兴趣吗?"

"你知道吗? 马叔叔的女儿考上了哈佛商学院, 将来找到好工作一定没问题! 你以后想要读研究生吗? 能申请到哈佛吗?"

另一些压力来自于父母为我的教育做出的牺牲, 比如, 为了让我上一个好高中, 父母花了很多钱买学区房。现在为了付我的大学学费和住宿费, 他们一直省吃俭用。

在这些压力下, 父母的关心和爱却成了我的负担, 好像让"听父母的话"成了理所当然的事情, 不听话就是不孝顺。

Hope Kids To Be Successful

Not allowed to get any grade less than an A.
Not allowed to attend a sleepover.
Not allowed to play computer games.
Not allowed to watch TV.

These four rules are part of the rules of "Chinese model parenting" that were introduced by Amy Chua, a professor of Yale Law School, in her book *Battle Hymn of the Tiger Mother*. Although my parents are not as strict as Amy Chua, they share the idea of "hoping your daughter to become a phoenix (to be successful)", which often brings me a lot of pressure.

Some of the pressure is from comparing me to other kids. For example,

"I heard that Uncle Li's daughter's SAT score is 1600. She is even younger than you are!"

"Look, Auntie Wang's son's major is computer science. He got a job with an annual pay of $100,000, right after graduating from college. Are you interested in computer science?"

"Did you know that Uncle Ma's daughter got into Harvard Business School, so she definitely will get a good job in the future! Do you want to go to graduate school in the future? Do you think that you can get into Harvard?"

Another source of pressure is the fact that my parents made sacrifices for my education. For example, in order for me to go to a good high school, my parents have spent a lot of money buying a house in the good school district. They always live frugally so they can pay for my college tuition and boarding fee.

Under this circumstance, my parents' care and love have become nothing but my burden. It seems that "obeying my parents" has become a norm, and if I don't obey them, I am an unfilial child.

生词 Vocabulary

Students are required to recognize and pronounce all the vocabulary listed. For the characters/words in italics and bold, students are also expected to know how to write.

1.	望子成**龙**	望子成龍	wàng zǐ chéng lóng	idm.	have high expectations of one's son
2.	望女成**凤**	望女成鳳	wàng nǚ chéng fèng	idm.	have high expectations of one's daughter
3.	**成绩**	成績	chéngjì	n.	score; grade
4.	低	低	dī	adj.	low
5.	于	於	yú	prep.	[indicating comparison] than, e.g., 低于; [indicating beginning or source] from, e.g., 来自于
6.	过夜	過夜	guòyè	v.	spend a night
7.	游戏	遊戲	yóuxì	n.	game
8.	**教授**	教授	jiàoshòu	n.	professor
9.	虎妈	虎媽	hǔmā	n.	tiger mom
10.	**介绍**	介紹	jièshào	v.	introduce

11.	中国式	中國式	Zhōngguó shì	n.	Chinese style
12.	**要求**	要求	yāoqiú	v./n.	request; require; requirement
13.	其中	其中	qízhōng	adv.	among
14.	严格	嚴格	yángé	adj.	strict
15.	**压力**	壓力	yālì	n.	pressure
16.	年薪	年薪	niánxīn	n.	annual salary; yearly income
17.	将来	將來	jiānglái	n.	future
18.	研究生	研究生	yánjiūshēng	n.	graduate student
19.	申请	申請	shēnqǐng	v.	apply
20.	**牺牲**	犧牲	xīshēng	v./n.	sacrifice
21.	**钱**	錢	qián	n.	money
22.	学区房	學區房	xuéqū fáng	n.	house in a good school district
23.	付	付	fù	v.	pay
24.	学费	學費	xuéfèi	n.	tuition
25.	住宿费	住宿費	zhùsù fèi	n.	room and board cost
26.	**省吃俭用**	省吃儉用	shěngchījiǎnyòng	ph.	live frugally
27.	负担	負擔	fùdān	n.	burden
28.	理所当然	理所當然	lǐsuǒdāngrán	idm.	naturally; to be expected as a matter of course

Proper Names

1.	耶鲁大学	耶魯大學	Yēlǔ dàxué	Yale University
2.	虎妈战歌	虎媽戰歌	Hǔmā zhàngē	Battle Hymn of the Tiger Mother
3.	哈佛商学院	哈佛商學院	Hāfó shāng xuéyuàn	Harvard Business School

Sentence Patterns / Grammar

1. 低于/ 高于: **lower/higher than . . . This pattern indicates comparison. 于 is used after an adjective, and it has the same meaning as 比 (meaning than).**

成绩不可以低于A。
Grades cannot be lower than A.

Examples:

1) 医生的年薪高于老师的年薪。
The annual salary of a doctor is higher than that of a teacher.
2) 毕业以后，你希望年薪不低于多少？
After graduation, how much do you hope your annual salary will be no less than?

2. A没有B (那么) adj: A is not as adj. as B.

This pattern is another way to make comparisons, indicating A is not as "adjective" as B or A is less "adjective" than B.

我的父母没有蔡美儿那么严格。
My parents are not as strict as Cai Mei'er.

Examples:

1) 中国大学的学费没有美国的那么贵。
Tuition fees in Chinese universities are not as expensive as in the United States.
2) 我的成绩没有哥哥的那么好。
My grades are not as good as those of my elder brother.

A比B + (更) + adj. "比" between two things indicates comparison, meaning "than". When 更 is used before the adjective, it indicates B is "adjective", but A is even more "adjective".

Examples:

1) 哥哥比我高。
My brother is taller than me.
2) 上海比纽约更大。
Shanghai is even bigger than New York.
3) 住校内比住校外方便。
Living on campus is more convenient than living off campus.

Adverbs of degree can be used in the 比 structure to indicate the degree that A is more adjective than B.

A 比 B+adj.+ "多了" or "得多": A is a lot more adj. than B.
A 比 B+adj.+ "一些": A is much more adj. than B.
A 比 B+adj.+ "一点": A is a little bit more adj. than B.

Examples:

1) 哥哥比我高多了。or 哥哥比我高得多。
My brother is a lot taller than me.

2) 中国的人口比美国的人口多多了or 多得多。
    The Chinese population is a lot bigger than that of the U.S.
3) 姐姐比我聪明一点。
    My elder sister is a little bit smarter than me.

Please note the following:

1) 很 cannot be used in the comparison.
    哥哥比我很高。(X)

2) 一样 (yīyàng, the same) cannot be used in the comparison.

    住校内比住校外一样方便。(X)
    一样 is often used in "A跟/和B + 一样 + adj.", meaning "A is as adj.
        as B".
    住校内和住校外一样方便。(✓)

3) The adjectives used in the comparison should not be negative.

    上海比纽约不大。(X)
    上海没有纽约大。or 上海不比纽约大。(✓)

3. 拿A跟B做比较: compare A with B, often used as "someone拿A跟B做比较"

父母喜欢拿我跟 "别人家的孩子" 做比较。
My parents like to compare me with "other people's kids" (kids who often
have been outstanding since childhood).

Examples:

1) 很多留学生常常会拿中国跟美国做比较。
    Many international students often compare China with the United States.
2) 不要拿自己的短处 (duǎnchù) 跟别人的长处做比较。
    Don't compare your own shortcomings with the strengths of others.

4. 一 + action 1 就 + action 2: "as soon as" or "once". This pattern indicates "As soon as the subject does action 1, then action 2 will happen", or "whenever the subject does action 1, they do action 2". The subjects of the two actions can be the same or different. If the subjects are the same, then you don't need to repeat the subject for the second action. If the subjects are different, then the second subject goes before "就".

王阿姨的儿子一毕业就拿到了年薪10万美金的工作。
Upon graduation, Aunt Wang's son got a job with an annual salary of 100,000
U.S. dollars.

Examples:

1) 我一回家就写作业。
    I will do my homework as soon as I get home.

2)　孩子们一回家, 妈妈就开始做晚饭。
As soon as the children got home, mother began to cook dinner.

"一 …… 就 ……" **can also be used to express "whenever" to indicate that a habitual action will happen whenever some other event or action happens. For example:**

1)　这两兄弟一见面就吵架, 但是一分开又很想念对方。
The two brothers would quarrel whenever they met, but they started to miss each other very much right after being separated.
2)　爸爸建议我学习上一有问题就要去找老师。
My father suggested that I should go to the teacher whenever I have any problems in my study.

5. 为 …… 做出 (的) 牺牲: make sacrifice for . . . / the sacrifice made for . . .; it is often used as "someone 为 something or somebody else 做出 (的) 牺牲".

另一些压力来自于父母为我的教育做出的牺牲。
Other pressures came from the sacrifices my parents made for my education.

Examples:

1)　大多数中国父母愿意为子女做出很多牺牲。
Most Chinese parents are willing to make many sacrifices for their children.
2)　有些子女不感谢 (gǎnxiè) 父母为他们做出的牺牲。
Some children don't feel grateful to their parents for the sacrifices their parents made for them.
3)　你愿意为谁或者什么做出牺牲? 是什么样的牺牲?
For whom or what are you willing to sacrifice? What kind of sacrifice?

6. 在 …… 压力下: under the pressure of . . .; it can be used at the beginning of a sentence or before the verb.

在这些压力下, 父母的关心和爱却成了我的负担。
Under these pressures, the care and love of my parents became my burden.

Examples:

1)　在高考的压力下, 很多孩子出现了心理问题。
Under the pressure of the college entrance examination, many children have psychological problems.
2)　州长 (zhōuzhǎng) 在巨大(jùdà) 的压力下辞职 (cízhí) 了。
The governor resigned under tremendous pressure.

III. Vocabulary and Grammar Exercise

1. Complete the sentences or answer the questions with the given patterns.

1) 低于 / 高于

    a. 上次考试我考了80分，这次考了90分。这次的成绩_____。

    b. 我希望毕业后的年薪_____10万美元。

2) 拿A跟B做比较; A没有B那么adj.; A比B + (更) + adj.;
A比B + adj. +多了 / 得多 / 一些/一点; A跟B一样adj.

    a. 拿大学生活跟高中生活做比较, 我觉得:

      • _____ (忙)

      • _____ (轻松 qīngsōng, relaxed)

      • _____ (好玩)

    b. 拿中国跟美国做比较,

      • _____ (人口; 多) 。

      • _____ (面积 miànjī, area; 大)

      • _____ (气候 qìhòu, climate; 好)

      • _____ (经济 jīngjì, economy; 发达 fādá, developed)

3) 一 + Event 1就 + Event 2

    a. 我常常_____。 (event 1: 回宿舍)

    b. 学生们_____。 (event 1: 放假)

4) 为 …… 做出 (的) 牺牲
中国父母会为子女做出哪些牺牲? 你觉得他们做出的这些牺牲有道理吗? 为什么?
如果以后你成了父母, 会为子女做出牺牲吗? 做出什么样的牺牲?

5) 在 …… 压力下
你最近有压力吗? 什么压力? 在这种压力下, 你会做什么? 不做什么?

2. 选择填空 Fill in the blanks.

毕业	申请	研究生	省吃俭用	孝顺	望子成龙	望女成凤
严格	成绩	年薪	牺牲	负担	学区房	

    很多中国父母 _望子成龙 望女成凤_ 他们对子女很 _严格_ , 希望孩子的学习 _成绩_ 好, 将来可以 _申请_ 到名校上大学。大学 _毕业_ 后可以找到 _年薪_ 高的工作或者读 _研究生_ 。为了实现 (shíxiàn) 这些愿望 (yuànwàng, wish), 这些父母愿意为孩子的教育做出很多 _牺牲_ : 比如, 花很多钱买 _学区房_ 他们在生活上却一直 _省吃俭用_ 。可是这些做法给孩子带来了很多压力。父母的爱和关心也成了 _负担_ 。孩子们觉得如果不听父母的话就是不 _孝顺_ 。唉, 这些父母和孩子都很不容易啊!

1)望子成龙 2)望女成凤 3)严格 4)成绩
5)申请 6)毕业 7)年薪 8)研究生 9)牺牲
10)学区房 11)省吃俭用 12)负担 13)孝顺

3. 小作文 Short essay:

写一篇200字左右的作文。在文章中，请先分析 (fēnxī) 一下中国式家庭教育方式 (fāngshì) 的利弊 (lìbì)，然后谈谈你对这种教育方式 (fāngshì) 的看法。请选用下面至少5-8个词汇和句型。

Please write an essay of about 200 characters. In your essay, please first analyze the merits and drawbacks of Chinese parenting, and then discuss your views on it. Please use at least five to eight words and all grammatical structures in the next section.

> 生词 (words): 望子成龙、望女成凤、严格、孝顺、省吃俭用、压力、负担、年薪、申请、理所当然
>
> 句型 (patterns): "比" sentences; A没有B那么adj; 拿A跟B做比较; 为 …… 做出 (的) 牺牲; 在 …… 压力下

IV. Post-reading Discussion

1. 你怎么看虎妈列出的这四条要求？你有这样的经历吗？如果你是父母，你会有什么样的要求？

   How do you view Tiger Mom's four rules? Did you have the same experiences? If you were a parent now, what kind of rules would you set up for your children?

2. 有的父母喜欢拿自己的孩子跟"别人家的孩子"做比较。你觉得这种做法怎么样？

   Some parents like to compare their own kids with "other kids". What do you think about it?

3. 你觉得什么时候父母的期望和爱会成为负担？

   When do you think parents' expectation and love would become a burden to a child?

4. 你生活中的压力主要来自于哪里？你是怎么面对这些压力的？

   What are sources of pressure in your life? How do you deal with these pressures?

5. 因为父母的爱和牺牲，孩子就一定要听父母的话吗？比如：在选专业、读研究生的问题上，"我" 应该听父母的话吗？为什么？

   Should children obey parents' wishes completely because of sacrifices their parents make for them? For example, should the author in the lesson text follow parents' wishes to choose his/her major or attend a graduate school? Why?

V. Presentational Task

采访 (cǎifǎng) 三个学生，问问他们的父母是怎么教育他们的？请从不同的方面谈谈，比如：学习、交朋友、选专业、谈恋爱等等。这些同学不一定要是华裔学生。然后根据采访的结果(jiéguǒ)，做一个口头报告 (kǒutóu bàogào)。在报告里，也要比较一下这些同学的父母的教育方法跟你父母的一样还是不一样？哪里一样？哪里不一样？

Interview three students about how their parents raised them. The interview could include but is not limited to studying, making friends, choosing majors, dating, and so on. The interviewees can be from any ethnic group. Then conduct an oral presentation based on your interview. In your presentation, you should also compare and include the differences and similarities between the interviewees' upbringing and yours.

Lesson Six 中文教育

Learning Objectives

In this lesson, you will learn to do the following:

1. Explain reasons for learning Chinese.
2. Narrate a story about Chinese learning experience.
3. Compare Chinese language education in the past and at present.
4. Write a brief biography of a historical figure.
5. Analyze the factors that influence Chinese language education in the U.S.

I. Warm-up: Pre-reading Discussion

1. 你为什么要学中文? 你觉得学中文最大的困难是什么?
   Why do you want to learn Chinese? What do you think is the biggest difficulty in learning Chinese?
2. 你觉得汉字难学吗? 你会写几个汉字?
   Do you think Chinese characters are difficult to learn? How many Chinese characters can you write?
3. 你猜猜看世界上有多少个汉字? 看得懂中文报纸需要认识多少个汉字?
   Can you guess how many Chinese characters there are in the world? How many Chinese characters do you need to recognize to understand Chinese newspapers?

II. Interpretive Task: Listening Comprehension

Please listen to the lesson dialogue and choose True (T) or False (F) for each of the following audio recordings of the statements.

1. (错) 2. (错) 3. (错) 4. (对) 5. (对)

Main Text

Part I 对话: 学中文的十个理由

Eric: Joy, 你的中文已经说得那么流利了, 为什么还要来上中文课?

DOI: 10.4324/9781003352228-10

Joy: 我要学中文因为我希望能够看懂中国餐馆里的中文菜单。

Eric: 是啊! 看懂菜单真的很重要, 去年我在上海带着一群不懂中文的美国朋友去吃牛排闹了一个大笑话。

Joy: 怎么了? 上海的牛排好吃吗?

Eric: 哎, 我们在当地的一个小饭馆, 看到墙上的菜单 "牛排饭" 真便宜, 所以我们一人点了一份。大家越吃越奇怪, 吃起来像鸡肉, 一点也不像牛肉。后来才知道是 "牛蛙" 不是 "牛排"!

Joy: 哈哈! 牛蛙是 "Bullfrog" 啊! 你的美国朋友肯定吓昏了吧! 我也只认识 "牛" 这个字啊!

Eric: 你不是从小就上中文学校吗? 怎么你也看不懂中文菜单、中文报纸呢?

Joy: 我小时候一点也不喜欢上中文学校, 功课又多又难。父母、老师都逼得很紧, 让我们的关系十分紧张。我从小学钢琴、画画, 星期六去中文学校, 我越来越讨厌这种生活, 特别是牺牲星期六的时间去中文学校!

Eric: 我的妈妈是新加坡人, 她在家里也和我说中文。对我来说, 学中文并不只是为了满足大学的语言要求, 也是为了和妈妈在新加坡的家人交流。我希望可以去中国学习中文、旅行、看懂中文电视、中国电影、听懂中国歌曲的歌词, 可以从另外一个文化视角来考虑问题。

Joy: 是啊 …… 现在会说双语的人更有吸引力, 科学研究说会说双语的人更聪明呢!

Eric: 嗯, 如果我把中文学好, 将来还可以教我的小孩, 让他们也可以变得更聪明!

Xué zhōngwén de shí ge lǐyóu

Eric: Joy, nǐ de Zhōngwén yǐjīng shuō de nàme liúlì le, wèishéme hái yào lái shàng Zhōngwénkè?

Joy: Wǒ yào xué Zhōngwén yīnwèi wǒ xīwàng nénggòu kàn dǒng Zhōngguó cānguǎn lǐ de Zhōngwén càidān.

Eric: Shì a! Kàn dǒng càidān zhēn de hěn zhòngyào, qùnián wǒ zài Shànghǎi dàizhe yīqún bù dǒng Zhōngwén de Měiguó péngyou qù chī niúpái nàole yīgè dà xiàohuà.

Joy: Zěnmele? Shànghǎi de niúpái hǎochī ma?

Eric: Āi, wǒmen zài dāngdì de yīge xiǎo fànguǎn, kàn dào qiáng shàng de càidān "niúpái fàn" zhēn piányi, suǒyǐ wǒmen yīrén diǎnle yī fèn. Dàjiā yuè chī yuè qíguài, chī qǐlái xiàng jīròu, yīdiǎn yě bù xiàng niúròu. Hòulái cái zhīdào shì "niúwā" bùshì "niúpái"!

Joy: Hāha! Niúwā shì "Bullfrog" a! Nǐ de Měiguó péngyou kěndìng xià hūnle ba! Wǒ yě zhǐ rènshi "niú" zhège zì a!

Eric: Nǐ bùshì cóngxiǎo jiù shàng Zhōngwén xuéxiào ma? Zěnme nǐ yě kànbudǒng Zhōngwén càidān, Zhōngwén bàozhǐ ne?

Joy: Wǒ xiǎoshíhòu yīdiǎn yě bù xǐhuān shàng Zhōngwén xuéxiào, gōngkè yòu duō yòu nán, fùmǔ, lǎoshī dōu bī de hěn jǐn, ràng wǒmen de guānxi shífēn jǐnzhāng. Wǒ cóngxiǎo xué gāngqín, huàhuà, xīngqīliù qù Zhōngwén xuéxiào, wǒ yuè lái yuè tǎoyàn zhè zhǒng shēnghuó, tèbié shì xīshēng xīngqīliù de shíjiān qù Zhōngwén xuéxiào!

Eric: Wǒ de māma shì Xīnjiāpōrén, tā zài jiālǐ yě hé wǒ shuō Zhōngwén. Duì wǒ lái shuō, xué Zhōngwén bìng bù zhǐshì wèile mǎnzú dàxué de yǔyán yāoqiú, yěshì wèile hé māma zài Xīnjiāpō de jiārén jiāoliú. Wǒ xīwàng kěyǐ qù Zhōngguó xuéxí Zhōngwén, lǚxíng, kàn dǒng Zhōngwén diànshì, Zhōngguó diànyǐng, tīng dǒng Zhōngguó gēqǔ de gēcí, kěyǐ cóng lìngwài yīgè wénhuà shìjiǎo lái kǎolǜ wèntí.

Joy: Shì a . . . xiànzài huì shuō shuāngyǔ de rén gèng yǒu xīyǐnlì, kēxué yánjiū shuō huì shuō shuāngyǔ de rén gèng cōngming ne!

Eric: Èn, rúguǒ wǒ bǎ Zhōngwén xué hǎo, jiānglái hái kěyǐ jiāo wǒ de xiǎohái, ràng tāmen yě kěyǐ biànde gèng cōngming!

生词 Vocabulary

Students are required to recognize and pronounce all the vocabulary listed. For the characters/words in italics and bold, students are also expected to know how to write.

1.	理由	理由	lǐyóu	n.	reason; justification, *rationale*
2.	流利	流利	liúlì	adj.	fluent
3.	能够	能夠	nénggòu	v.	to be able to; can
4.	餐馆	餐館	cānguǎn	n.	restaurant
5.	菜单	菜單	càidān	n.	menu
6.	群	群	qún	mw.	group; herd
7.	当地	當地	dāngdì	adj.	local
8.	墙	牆	qiáng	n.	wall
9.	**便宜**	便宜	piányi	adj.	cheap; inexpensive
10.	肯定	肯定	kěndìng	adv.	surely; certainly
11.	吓昏	嚇昏	xiàhūn	v.	faint from fear; shell-shocked
12.	报纸	報紙	bàozhǐ	n.	newspaper
13.	逼	逼	bī	v.	force; compel
14.	紧	緊	jǐn	adj.	tight; strict
15.	**关系**	關係	guānxi	n.	relation; relationship
16.	**紧张**	緊張	jǐnzhāng	adj.	nervous; intense; tense
17.	钢琴	鋼琴	gāngqín	n.	piano
18.	画画	畫畫	huàhuà	v.o.	draw a picture
19.	越来越	越來越	yuèláiyuè	adv	more and more
20.	讨厌	討厭	tǎoyàn	v./adj.	dislike; loathe; annoying; troublesome
21.	满足	滿足	mǎnzú	v.	satisfy

22.	旅行	旅行	lǚxíng	v./n.	travel; journey; trip
23.	电影	電影	diànyǐng	n.	movie
24.	歌曲	歌曲	gēqǔ	n.	song
25.	歌词	歌詞	gēcí	n.	song lyric
26.	视角	視角	shìjiǎo	n.	viewpoint; perspective
27.	**考虑**	考慮	kǎolǜ	v./n.	consider; consideration
28.	吸引力	吸引力	xīyǐnlì	n.	attractiveness
29.	科学	科學	kēxué	n.	science; scientific knowledge
30.	**研究**	研究	yánjiū	n./v.	research; study
31.	**聪明**	聰明	cōngming	adj.	intelligent; smart

Sentence Patterns / Grammar

1. 又 adj./verb 又 adj./verb: both . . . and . . .

The two words used to highlight the certain traits should both be positive or both be negative.

中文学校的功课又多又难。
The homework in Chinese school is so many and difficult.

Examples:

1) 他的宿舍又乱 (luàn) 又脏 (zāng)。
His dorm is messy and dirty.
2) 她又会说日语又会说韩语。
She can speak both Japanese and Korean.

2. 越来越 adj./stative verb: more and more adj./stative verb over time

我越来越讨厌这种生活, 特别是牺牲星期六的时间去中文学校。
I hate this kind of life more and more, especially when I sacrifice Saturdays to go to Chinese school.

Examples:

1) 开学两个月了, Joy越来越习惯大学生活。
It's been two months since school started. Joy is more and more used to college life.
2) 我跟室友谈不来, 最近我们的关系越来越紧张。
I do not get along well with my roommate. Recently, our relationship has become increasingly tense.

越 …… 越 …… **the more . . . the more; it is typical that verbs follow the first "yue", while adjectives or emotion verbs follow the second "yue". The subjects before the first "yue" and the second "yue" could be different.**

大家越吃越奇怪, 吃起来像鸡肉, 一点也不像牛肉。
The more everyone eats it, the stranger they feel. It tastes like chicken, not like beef at all.

Examples:

1) 她的中文进步 (jìnbù) 很大, 越说越流利。
   She has made great progress in Chinese, and the more she speaks, the more fluent she is.
2) 妈妈越逼我学钢琴, 我越讨厌学。
   The more my mother forced me to learn piano, the more I hated it.

When the verbs/verb phrases/adjectives are negative, it is more appropriate to translate the patterns as "less and less" and "the less . . .".

Examples:

1) Joy 的妈妈觉得 Joy 越来越不关心父母。
   Joy's mother feels that Joy is less and less caring about her parents.
2) 父母越严格, 她越不想好好学。
   The stricter her parents are, the less she wants to study hard.

3. 对someone来说: to/for someone

This pattern is different from "在 someone 看来". While "对 someone 来说" indicates the person is involved and the feeling or the opinion is more based on personal experience. "在 someone 看来" is expressing the person's opinion more as an outsider and is often used in a formal discussion. For example, "对我来说, 跟她交流特别难, 她好像听不懂我说的话。" vs. "在我看来, 中美关系会越来越好。"

对我来说, 学中文并不只是为了满足大学的语言要求, 也是为了和妈妈在中国的家人交流。
For me, learning Chinese is not only to meet the language requirements of universities but also to communicate with my mother's family in China.

Examples:

1) 对我来说, 年薪 10 万美金的工作非常有吸引力。
   For me, a job with an annual salary of $100,000 is very attractive.
2) 对中文不好的人来说, 要看懂中文菜单太难了。
   For people who are not good at Chinese, it is too difficult to understand Chinese menus.

4. (并) 不只是 …… 也是 …… more than . . . it is also . . .

"并" is often used to strengthen the tone.

对我来说, 学中文并不只是为了满足大学的语言要求, 也是为了和妈妈在中国的家人沟通。

For me, learning Chinese is indeed more than meeting the language requirements of universities; it is also for communicating with my mother's family in China.

Examples:

1) 我家的狗狗不只是宠物, 也是我的家人。
   Our doggie is more than a pet; it is also my family.
2) 大学并不只是学习的地方, 也是一个认识新朋友的地方。
   College is indeed not just a place to study but also a place to meet new friends.

5. 把 . . . + V + resultative complement

This "ba structure" is used to describe the disposal of an object and the result that the action leads to.

如果我把中文学好, 将来还可以教我的小孩。
If I learn Chinese well, I can teach my children in the future.

Examples:

1) 我把这个汉字写错了。
   I wrote this Chinese character wrong.
2) 我先把这个问题想清楚, 然后再跟你讨论。
   Let me think it through first, and then discuss with you.

III. Vocabulary and Grammar Exercise

1. Radical Recognition

Please identify the radicals of the following characters. Write down the radical and its meaning.

Examples: 好 → (女) woman

食 1) 餐 → (shí) *eat*　　　　　 𠆢 2) 馆 → (shí) *eat*

欠 3) 歌 → (qiàn) *owe*　　　　 禾 4) 利 → (hé) *grain*

彡 5) 影 → (shān) *bristle*　　　　 耳 6) 聪 → (ěr) *ear*

糸 7) 紧 → (mì) *silk*　　　　　 辶 8) 逼 → (chuò) *go*

目 9) 盲 → (mù) *eye*　　　　　 纟 10) 纸 → (mì) *silk*

2. Word-building Exercises

For each of the characters in the next example, write three more words that include that character.

1) 馆：餐馆 _fàn guǎn guǎn zi shǐ guǎn_
2) 定：肯定 _què dìng guī dìng dìng wèi_
3) 歌：歌曲 _tīng gē chàng gē gē cí_
4) 单：菜单 _jiǎn dān mǎi dān dān cí_
5) 影：电影 _yǐng xiǎng yīn yǐng yǐng piàn_

(handwritten) 饭馆 馆子 使馆　确定 规定 定位
听歌 唱歌 歌词
简单 买单 单词　阴影
影响 影片

3. Matching Exercise: Please match Pinyin and characters

1) 理由
2) 流利
3) 餐馆
4) 文盲
5) 关系
6) 讨厌
7) 满足
8) 要求
9) 考虑
10) 研究

a. kǎolǜ
b. wénmáng
c. yánjiū
d. mǎnzú
e. yāoqiú
f. liúlì
g. lǐyóu
h. cānguǎn
i. tǎoyàn
j. guānxi

(handwritten answers) 1) 考虑 2) 吸引力 3) 研究
4) 聪明 5) 视角 6) 讨厌
7) 逼 8) 电影 9) 歌曲
10) 旅行

4. Fill in the blanks with the appropriate words

讨厌　吸引力　考虑　聪明　电影　逼　歌曲　研究　旅行　视角

很多父母现在 _kǎo lǜ_ 让孩子学习两种语言，因为一方面，会说双语的人更有 _xī yǐn lì_；另一方面，根据科学 _yán jiū_，会说双语的人更 _cōng míng_，而且会另一种语言也可以从另外一个文化 _shì jiǎo_ 考虑问题。但是怎么学外语对很多人来说却是一个大问题。比如，要是孩子 _tǎo yàn_ 学外语，父母应该 _bī_ 孩子吗？看外语 _diàn yǐng_，听外语 _gē qǔ_ 是一种好方法吗？去那个国家 _lǚ xíng_ 对学外语有帮助吗？

5. Complete the following sentences with the given correlatives and words

1) 又……又……

   a. 昨天我跟室友去了一家新餐馆吃饭，那家餐馆＿＿＿＿＿＿＿（便宜）。
   b. 她学习日语学了很多年，现在说得＿＿＿＿＿＿＿＿＿＿（流利）。
   c. 我们这个社团很好玩，＿＿＿＿＿＿＿＿＿＿（唱歌chànggē）。

2) 越来越adj/stative verb

   a. 这个学期我选的课＿＿＿＿＿＿＿（难），让＿＿＿＿＿＿＿（压力）。
   b. 我跟我室友的生活习惯很不一样，也谈不来，现在我们＿＿＿＿＿＿＿＿（紧张）。

越 …… 越 ……

    a. 中国歌曲我越听越_____。

    b. 妈妈很想知道我在忙什么, 可是她_____(问), 我_____(说)。

3) 对someone来说

    a. 对_____(年薪) 的人来说, 这里的学区房太贵了。

    b. _____, 加女儿的脸书可以让她看到女儿的生活, 就不用那么担心了。

4) (并) 不只是 …… 也是 ……

    a. 她选这个工作不只是因为_____, 也是_____(兴趣)。

    b. 我常常跟父母视频聊天, 这_____(联系), _____(担心)。

5) 把 …… + V + resultative complement

    a. 我把方言_____(会) 了以后就能跟外公交流了。

    b. 今天的功课不太多, 我半个小时就_____(完)。

IV. Post-reading Discussion

1. 你可以找出课文这段对话中学中文的十个理由吗?
   Can you find ten reasons for learning Chinese in the dialogue of this lesson?
2. 你吃过什么奇怪的菜吗? 是什么? 在哪儿吃的?
   Have you eaten any strange dishes? What was it? Where did you eat it?
3. 你小时候上过什么才艺班 (cáiyì bān) 或兴趣班 (xìngqù bān) 吗? 在哪儿的? 喜欢吗?
   What talent class or interest class did you attend when you were a child? Where was it? Did you like it?
4. 你上过中文学校吗? 上了几年? 你喜欢吗? 为什么?
   Have you ever attended a Chinese school? For how many years? Did you like it? Why?
5. 你觉得上中文学校有什么优点 (yōudiǎn) 和缺点 (quēdiǎn)?
   In your opinion, what are the advantages and disadvantages of going to Chinese school?
6. 如果以后你有孩子, 你也会送你的孩子上中文学校吗? 为什么?
   If you had kids, would you also send them to Chinese schools? Why?

V. Interpersonal Tasks

1. 两两对话 (liǎngliǎng duìhuà) Pair-work

我为什么要学中文? 请参考课文和自己学中文的经验, 编演 (biānyǎn) 一段对话。

Why should I learn Chinese? Find a partner and present a dialogue of some of the reasons why you learn Chinese. Please refer to the text and your own experience.

2. 采访 (cǎifǎng) Interview

请采访一下你学其他外语 (西班牙语、法语、德语、日语、韩语等等) 的朋友, 问他们学这个外语的十个理由。

Please interview other foreign language learners (such as Spanish, French, German, Japanese, Korean, etc.) and ask them ten reasons for learning this foreign language.

我学＿＿＿＿＿＿＿＿＿的十个理由   受访者的名字: ＿＿＿＿＿＿＿＿＿

1	
2	
3	
4	
5	
6	
7	
8	
9	
10	

Part II 短文: 戈鲲化

I. Warm-up: Pre-reading Discussion

1. 你听说过戈鲲化这个人吗? 你知道他是做什么的吗?
   Have you ever heard of Ge Kunhua? Do you know what he did?
2. 你知道《佩奇法案》和《排华法案》吗? 它们是什么样的法案?
   Do you know the Page Act and the Chinese Exclusion Act? What kind of bills are they?
3. 你觉得美国的中文教育发展得怎么样? 你是怎么知道的?
   What do you think of the development of Chinese education in the United States? How did you know?

II. Interpretive Task: Listening Comprehension

Please listen to the text and choose True (T) or False (F) for each of the following audio recordings of the statements.

1. (对)   2. (错)   3. (对)   4. (错)   5. (对)

戈鲲化 (1838–1882) 是历史上第一个从中国来美国大学教中文的老师。1879–1882年，他在哈佛大学教中文的时候一共只有五个学生。戈鲲化来美国的时候，大多数中国移民都是从事建筑铁路，经营餐馆和洗衣店的工作，他们受到很严重的歧视。1875年，美国政府通过一项法律叫《佩奇法案》(Page Act)，这项法案禁止中国妇女入境美国。1882年，美国政府又通过了《排华法案》(The Chinese Exclusion Act)。根据这项法案，美国从1882年到1943年禁止所有的中国移民进入美国。许多美国人认为华人低人一等，难怪戈鲲化只有五个学生。

1830年以前，美国大学教的外语只有拉丁文和希腊文。第二次世界大战以后，中文才慢慢地受到了重视。从1980 年到2000年这段时期，由于中国的经济越来越发达，越来越多的美国人想跟中国做生意，所以都想学中文。然而，最近几年由于政治原因，许多亚裔受到歧视。因此，戈鲲化的故事告诉我们，美国中文教育的发展跟政治和经济有直接的关系。

Ge Kunhua (1838–1882) was the first teacher from China to teach Chinese in American universities in history. From 1879 to 1882, when he was teaching Chinese at Harvard University, there were only five students. When Ge Kunhua came to the United States, most Chinese immigrants were engaged in railway construction, restaurants, and laundries, and they were severely discriminated against. In 1875, the American government passed a bill called *The Page Act*, which prohibited Chinese women from entering the United States. In 1882, the American government passed *The Chinese Exclusion Act*. According to this bill, the United States banned all Chinese immigrants from entering the United States from 1882 to 1943. Many Americans think that Chinese are inferior. No wonder Ge Kunhua only had five students.

Before 1830, the only foreign languages taught in American universities were Latin and Greek. After the Second World War, Chinese was slowly taken seriously. From 1980 to 2000, as China's economy became more and more developed, an increasing number of Americans wanted to do business with China, so they all wanted to learn Chinese. However, due to political reasons, many Asians have been discriminated against in recent years. Therefore, the story of Ge Kunhua tells us that the development of Chinese education in the United States is directly related to politics and economy.

生词 Vocabulary

Students are required to recognize and pronounce all the vocabulary listed. For the characters/words in italics and bold, students are also expected to know how to write.

1.	历史	歷史	lìshǐ	n.	history
2.	从	從	cóng	prep.	from; since
3.	大多数	大多數	dàduōshù	n.	the majority
4.	**从事**	從事	cóngshì	v.	go in for; deal with (a profession)
5.	建筑	建築	jiànzhù	v./ n.	build; building; architecture
6.	铁**路**	鐵路	tiělù	n.	railroad

7.	**经营**	經營	jīngyíng	v.	manage; run
8.	洗衣店	洗衣店	xǐyīdiàn	n.	laundromat
9.	**受到**	受到	shòudào	v.	be given; suffer the effects of
10.	严重	嚴重	yánzhòng	adj.	serious; critical
11.	**歧视**	歧視	qíshì	v./n.	discriminate; discrimination
12.	**政府**	政府	zhèngfǔ	n.	government
13.	通过	通過	tōngguò	v.	pass; adopt
14.	项	項	xiàng	mw.	for rules, laws, projects
15.	**法律**	法律	fǎlǜ	n.	law
16.	禁止	禁止	jìnzhǐ	v.	prohibit
17.	妇女	婦女	fùnǚ	n.	women
18.	入境	入境	rùjìng	v.o.	enter a country
19.	**所有的**	所有的	suǒyǒu de	adj.	all
20.	进入	進入	jìnrù	v.	enter
21.	认为	認為	rènwéi	v.	think; believe
22.	低人一等	低人一等	dīrényìděng	ph.	be inferior to others
23.	难怪	難怪	nánguài	adv.	no wonder
24.	**重视**	重視	zhòngshì	v.	value; attach importance to
25.	时期	時期	shíqī	n.	period (of time)
26.	发达	發達	fādá	adj.	developed
27.	生意	生意	shēngyì	n.	business; trade
28.	然而	然而	rán'ér	conj.	but; however
29.	政治	政治	zhèngzhì	n.	politics
30.	**原因**	原因	yuányīn	n.	reason
31.	**亚裔**	亞裔	yàyì	n.	of Asian descent
32.	**因此**	因此	yīncǐ	conj.	therefore; consequently
33.	发展	發展	fāzhǎn	v./n.	develop; development
34.	直接	直接	zhíjiē	adj./adv.	direct; directly
35.	由于	由於	yóuyú	prep.	because of; owing to

Proper Names

1.	戈鲲化	戈鯤化	Gē Kūnhuà	Kunhua Ge (1838–1882) was the first Chinese teacher who came from China to teach at an American university.
2.	哈佛大学	哈佛大學	Hāfó dàxué	Harvard University
3.	佩奇法案	佩奇法案	Pèiqí fǎ'àn	Page Act
4.	排华法案	排華法案	Páihuá fǎ'àn	The Chinese Exclusion Act
5.	第二次世界大战	第二次世界大戰	Dì'èr cì shìjiè dàzhàn	The World War II
6.	拉丁文	拉丁文	Lādīngwén	Latin
7.	希腊文	希臘文	Xīlàwén	Greek

Sentence Patterns / Grammar

1. 从 ⋯⋯ 到 ⋯⋯ from . . . to . . .

从1980年到2000年这段时期, 由于中国的经济越来越发达, 越来越多的美国人想跟中国做生意, 所以都想学中文。

From 1980 to 2000, as China's economy became more and more developed, an increasing number of Americans wanted to do business with China, so they all wanted to learn Chinese.

Examples:

1) 我们从星期一到星期五都有中文课。
   We have Chinese classes from Mondays to Fridays.
2) 从第一课到第六课, 我们讨论了很多, 比如, 方言、中文学习、中国式教育。
   We have discussed a lot from Lessons 1 to 6, such as Chinese language varieties, Chinese language learning, and Chinese parenting.

2. 受到 ⋯⋯ suffer from . . . or is received . . .

This pattern can be used in a positive or negative situation. It literally means "receive", but the things that are received have to be abstract, not concrete things.

《排华法案》以后, 中国移民受到很严重的歧视。
After the Chinese Exclusion Act, Chinese immigrants suffered from discrimination.

第二次世界大战以后, 中文慢慢地受到了重视。
After World War II, the Chinese language gradually received attention.

Examples:

1) 来公司 (gōngsī) 一年以后, 他慢慢地受到了老板 (lǎobǎn) 的重视。
   After one year at the company, he slowly received attention from his boss.
2) 在美国, 有的时候少数族裔 (shǎoshù zúyì) 还受到歧视。
   In the U.S., sometimes ethnic minorities still suffer from discrimination.

3. 跟 + Noun + Verb: do something with someone

Unlike English, the word order in Chinese is different. The verb should go after "with someone".

美国人想跟中国做生意。
Americans would like to do business with China.

Examples:

1) 我想跟我的室友聊天。
   I want to chat with my roommate.
2) 我跟妈妈一起去买东西了。
   I went shopping with my mom.

4. 因此, sentence : Therefore . . .

The sentence 因此 leads usually summarizes the previous statement. 因此 is often placed at the beginning of the sentence.

因此, 戈鲲化的故事告诉我们, 美国中文教育的发展跟政治和经济有直接的关系。
Therefore, from the story of Ge Kunhua, we know that the development of Chinese education in the United States is directly related to politics and economy.

Examples:

1) 他觉得中文学校又难又没意思, 在那里也没学到什么东西。因此, 他以后就不去上中文学校了。
   He found that Chinese school was difficult and not interesting, and he also felt that he did not learn anything from there. Therefore, he doesn't go to Chinese school anymore.
2) 中国人刚到美国的时候, 从事很多低人一等的工作, 没有什么教育。因此, 中国人常常受到歧视。
   When Chinese first came to the U.S., many worked in low-ranking jobs and without much education. Therefore, Chinese people often suffered from discrimination.

5. A跟B有 …… 的关系: A is related to B/ A has something to do with B

关系 here means relation. It is used to express a relationship between situation A and situation B. The word order in Chinese is very different from English.

美国中文教育的发展跟政治和经济有直接的关系。
The development of Chinese language education in the U.S. is directly related to politics and economy.

Examples:

1) 他考试考得不好，跟他的学习方法有很大的关系。
   He did poorly in tests, and that has a lot to do with his way of studying.
2) 他决定不去中国，跟喜不喜欢中国没有关系。
   He had decided not to go to China, and it has nothing to do with whether he likes China or not.

III. Vocabulary and Grammar Exercise

1. Make at least five sentences with the characters provided. You can use the same character repeatedly as long as you use 15 different characters in total.

的	原	越	紧	学
所	系	受	来	是
关	人	生	中	校
到	视	他	因	张
跟	有	从	歧	国

Example: 有的学生受到歧视。

1)
2)
3)
4)
5)

1) 最近 2) 政治 3) 压力
4) 经济 5) 因此 5) 从事
6) 收到 7) 看来 8) 原因

2. 选择填空 Fill in the blanks.

因此   经济   看来   从事   原因   政治   最近   受到   压力

1) ___zuì jìn___，中国和美国的___zhèng zhì___关系越来越紧张。由于这个___yā lì___，中国学生来美国学习，美国学生去中国都越来越不容易。
2) 由于疫情 (yìqíng, pandemic)，全世界的___jīng jì___都不太好，所以很多人没有工作。___yīn cǐ___，这个问题现在___cóng shì___全世界政府的重视。
3) 她___shì___教育的工作，在她___kàn lái___，很多孩子的___yuán yīn___是父母造成 (zàochéng, cause) 的。

3. 完成下面的对话

Complete the following dialogues with given words or patterns in Pinyin or characters.

1) A: 你是哪里人?
   B: wǒ shì huá yì měi guó rén, cóng jiā zhōu lái dào zhè lǐ。(从)
   A: 你觉得 jiā zhōu (place you wrote previously) 怎么样?
   B: wǒ jué dé jiāzhōu hǎoxiàng yuè lái yuè rè 。(越来越)
   A: 哦, 是吗? 为什么?
   B: kě néng gēn qìhòu biànhuà yǒu guān xì 。(跟……
      有关系)
   A: 在那里人们喜欢做什么?
   B: dà duō shù rén xǐhuān qù hǎibiān wán 。(大多数)

2) A: 请问你是从事什么工作的?
   B: wǒ shì cóng shì lǜ shī 。(从事)
   A: 哦, 你觉得 lǜ shī (job you wrote previously) 怎么样?
   B: yǎ lì duō de rén wèi lǜshī hěn róngyì shòudào fāmiàn de。(受到
      …… 的重视)　　　　　　　　　　　zhòng shì
   A: 哦, 你认为以后会怎么样呢?
   B: wǒ yě bù zhīdào, jiù xīwàng gōngxiáng huì jìn bù 。

      (There is no single correct answer, as long as it is logical.)

4. 小作文 Short essay: 写一个跟戈鲲化的对话

Imagine you were a student of 戈鲲化's. What would your conversation with him be like? Write a dialogue between you and 戈鲲化, and each person should have at least five lines. Please include all the provided patterns and words in your dialogue.

因此, sentence;
跟 + noun + verb;
才 + verb;
越来越;
不管 …… 都 ……

IV. Post-reading Discussion

1. 早期的中国移民从事什么工作?
   What did the early Chinese immigrants do for a living?
2. 你听过《佩吉法案》和《排华法案》吗? 这两个法案有什么不同?
   Have you heard of the Peggy Act and the Chinese Exclusion Act? What is the difference between the two bills?
3. 为什么第二次世界大战以后, 中文才在美国慢慢地受到重视?
   Why did Chinese get more attention in America after World War II?

4. 你知道哪些美国名人在学或者学过中文？请举例。

   Do you know which American celebrities are studying or have studied Chinese? Please give examples.

5. 很多人认为戈鲲化在美国教中文是失败的, 你认为呢？你从他的故事中学到了什么？

   What is your opinion on the belief that Ge Kunhua was unsuccessful in teaching Chinese in the United States? What insights have you gained from his story?

V. Interpersonal Tasks

1. 请从下面选一个任务进行采访 (cǎifǎng)。   Please choose any of the following tasks for the interview.

1) 请采访一位中文老师: (a) 为什么要来美国教中文？(b) 他们所在的中文项目现在有多少学生和老师？(c) 目前美国的中文教育发展得怎么样？面临着什么挑战？应该如何战胜 (zhànshèng) 这些挑战？(d) 美国的中文教育未来 (wèilái) 会继续 (jìxù) 发展吗？为什么？

   Please interview a Chinese teacher and ask the following: (a) Why did they come to the United States to teach Chinese? (b) How many students and teachers are there in their Chinese program? (c) How is the current development of Chinese education in the United States? What are the challenges? How should these challenges be overcome? (d) Will American Chinese education continue to develop in the future? Why?

2) 请采访你的父母或者华裔朋友, 问问他们: (a) 听说过《佩吉法案》和《排华法案》吗？这两个法案有什么规定？对美国的华裔有什么影响 (yǐngxiǎng)? (b) 在工作中或生活中受到过歧视吗？是什么样的歧视？他们是如何应对歧视的？(c) 华裔应该怎样做才能不再被歧视？

   Conduct an interview with either your parents or Chinese American friends, asking the following questions: (a) Are they aware of the *Peggy Act* and the *Chinese Exclusion Act*? If so, what are the key provisions of these two laws and what impact have they had on Chinese Americans? (b) Have they experienced discrimination in the workplace or in their daily lives? If so, what form did this discrimination take and how did they handle it? (c) In their opinion, what actions should Chinese Americans take to combat discrimination?

VI. Presentational Tasks

1. 口头报告 (kǒutóu bàogào) Oral Presentation

根据你上面的采访, 做一个3-5分钟的口头报告, 分享你的采访结果和你的反思 (fǎnsī)。

Based on your interview, make a three-to-five-minute oral presentation to share your interview results and your reflections.

2. **研究报告** (yánjiū bàogào) Research Report

请查阅相关资料, 研究一下, 除了《佩吉法案》和《排华法案》以外, 美国历史上还有哪些歧视法案或者政策是针对华裔或者亚裔的? 这些带有歧视的法案和政策对华裔 / 亚裔有什么影响 (yǐngxiǎng)? 请写一篇350字左右的小报告总结一下你的研究结果和你的反思。

Please conduct research to identify other discriminatory laws or policies in the history of the United States are aimed at Chinese or Asian Americans in addition to the *Peggy Act* and the *Chinese Exclusion Act*. What impacts did these discriminatory laws and policies have on Chinese/Asian Americans? Then write a short report of about 350 words to summarize your research results and your reflections.

Unit Four

移民故事

Lesson Seven 移民故事

Learning Objectives

In this lesson, you will learn to do the following:

1. Describe diet preferences in different cultures.
2. Narrate immigrants' stories.
3. Discuss personal challenges of living in a new culture.
4. Demonstrate knowledge of Chinese American immigration history.
5. Express opinions about American immigration policies.

I. Warm-up: Pre-reading Discussion

1. 你有什么样的饮食习惯？早餐、午餐、晚餐常常吃什么？
   What kind of eating habits do you have? What do you often eat for breakfast, lunch, and dinner?
2. 你知道有哪些方式 (fāngshì) 可以移民美国吗？
   Do you know in what ways people can immigrate to America?
3. 要是你移民去一个新的国家，你可能会担心哪些事情？
   What might you worry about if you immigrate to a new country?

II. Interpretive Task: Listening Comprehension

Please listen to the lesson dialogue and choose True (T) or False (F) for each of the following audio recordings of the statements.

1. (对) 2. (错) 3. (错) 4. (对) 5. (对)

Main Text

Part I 对话： 初到美国

Joy: 爸爸妈妈，今天我的室友告诉我，她父母打算通过EB2投资移民到美国来，可是又担心来了以后不习惯美国的生活，而且他们的英语说得不好，也担心不能跟美国人交流。你们来美国以前也有过这样的担心吗？

DOI: 10.4324/9781003352228-12

妈妈：　有啊! 而且刚来美国的时候, 我真的很不习惯这里的生活, 特别是美国的饮食。中国人觉得 "早餐要吃好、午餐要吃饱、晚餐要吃少"。可是美国人常常不吃早餐, 只喝一杯咖啡。即使吃早餐, 也只是冰牛奶和麦片。午餐也很简单, 不是三明治就是汉堡。可是他们的晚餐却吃得很好! 我中午在学校吃了几天汉堡就受不了了, 后来只好自己带中餐去学校吃。

爸爸：　我倒是觉得汉堡挺好吃的, 也很方便。只是刚来美国留学的时候, 我英语不太好, 不会点餐, 也闹过不少笑话。有一次, 我在麦当劳点土豆饼, 可是服务员说他们没有这个东西。

Joy：　啊? 怎么回事儿? 卖完了?

妈妈：　不是, 因为你爸说的是 "potato cookie"! 哈哈。

Joy：　哈哈, 原来是这样! 难怪人家说没有。

爸爸：　是啊。那时候我也不知道什么是 "ketchup", 我一直说 "tomato sauce"。哈哈。还有一次, 我在一家超市买了很多东西, 付钱的时候, 人家问我要不要 "cash back", 我还以为人家要给我钱呢!

Joy：　哈哈, 太好笑了。

妈妈：　是啊, 现在觉得是很好笑。可是当时没有朋友, 也没有车, 感觉美国真的是 "好山好水、好寂寞啊!"

爸爸：　嗯。好在后来我们很快融入了 "大熔炉" 的生活。特别是认识你妈以后, 就更不觉得无聊啦! 哈哈哈。

Chūdào měiguó

Joy：　Bàba māma, jīntiān wǒ de shìyǒu gàosu wǒ, tā fùmǔ dǎsuàn tōngguò EB2 tóuzī yímín dào Měiguó lái, kěshì yòu dānxīn láile yǐhòu bù xíguàn Měiguó de shēnghuó, érqiě tāmen de Yīngyǔ shuō de bù hǎo, yě dānxīn bùnéng gēn Měiguó rén jiāoliú. Nǐmen lái Měiguó yǐqián yě yǒuguò zhèyàng de dānxīn ma?

Māma：　Yǒu a! Érqiě gāng lái Měiguó de shíhòu, wǒ zhēnde hěn bù xíguàn zhèlǐ de shēnghuó, tèbié shì Měiguó de yǐnshí. Zhōngguó rén juéde "zǎocān yào chī hǎo, wǔcān yào chī bǎo, wǎncān yào chī shǎo". Kěshì Měiguó rén chángcháng bù chī zǎocān, zhǐ hē yībēi kāfēi. Jíshǐ chī zǎocān, yě zhǐshì bīng niúnǎi hé màipiàn. Wǔcān yě hěn jiǎndān, bùshì sānmíngzhì jiùshì hànbǎo. Kěshì tāmen de wǎncān què chī de hěn hǎo! Wǒ zhōngwǔ zài xuéxiào chīle jǐ tiān hànbǎo jiù shòubùliǎole, hòulái zhǐhǎo zìjǐ dài zhōngcān qù xuéxiào chī.

Bàba：　Wǒ dàoshi juéde hànbǎo tǐng hǎochī de, yě hěn fāngbiàn. Zhǐshì gāng lái Měiguó liúxué de shíhòu, wǒ Yīngyǔ bù tài hǎo, bù huì diǎn cān, yě nàoguò bù shǎo xiàohuà. Yǒu yīcì, wǒ zài Màidāngláo diǎn tǔdòubǐng, kěshì fúwùyuán shuō tāmen méiyǒu zhège dōngxī.

Joy：　Á? Zěnme huí shì'er? Mài wán le?

Māma：　Bùshì, yīnwèi nǐ bà shuō de shì "potato cookie"! Hāha.

Joy：　Hāha, yuánlái shì zhèyàng! Nánguài rénjiā shuō méiyǒu.

Bàba: Shì a. Nà shíhòu wǒ yě bù zhīdào shénme shì "ketchup", wǒ yīzhí shuō "tomato sauce". Hāha. Hái yǒu yīcì, wǒ zài yījiā chāoshì mǎi le hěnduō dōngxi, fù qián de shíhòu, rénjiā wèn wǒ yào bu yào "cash back", wǒ hái yǐwéi rénjiā yào gěi wǒ qián ne!

Joy: Hāha, tài hǎoxiàole.

Māma: Shì a, xiànzài juéde shì hěn hǎoxiào. Kěshì dāngshí méiyǒu péngyou, yě méiyǒu chē, gǎnjué Měiguó zhēn de shì "hǎo shān hǎo shuǐ, hǎo jìmò a!"

Bàba: Èn. Hǎo zài hòulái wǒmen hěn kuài róngrù le "dà rónglú" de shēnghuó. Tèbié shì rènshi nǐ mā yǐhòu, jiù gèng bù juéde wúliáo la! Hāhaha.

生词 Vocabulary

Students are required to recognize and pronounce all the vocabulary listed. For the characters/words in italics and bold, students are also expected to know how to write.

1.	**初**	初	chū	adv.	at the beginning
2.	**投资**	投資	tóuzī	v./n.	invest; investment
3.	**饮食**	飲食	yǐnshí	n.	diet
4.	早**餐**	早餐	zǎocān	n.	breakfast
5.	午餐	午餐	wǔcān	n.	lunch
6.	晚餐	晚餐	wǎncān	n.	dinner
7.	**喝**	喝	hē	v.	drink
8.	杯	杯	bēi	mw.	cup; cupful; glassful
9.	咖啡	咖啡	kāfēi	n.	coffee
10.	即使	即使	jíshǐ	conj.	even if
11.	冰	冰	bīng	n./adj.	ice; icy
12	牛奶	牛奶	niúnǎi	n.	milk
13	麦片	麥片	màipiàn	n.	cereal
14.	三明治	三明治	sānmíngzhì	n.	sandwich
15.	汉堡	漢堡	hànbǎo	n.	hamburger
16.	受不了	受不了	shòubùliǎo	v.	be unable to endure; cannot stand/bear
17.	**点餐**	點餐	diǎncān	v.o.	order food
18.	土豆饼	土豆餅	tǔdòubǐng	n.	hash brown
19.	服务员	服務員	fúwùyuán	n.	waiter; waitress
20.	**卖**	賣	mài	v.	sell

21.	家	家	jiā	mw.	individual measure for a family; individual measure for institutions and enterprises
22.	超市	超市	chāoshì	n.	supermarket
23.	寂寞	寂寞	jìmò	adj.	lonely
24.	融入	融入	róngrù	v.	adapt to; mingle with
25.	熔炉	熔爐	rónglú	n.	melting pot

Sentence Patterns / Grammar

1. 不是 …… 就是 …… : "if it's not . . . it's . . ."

To describe a situation as being one of only two possibilities.

在学校午餐很简单, 不是三明治就是汉堡。
Lunch at school is very simple, either sandwiches or hamburgers.

Examples:

1) 我的室友常常不在, 他不是去上课就是去图书馆读书。
   My roommate is often not home. He either goes to class or goes to the library to study.
2) 大学生不是吃学校食堂 (shítáng) 就是点外卖 (wàimài), 根本没有时间做饭。
   College students either eat in the school cafeteria or order takeout and have no time to cook.

2. 受不了 : be unable to endure; cannot stand/bear

"不+了" is the negative form of "得+了"。 The negative form is more used than the positive form. Many verbs and some adjectives can take "不+了" as the complement.

我中午在学校吃了几天汉堡就受不了。
I can't stand eating hamburgers at school for a few days at noon.

Examples:

1) 这里太吵, 真让人受不了!
   It's too noisy here, it's unbearable!
2) 今年夏天天气很反常 (fǎncháng), 热得让人受不了!
   This summer's weather is abnormal, and it's unbearably hot!

3. 只好: it is an adverb used to indicate that the option "no choice but to" is not liked by the speaker.

后来只好自己带中餐去学校吃。
Later, I had to bring my own Chinese food to school.

Examples:

1) 我坐飞机忘了做核酸检测 (hésuān jiǎncè), 只好取消 (qǔxiāo) 了出国旅行。
I forgot to do the RT-PCR test before air travel and had to cancel my trip abroad.
2) 学校食堂 (shítáng) 都关门 (guānmén) 了, 我们只好自己做饭了。
School cafeterias are closed, so we have to cook by ourselves.

4. 倒是: on the contrary, but actually, and usually used in conversations to indicate an opposite opinion to the other speaker or something not expected.

我倒是觉得汉堡挺好吃的, 也很方便。
I think hamburgers are delicious and convenient.

Examples:

1) A: 学中文实在太无聊了!
Learning Chinese is so boring!
B: 不会啊! 我倒是觉得很有意思呢!
No at all! I think it is actually very interesting!
2) A: 在中国, 什么都很便宜!
In China, everything is cheap!
B: 真的吗? 我倒是觉的房价 (fángjià) 比美国贵多了!
Really? I think the house price is much more expensive than that in America!

*却 is an adverb inserted between the subject and predicate of a sentence. Its function of indicating contrast is similar to that of 但是, 可是, and 不过。

Example:

中国物价 (wùjià) 很便宜, 但是房价 (fángjià) 却比美国贵多了。
Things in China are very cheap, but houses are much more expensive than those in America!

5. 难怪: no wonder

It can be used to express that the speaker finds something unsurprising. It is used to convey the speaker's newfound understanding of a situation.

原来是这样! 难怪人家说没有。
That's it! No wonder they say no.

Examples:

1) 他是你弟弟？难怪你们两个人这么像！
   Is he your brother? No wonder you two are so alike!
2) 你做菜忘了放盐 (yán)？难怪那么难吃！
   Did you forget to put salt in your cooking? No wonder it tastes so bad!

III. Vocabulary and Grammar Exercise

1. Radical Recognition

Please identify the radicals of the following characters. Write down the radical and its meaning.

Examples: 好 → （女）<u>woman</u>

⼇ 1) 寂 → (mián) <u>roof</u>　　　　火 2) 熔 → (huǒ) <u>fire</u>

口 3) 咖 → (kǒu) <u>mouth</u>　　　木 4) 杯 → (mù) <u>tree</u>

宀 5) 寞 → (mián) <u>roof</u>　　　贝 6) 资 → (bèi) <u>shell</u>

饣 7) 饼 → (shí) <u>eat</u>　　　⺮ 8) 简 → (zhú) <u>bamboo</u>

冫 9) 冰 → (bīng) <u>ice</u>　　　走 10) 超 → (zǒu) <u>walk</u>

2. Word-building Exercises

For each of the characters in the next example, write three more words that include that character.

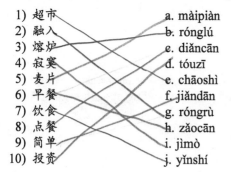

1) 饼: 土豆饼 jiān bǐng, juǎn bǐng, bǐng gān
2) 餐: 点餐 cān guǎn, cān tīng, jiān cān
3) 投: 投资 tóu piào, tóu sù, tóu fàng
4) 晚: 晚餐 wǎn shàng, wǎn ān, jīn wǎn
5) 超: 超市 chāo guò, chāo jí, chāo hǎo

餐馆, 餐厅, 煎餐
投票, 投诉, 投放
晚上, 晚安, 今晚
超过, 超级, 超好

3. Matching Exercise: Please match Pinyin and characters

1) 超市　　　a. màipiàn
2) 融入　　　b. rónglú
3) 熔炉　　　c. diǎncān
4) 寂寞　　　d. tóuzī
5) 麦片　　　e. chāoshì
6) 早餐　　　f. jiǎndān
7) 饮食　　　g. róngrù
8) 点餐　　　h. zǎocān
9) 简单　　　i. jìmò
10) 投资　　　j. yǐnshí

4. Fill in the blanks with the appropriate words

饮食　闹笑话　习惯　汉堡　寂寞　熔炉　点餐　无聊　融入　交流

1) 许多移民担心来了美国以后不 _习惯_ 美国的生活, 特别是美国人的 _饮食_ , 像牛奶、三明治和 _汉堡_ 。英文也说得不好, 不能和美国人 _交流_ 。

2) 许多移民刚开始到美国没有车, 也没有朋友, 常常觉得很 _寂寞_ 。去餐馆吃饭的时候也不会 _点餐_ , 所以常常 _闹笑话_ 。后来这些移民很快地 _融入_ 美国这个大 _熔炉_ 的生活以后就不觉得 _无聊_ 了。

5. Complete the following sentences with the given correlatives and words

1) 不是 …… 就是 ……

   a. 老师: 感恩节 (Gǎn'ēn jié, Thanksgiving) 的时候大家都做什么呢?
      学生: 感恩节的时候, 我们不是＿＿＿＿＿＿就是＿＿＿＿＿＿。

   b. 我妈妈总是很操心, 她不是＿＿＿＿＿＿＿＿＿＿就是
      ＿＿＿＿＿＿＿＿。

2) 倒是

   a. Joy: 开车实在太难了!
      Eric: 不会啊! 很多人觉得开车很难, ＿＿＿＿＿＿＿＿＿＿。

   b. 妈妈: 投资股票 (gǔpiào, stocks) 太危险 (wēixiǎn, risky) 了!
      爸爸: 有些人觉得投资股票风险 (fēngxiǎn; risk) 太大, ＿＿＿＿＿＿。

   c. 女儿: 大家都说吃素好处很多。
      妈妈: 很多人认为吃素 (chīsù, vegetarian) 对身体好, ＿＿＿＿＿＿。

3) 难怪

   a. 你的手机没电了, 难怪＿＿＿＿＿＿＿＿＿＿＿＿＿。

   b. 他是北京人? 难怪＿＿＿＿＿＿＿＿＿＿＿＿。

   c. 他考上了医学院 (yīxué yuàn, medical school), 难怪＿＿＿＿＿＿＿。

IV. Post-reading Discussion

1. 你觉得移民来美国的人可能会碰到什么困难?
   What difficulties do you think immigrants may encounter in the United States?

2. 你觉得移民可以怎么更快更好地融入美国的生活?
   How do you think immigrants can adapt to American life faster and better?

3. 你的家人移民到美国后, 融入了美国的生活吗? 他们有什么样的饮食习惯?
   After your family immigrated to the United States, did they adapt to life in the United States? What kind of eating habits do they have?

4. 你在别的国家生活过吗?你习惯那儿的生活吗?有没有什么是你受不了的?
   Have you ever resided in a foreign country? Are you accustomed to the lifestyle in that country? Is there anything about it that you find unbearable?

5.   你用外语点过餐吗? 闹过笑话吗? 或者你听说过谁用外语点餐闹过笑话吗?
Have you ordered a meal in a foreign language? Have you personally or have
you heard of someone else who made a mistake or had a humorous situation
when ordering in a foreign language?

V. Interpersonal Tasks

1. 角色扮演 (juésè bànyǎn) Role-play

好好学习重要, 可是好好吃饭也很重要。开学两个多月了, 你的家人想知道你在
学校的饮食习惯怎么样, 吃得好不好, 学校的餐厅好不好, 吃不吃得惯等等。今
天他们跟你视频聊天, 问了你很多问题, 也给你提了一些建议 (jiànyì)。请跟你
的同学一起, 从下面选至少10个词和5个句型完成这个对话。

It is important to study hard, but it is also important to eat well. It's been more
than two months since school started. Your family wants to know how your eating
habits at school are, whether you eat well, whether the school restaurant is good,
whether you are used to the food and so on. Today they video-chat with you, ask
you a lot of questions, and also give you some suggestions.

Please work with one or two of your classmates and choose at least ten words
and five patterns from the following to make a dialogue.

生词(words): 饮食、早餐、午餐、晚餐、喝、咖啡、牛奶、麦片、三明
治、汉堡、超市、点餐、感觉

句型(patterns): 即使 …… 也 ……; 不是 …… 就是 ……; 受不了; …… 只是
……; 只好 ……; 倒是 ……; 好在 ……; 难怪 ……

2. 采访 (cǎifǎng) Interview

请采访一个中国留学生, 问问 (1) 他们为什么决定来美国留学; (2) 来美国以
前, 他们担心什么; (3) 刚来美国的时候, 他们碰到了哪些困难, 最大的困难是
什么; (4) 他们觉得中美饮食有哪些不同; (5) 现在他们习惯了美国的生活吗?
特别在饮食上习惯了吗; (6) 他们感觉美国的生活怎么样? 像课文里说的 "好
山好水好寂寞" 吗? (7) 你们自己的问题。

Please interview a Chinese student and ask (1) why they decided to study in the
United States; (2) what worried them before coming to the United States; (3) what
difficulties they encountered when they first came to the United States, and what
were the biggest difficulties; (4) in their opinion, what the differences are between
Chinese and American diets; (5) if they are accustomed to life in the United States
now, particularly with regards to food; 6) how they feel about life in the United
States, if it is like what is said in the text "good mountains, good rivers and so
lonely"; (7) Additional questions of your choice.

Part II 短文: 纸儿女

I. Warm-up: Pre-reading Discussion

1.   请你说说你家人或者朋友的移民故事。
Share any of your family member's or friend's immigration stories with us.

2. 你觉得移民来美国难不难? 要移民来美国得做什么?
   Do you find immigrating to the U.S. hard? What does one need to do to immigrate to the U.S.?
3. 你对美国现在的移民政策有什么看法?
   What is your opinion about the immigration policy in the U.S.?

II. Interpretive Task: Listening Comprehension

Please listen to the text and choose True (T) or False (F) for each of the following audio recordings of the statements.

1. (错)   2. (错)   3. (对)   4. (错)   5. (错)

你听说过 "纸儿子"、"纸女儿" 吗? 你觉得他们是什么样的人?

1882年的《排华法案》禁止华工移民美国, 但商人、学生或者美国公民的孩子可以进入美国。1906年, 旧金山发生了大地震, 市政厅着火, 烧毁了大量移民的出生记录。在这种情况下, 很多华人声称自己是在美国出生的, 是美国公民, 但他们的出生记录被烧毁了。他们还说, 地震前, 他们回过中国好几次, 在中国结了婚, 而且和妻子生了好几个孩子。这样, 他们就可以得到移民名额, 不但能把自己的妻子和孩子接到美国来, 而且还可以把名额卖给其他人, 说他们是自己的"儿子" 或者 "女儿", 帮他们移民到美国。这些买假身份的人就是"纸儿女"。买"纸儿女"的身份要花很多钱, 而且到美国以后, 要先在旧金山的天使岛通过移民局的严格审问才能进入美国。但即使是这样, 从1910年到1940年, 还是有很多的华人以"纸儿女"的身份进入了美国。

他们进入美国以后的生活会是什么样的呢?

Paper Sons and Paper Daughters

Have you heard of "paper sons and paper daughters?" What kind of people do you think they are?

The Chinese Exclusion Act of 1882 prohibited Chinese workers from immigrating to the United States, but the children of businessmen, students, or American citizens could still enter the U.S. In 1906, a big earthquake happened in San Francisco, and the city hall caught fire, which destroyed the birth records of a large number of immigrants. Under such circumstances, many Chinese claimed that they were born in the U.S., and were American citizens, but the fire destroyed their birth records. These Chinese men also claimed that before the earthquake, they had traveled back to China several times and got married in China and had several children with their wives. In this way, they were able to obtain the immigration quota for their family. They not only were able to bring their wives and children to the U.S. but also were able to sell their quota to other people, claiming them as their own "sons" or "daughters" to help these people immigrate to the U.S. These people who bought fake identities were called "paper sons and paper daughters". It cost a lot of money to buy an identity of "paper sons and paper daughters", and after arriving in the U.S., these people had to first go through a strict interrogation by the Immigration Bureau on Angel Island in San Francisco before entering the U.S. Even so, there were still many Chinese entering the U.S. as "paper sons and paper daughters" from 1910 to 1940.

What would their life be after entering the U.S.?

生词 Vocabulary

Students are required to recognize and pronounce all the vocabulary listed. For the characters/words in italics and bold, students are also expected to know how to write.

1.	**纸**	紙	zhǐ	n.	paper
2.	**商人**	商人	shāngrén	n.	merchant
3.	**公民**	公民	gōngmín	n.	citizen
4.	地震	地震	dìzhèn	n.	earthquake
5.	市政厅	市政廳	shìzhèngtīng	n.	city hall
6.	着火	著火	zháohuǒ	v.	on fire; catch fire
7.	烧毁	燒毀	shāohuǐ	v.	destroy by fire
8.	声称	聲稱	shēngchēng	v.	claim
9.	名额	名額	míng'é	n.	quota
10.	**假**	假	jiǎ	adj.	fake
11.	**身份**	身份	shēnfèn	n.	identity
12.	移民局	移民局	yímínjú	n.	Immigration Office
13.	审问	審問	shěnwèn	n./v.	interrogation; interrogate

Sentence Patterns / Grammar

1. 在这种情况下: "under the circumstance" or "in this case", often used as the beginning of a sentence to refer to a circumstance or a situation that is previously mentioned.

在这种情况下, 很多华人声称自己是在美国出生的, 是美国公民, 但他们的出生记录被烧毁了。
Under such circumstances, many Chinese claimed to be born in the United States and American citizens, but their birth records were burned.

Examples:

1) 大火烧毁了很多人的出生记录。在这种情况下, 政府只好相信这些华人是美国公民。
The fire destroyed many people's birth records. Under such circumstances, the government has to believe that these Chinese are American citizens.

2) 房子突然着火了。在这种情况下, 你会怎么做?
The house suddenly caught fire. In this case, what would you do?

2. verb + resultative complement: the resultative complements can be adjectives like 好、晚、光、干净 or monosyllabic verbs like 完、会、到 to indicate the result of an action.

烧毁 destroy by fire　　来晚 come late　　　吃光 eat up
打扫干净 clean up　　　写完 finish writing　　找到 find
学会 learn

市政厅着火, 烧毁了大量移民的出生记录。
The city hall caught fire and destroyed the birth records of a large number of immigrants.

Examples:

1) 我把房间打扫干净了。
   I cleaned up the room.
2) 奶奶希望我学会她的方言。
   Grandma wants me to learn her regional language.

3. ⋯⋯ 这样 + (subject) + 会/才 ⋯⋯ "in this way; thus", often used at the beginning of a sentence or a clause to indicate "only in this way (the way mentioned in the previous sentence or clause) can or will something happen".

他们还说, 地震前, 他们回过中国好几次, 在中国结了婚, 而且和妻子生了好几个孩子。这样, 他们才可以得到移民名额。
They also said that before the earthquake, they had returned to China for several times. They got married in China, and had several children with their wives. In this way, they could get the immigrant quota.

Examples:

1) 你要多跟中国人练习说中文, 这样你的中文会越来越好。
   You should practice speaking Chinese with Chinese people. In this way, your Chinese will get better and better.
2) 父母希望我把中文学好, 这样我才能和他们更好地交流。
   My parents want me to learn Chinese well so that I can communicate with them better.

4. 以 ⋯⋯ 的身份: with the identity of; as . . .; often used as "someone 以 ⋯⋯ 身份 + verb" to emphasize the identity that someone has when doing something.

从1910年到1940年, 还是有很多的华人以"纸儿女"的身份进入了美国。
From 1910 to 1940, many Chinese entered the United States as "paper sons and paper daughters".

Examples:

1) 我以朋友的身份告诉你, 千万不要用假身份参加考试。
   I tell you as a friend, never take an exam under a false identity.
2) 很多人都是以留学生的身份进入美国的。
   Many people enter the United States as international students.

III. Vocabulary and Grammar Exercise

1. Complete the following sentences with the given patterns.

1) 在这种情况下

   a. 最近新冠疫情 (xīnguān yìqíng, Covid-19 pandemic) 越来越严重(yánzhòng, serious)了。在这种情况下, _____。
   b. 这个华裔孩子听不懂中文, 不能跟爷爷奶奶交流。在这种情况下, _____。

2) verb + resultative complement (like 好、完、到、晚, etc.)

   a. 我的车坏了, 所以上课_____了。(来)
   b. 奶奶做的饭太好吃了。我几口就把饭都_____了。(吃)
   c. 妈妈说我的出生记录_____了, 让我不要担心。(找)

3) …… 这样 + (subject) +会/才 ……

   a. 学校让大家都要戴口罩 (dài kǒuzhào, wear a mask), 因为这样 _____。
   b. 新生最好都住在校内。这样_____。

4) 以 …… 身份

   a. 很多子女都希望父母能_____跟他们平等地 (píngděngde, equally) 交流。(朋友)
   b. 20年前, 我的父母从中国来美国读研究生, 他们当时是_____进入美国的。(学生)

2. 选择填空 Fill in the blanks.

在这种情况下	出生记录	身份	名额	公民	假	严格	声称

如果你是在美国出生的, 那么你可以用你的____1____自动 (zìdòng, automatically) 成为美国____2____。如果你不是在美国出生的, 那你必须通过移民局的____3____审查 (shěnchá, investigation)。如果你____4____自己的父母是美国人, 那么当他们发现你的____5____是____6____的, 你得马上离开美国。另外, 为了限制 (xiànzhì, limit) 移民的数量 (shùliàng, number), 美国每年都会有一定的移民____7____。____8____, 很多申请者 (shēnqǐngzhě, applicants) 要等很长时间才能入籍 (rùjí, acquire citizenship)。

1)出生记录 2)公民 3)严格 4)声称
5)身份 6)假 7)名额 8)在这种情况下

3. 小作文 Short essay:

假设你是一个纸儿子或者纸女儿, 请用下面至少8个词和所有的句型写一个最少300字的小故事, 说一说你是怎么移民到美国的, 你经历 (jīnglì) 了什么, 你的感受 (gǎnshòu) 是什么样的。

　Imagine you were a paper son or a paper daughter. Please use the following words (at least eight words) and all the patterns to write an essay of no less than 300 characters to tell the story of your immigration to the United States, what you went through, and how you felt.

　生词 (words): 地震、烧毁、《排华法案》、禁止、出生记录、声称、名额、移民局、审问、假身份

　句型 (patterns): 在这种情况下; ……这样+(subject)+会/才……; 以……身份

IV. Post-reading Discussion

1. 什么是 "纸儿女"?
   What does "paper sons and paper daughters" mean?
2. 为什么会有 "纸儿女"?
   Why did "paper sons and paper daughters" exist?
3. "纸儿女" 要怎么样才可以进入美国?
   How could "paper sons and paper daughters" enter the U.S.?
4. 你对 "纸儿女" 有什么看法?
   What is your opinion of "paper sons and paper daughters"?
5. 你对现在美国政府处理 (chǔlǐ) 墨西哥 (Mòxīgē) 移民的政策 (zhèngcè) 有什么想法?
   What is your opinion of the current policy of the U.S. government regarding Mexican immigrants?

V. Presentational Task

请从两个任务中选择一项任务 (Pick one of the two tasks)

1. 请你跟同组的同学查一查天使岛 (Tiānshǐdǎo) 的历史, 然后一起设计 (shèjì) 一个天使岛的导游 (dǎoyóu) 海报 (hǎibào)。海报里要有图片 (túpiàn), 介绍 (jièshào) 一点天使岛的历史, 为什么要去天使岛旅游 (lǚyóu), 还有天使岛对移民的重要性 (zhòngyàoxìng)。
   Please check the history of Angel Island in California. With your group, design a poster of touring Angel Island. In your poster, you should include pictures, a bit of the history of the island, reasons for visiting there, and its significance to immigrants.

2. 两人一组, 上纽约华人博物馆的网站, 看一段有关移民的视频, 做一个三分钟的中文报告, 说一说你们看了什么故事和你们的感想。
   As a group, research the Museum of Chinese in America website and watch a video clip featuring immigrant stories. Give a three-minute oral presentation in Chinese, discussing the story watched and sharing your personal reflections.

Lesson Eight　中国版图

Learning Objectives

In this lesson, you will learn to do the following:

1. Name major dynasties in Chinese history.
2. Describe a place in details.
3. Give directions to a place.
4. Demonstrate knowledge of geography of China.
5. Discuss the concept of "hometown".

I. Warm-up: Pre-reading Discussion

1. 你听说过秦始皇这个历史人物吗? 他是谁?
   Are you familiar with the historical figure of Qin Shihuang? If so, can you provide a brief overview of who he is?
2. 中国分北方和南方, 你知道怎么分吗? 美国呢?
   China is divided into the north and the south. Do you know how they are divided? What about America?
3. 你听过中国的哪些朝代? 这些朝代有哪些有名的人?
   What dynasties have you heard of China? What are some famous people in these dynasties?

II. Interpretive Task: Listening Comprehension

Please listen to the lesson dialogue and choose True (T) or False (F) for each of the following audio recordings of the statements.

1. (对)　2. (错)　3. (对)　4. (错)　5. (错)

Main Text

Part I 对话：　中国的版图

Joy: 　　　老师, 课本上说长城以前是用来保护中国的, 不让北边的少数民族打进来。长城这么重要呀? 中国这么大, 一直是这样吗?

DOI: 10.4324/9781003352228-13

老师:	商周时代中国的版图很小,只有今天北方的几个省。到了秦始皇统一中国后,版图才扩大,往南到今天的广东和广西省,往西南到今天的四川省。后来中国的版图经过了很多朝代,就越来越大了,用长城保护中国的想法也渐渐地变了。
Melinda:	美国以前也没有今天这么大,是经过几次战争以后,才变成现在的样子。中国到了什么时候才有今天这么大?
老师:	是到了清朝的时候,版图跟今天的中国差不多大,但是蒙古现在已经不是中国的一部分了。中国历史上的元朝和清朝都是由当时北边的少数民族建立的。其实更早在唐朝的时候,中国非常强大,连外国的国王也要来中国朝拜中国的皇帝呢!
Melinda:	美国每个州都有一个capital,中国的省也有吗?
老师:	在美国,我们叫"州府"。可是在中国,我们叫"省会",每个省都有一个。中国的首都是北京。
Joy:	北京一直是中国的首都吗?
老师:	不是。但是北京是好几个朝代的首都,比如:元朝、明朝和清朝。

Zhōngguó de bǎntú

Joy:	Lǎoshī, kèběn shàng shuō Chángchéng yǐqián shì yòng lái bǎohù Zhōngguó de, bù ràng běibian de shǎoshù mínzú dǎ jìnlái, Chángchéng zhème zhòngyào ya? Zhōngguó zhème dà, yīzhí shì zhèyàng ma?
Lǎoshī:	Shāng Zhōu shídài Zhōngguó de bǎntú hěn xiǎo, zhǐyǒu jīntiān běifāng de jǐ gè shěng. Dàole Qínshǐhuáng tǒngyī Zhōngguó hòu, bǎntú cái kuòdà, wǎng nán dào jīntiān de Guǎngdōng hé Guǎngxī shěng, wǎng xīnán dào jīntiān de Sìchuān shěng. Hòulái Zhōngguó de bǎntú jīngguò le hěnduō cháodài, jiù yuèláiyuè dà le, yòng Chángchéng bǎohù Zhōngguó de xiǎngfǎ yě jiànjiàn de biànle.
Melinda:	Měiguó yǐqián yě méiyǒu jīntiān zhème dà, shì jīngguò jǐ cì zhànzhēng yǐhòu, cái biàn chéng xiànzài de yàngzi. Zhōngguó dàole shénme shíhòu, cái yǒu jīntiān zhème dà?
Lǎoshī:	Shì dàole Qīngcháo de shíhòu, bǎntú cái gēn jīntiān de Zhōngguó chàbuduō dà, dànshì Měnggǔ xiànzài yǐjīng bùshì Zhōngguó de yībùfèn le. Zhōngguó lìshǐ shàng de yuáncháo hé Qīngcháo, dōu shì yóu dāngshí běibian de shǎoshù mínzú jiànlì de, qíshí gèngzǎo zài Tángcháo de shíhòu, Zhōngguó fēicháng qiángdà, lián wàiguó de guówáng yě yào lái Zhōngguó cháobài Zhōngguó de huángdì ne!
Melinda:	Měiguó měi gè zhōu dōu yǒu yīge capital, Zhōngguó de shěng yěyǒu ma?
Lǎoshī:	Zài Měiguó wǒmen jiào "zhōu fǔ", kěshì zài Zhōngguó wǒmen jiào "shěnghuì", měi ge shěng dōu yǒu yīge. Zhōngguó de shǒudū shì Běijīng.

Joy: Běijīng yī zhí shì Zhōngguó de shǒudū ma?

Lǎoshī: Búshì. Dànshì Běijīng shì hǎojǐgè cháodài de shǒudū, bǐrú, Yuáncháo, Míngcháo hé Qīngcháo.

生词 Vocabulary

Students are required to recognize and pronounce all the vocabulary listed. For the characters/words in italics and bold, students are also expected to know how to write.

1.	版图	版圖	bǎntú	n.	domain; territory
2.	**课本**	課本	kèběn	n.	textbook
3.	**保护**	保護	bǎohù	n./v.	protect; protection; defend
4.	**北边**	北邊	běibian	n.	north; north side; northern part; to the north of
5.	**少数民族**	少數民族	shǎoshùmínzú	n.	minority; ethnic group
6.	时代	時代	shídài	n.	age; era; epoch
7.	统一	統一	tǒngyī	n./adj.	unity; unified; unitary
8.	省	省	shěng	n./v.	province; save
9.	**扩大**	擴大	kuòdà	v.	expand; enlarge; broaden one's scope
10.	经过	經過	jīngguò	v.	pass; go through
11.	朝代	朝代	cháodài	n.	dynasty
12.	渐渐	漸漸	jiànjiàn	adv.	gradually
13.	战争	戰爭	zhànzhēng	n.	war; conflict
14.	部分	部分	bùfen	n.	part; share; section; piece
15.	由	由	yóu	prep.	by; from
16.	**建立**	建立	jiànlì	v.	establish; set up; found
17.	强大	強大	qiángdà	adj.	powerful; strong
18.	国王	國王	guówáng	n.	king
19.	朝拜	朝拜	cháobài	v.	worship; pilgrimage

20.	皇帝	皇帝	huángdì	n.	emperor
21.	州	州	zhōu	n.	state (e.g., of the United States)
22.	**州府**	州府	zhōufǔ	n.	state capital
23.	**省会**	省會	shěnghuì	n.	provincial capital
24.	首都	首都	shǒudū	n.	capital

Proper Names

1.	长城	長城	Chángchéng	the Great Wall
2.	商周	商周	Shāng Zhōu	the earliest named Chinese dynasties
3.	秦始皇	秦始皇	Qín Shǐhuáng	the first emperor of a unified China
4.	广西	廣西	Guǎngxī	Guangxi province in south China
5.	清朝	清朝	Qīngcháo	Qing dynasty (1644–1911)
6.	唐朝	唐朝	Tángcháo	Tang dynasty (618–907)
7.	蒙古	蒙古	Měnggǔ	Mongolia
8.	元朝	元朝	Yuáncháo	Yuan dynasty (1271–1368)
9.	明朝	明朝	Míngcháo	Ming dynasty (1368–1644)

Sentence Patterns / Grammar

1. 往 + direction + verb: verb toward the direction

秦朝版图往南到今天的广东和广西省,往西南到今天的四川省。

The territory Qin Dynasty went south to today's Guangdong and Guangxi provinces, and southwest to today's Sichuan Province.

Examples:

1) A: 你知道四川餐馆怎么走吗?
   B: 知道啊, 先往南走, 然后往右拐, 过一个街区 (jiēqū) 就到了。
   A: Do you know how to get to the Sichuan restaurant?
   B: Yes, go south first, then turn right, and you will be there after one block.

2) 你往外看, 那儿有一只狗。
   Look out, there is a dog.

2. 渐渐地 + verb: Verb gradually . . .

When using 渐渐 to describe a situation, the situation is gradually happening beyond one's control. The verb or verb phrases after 渐渐 should indicate the change resulted from the gradual process. Hence, often the verb "变" or "verb + resultative" structure is used together with 渐渐.

用长城保护中国的想法也渐渐地变了。
The idea of using the Great Wall to protect China has gradually changed.

Common mistakes:

我渐渐学习中文。(X)→我渐渐学会了中文。(✓)
我渐渐看书。(X)→我渐渐看懂了这本书。(✓)

Examples:

1) 我上了中文课以后渐渐地能够听懂中文歌曲了。
   After I took Chinese classes, I can gradually understand Chinese songs.
2) 这几年他们在当地认识了越来越多的朋友,渐渐地融入了美国"大熔炉"的生活。
   In the past few years, they have made more and more friends locally and gradually adapted to the life of the American "melting pot".

3. 每 …… 都 ……: every . . .

在美国,每个州都有一个州府。在中国,每个省都有一个省会。
In America, every state has a state capital. In China, every province has a provincial capital.

Examples:

1) 他的妈妈很严格,每天都要求他学习两个小时的外语。
   His mother is very strict and requires him to learn two hours of foreign language every day.
2) 这个学期每门课都很重,有很多功课。
   This semester the workload of every course is very heavy, and there is a lot of homework.

4. 后来 vs. 以后 vs. 然后

后来 means "later" and can refer only to the past events.
以后 means "in the future" and can refer only to the future events.
然后 means "and then . . ." It is a conjunction and is often used in the pattern "先 …… 然后 ……", referring to the sequence of actions.

Examples:

1) 商周时代中国的版图很小。<u>后来</u>中国的版图经过了很多朝代,就越来越大了。

China in the Shang and Zhou eras had a very small territory. Later, China's territory has gone through many dynasties, and it has become bigger and bigger.

2) 她考上了哈佛商学院,<u>以后</u>找到好工作肯定没问题。

She was admitted to Harvard Business School, and it will be no problem to find a good job in the future.

3) 奶奶,明天你坐飞机,先排队过机场安检,<u>然后</u>去登机口 (dēngjīkǒu),有问题就问机场工作人员。

Grandma, when you fly tomorrow, you should first queue up for the airport security check, then go to the boarding gate. Ask the airport staff if you have any questions.

5. 北方 vs. 北边

1) In general, 北方 means the northern area of a country, and 南方 means the southern area of a country. For instance, 中国北方、美国南方、北方方言。

2) 北边 could mean "the northern area of a place that is smaller than a country, such as a state or a city". For instance, 芝加哥北边有很多好吃的餐馆。北边 could also mean "to the north of . . ." For example, 加拿大(Jiānádà)在美国的北边。图书馆在宿舍的北边。"南边、东边 and 西边" have the same uses as "北边".

3) Please note 东方 and 西方 have distinct meanings and generally refer to *eastern (countries)* and *western (countries)* respectively. For example, 东方人跟西方人的饮食习惯不同。"东部"and "西部"refer to the eastern and western area of a country, a state, or a province.

6. 变成 vs. 变得

变成 is followed by nouns or noun phrases, while 变得 is followed by adjectives or adjective phrases.

Examples:

1) 美国的版图经过几次战争以后,才<u>变成现在的样子</u>。
The territory of the United States became what it is now after several wars.

2) 汉语拼音的出现让外国人学习中文<u>变得容易多了</u>。
The appearance of Chinese Pinyin has made it easier for foreigners to learn Chinese.

III. Vocabulary and Grammar Exercise

1. Radical Recognition

Please identify the radicals of the following characters. Write down the radical and its meaning.

Examples: 好 → (**女**) <u>woman</u>

口 1) 图 → (*wéi*) <u>enclosure</u>   刂 2) 刚 → (*dāo*) <u>knife</u>

戈 3) 战 → (*qē*) <u>spear</u>   纟 4) 统 → (*mì*) <u>silk</u>

广 5) 府 → (*guǎng*) <u>shelter</u>   扌 6) 护 → (*shǒu*) <u>hand</u>

走 7) 越 → (*zǒu*) <u>walk</u>   彳 8) 往 → (*chì*) <u>step</u>

阝 9) 都 → (*yì*) <u>city</u>   亅 10) 争 → (*jué*) <u>hook</u>

2. Word-building Exercises

For each of the characters in the next example, write three more words that include that character.

1) 图: 版图 图片, 地图, 图表 *tú piàn dì tú tú biǎo*
2) 课: 课本 上课, 课文, 课堂 *chàng tǐ kè wén kè táng*
3) 朝: 朝代 朝向, 朝上, 朝下 *cháo xiàng cháo shàng cháo xià*
4) 保: 保护 保留, 保安, 保证 *bǎo liú bǎo ān bǎo zhèng*
5) 法: 想法 看法, 方法, 法国 *kàn fǎ fāng fǎ fǎ guó*

3. Matching Exercise: Please match Pinyin and characters

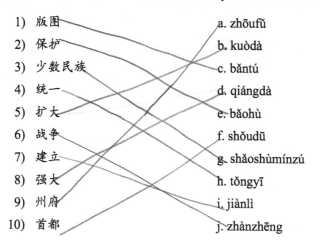

1) 版图   a. zhōufǔ
2) 保护   b. kuòdà
3) 少数民族   c. bǎntú
4) 统一   d. qiángdà
5) 扩大   e. bǎohù
6) 战争   f. shǒudū
7) 建立   g. shǎoshùmínzú
8) 强大   h. tǒngyī
9) 州府   i. jiànlì
10) 首都   j. zhànzhēng

4. Fill in the blanks with appropriate words

朝拜 统一 部分 时代 国王 扩大 朝代 少数民族 强大 清朝

商周___1___中国的版图很小。到了秦始皇___2___中国后，版图
才___3___。后来中国的版图经过了很多___4___，就越来越大了。

1) 时代 2) 统一 3) 扩大 4) 朝代 5) 清朝
6) 部分 7) 少数民族 8) 强大

到了_____5_____的时候, 版图跟今天的中国差不多大, 但是蒙古现在已经不是中国的一_____6_____了。中国历史上的元朝和清朝, 都是由当时的_____7_____建立的。更早在唐朝的时候, 中国非常_____8_____, 连外国的_____9_____也要来中国_____10_____中国的皇帝。

5. Complete the following sentences with the given correlatives and words

1) 往 + **direction** + **verb**:

请看下面的地图, 你知道_____怎么走吗?
Useful patterns: 先 ⋯⋯ 然后 ⋯⋯ 再 / 然后再; 过 ⋯⋯ ; ⋯⋯ 就到了

Example:

A: 你知道公共汽车站 (gōnggòngqìchē zhàn) 怎么走吗?
B: 你先往前走, 过两个街区 (jiēqū, block), 然后往右拐, 再往前走一点就到了, 公共汽车站在你的左边。

Figure 33 Map

2) 渐渐地 + **verb**

a. 父母为我的教育做出的牺牲给了我很大的压力, 他们的关心和爱_____。(负担)

b. 我哥哥常常让我做这做那, 帮他做事 _____。
(理所当然)

3) 每 …… 都 ……

    a. 美国＿＿＿＿＿＿＿＿＿＿＿＿＿＿＿＿＿＿＿＿有麦当劳吗? (地方)

    b. 我特别喜欢喝咖啡,＿＿＿＿＿＿＿＿＿＿＿＿＿。(早餐)

4) 后来 vs. 以后 vs. 然后

    a. 刚开始我选的专业是计算机,可是我根本没有兴趣,所以＿＿＿换 (huàn) 了专业。

    b. 妈妈一直跟我说: "你现在不懂为什么我有望子成龙的想法, ＿＿＿＿你就懂了。"

    c. 1830年以前,美国大学教的外语只有拉丁文和希腊文,＿＿＿＿＿中文 才渐渐地受到了重视。

    d. 我们明天早上去看长城,＿＿＿＿＿下午去饭馆吃北京烤鸭 (kǎoyā)。

5) 方 vs. 边

    a. 中国南＿＿＿＿冬天的时候没有暖气,北＿＿＿＿人去了很不习惯。

    b. 我的宿舍在校园的北＿＿＿＿,可是教室在校园的南＿＿＿＿,每天上课都 很不方便。

    c. 墨西哥 (Mòxīgē) 在美国的南＿＿＿＿。

    d. 东西＿＿＿＿看问题的视角常常很不同。

6) 变成 vs. 变得

    a. 因为大火,原来的咖啡店烧毁了,后来变成了＿＿＿＿＿＿＿＿＿。

    b. 有了视频聊天以后,跟家人朋友联系变得＿＿＿＿＿＿＿。

    c. 上大学以前我＿＿＿＿,但是上大学以后我变得＿＿＿,变成了＿＿＿, 比如,＿＿＿。

7) 中国地图

    1) Look up the Chinese map on the Internet, then fill in the names of the provinces (either in Pinyin or Chinese characters) in the first map on the next page and color the regions of China in different colors.

    2) Fill in the names of cities in the second map on the next page (either in Pinyin or Chinese characters).

IV. Post-reading Discussion

1. 中国很早就开始跟外国交流了吗? 你觉得中国文化受到外国文化的影响 (yǐngxiǎng) 了吗?

    Has China started to communicate with foreign countries very early? Do you think Chinese culture is influenced by foreign cultures?

2. 你认为在美国K-12应不应该教中国历史?为什么?

    Do you think Chinese history should be taught in the K-12 schools in the U.S.? Why?

Figure 34 Maps

3. 还没读课文以前, 你觉得中国的版图一直是一样的吗? 为什么?
   Before reading the text, do you think the territory of China has always been the same? Why?

4. 你去过长城吗? 你对长城有什么了解? 请你谈谈你眼中的长城。
   Have you ever been to the Great Wall? What do you know about the Great Wall? Please talk about the Great Wall in your eyes.

V. Presentational Task

1. 制作一本关于你父母家乡的电子书, 和你的同学一起分享。

   在你的书中, 请包括: 家乡的位置、人口、省会、天气、著 (zhù) 名的人物、著名的地方、有名的食物、家族历史和记忆(照片)。
   Make an e-book about your parents' hometown and share it with your classmates.

In your book, please include location, population, provincial capital, weather of their hometown, famous people, famous places, famous food, family history, and memory (photo).

2. 做一个3-5分钟的口头报告或者小视频《我的老家》,介绍一下:你的老家在哪里? 面积 (miànjī) 多大? 有多少人口? 气候 (qìhòu) 怎么样? 有什么重要的历史和文化? 有什么有名的景点 (jǐngdiǎn)? 有什么有特色 (tèsè) 的饮食和风俗习惯等等。

Make a three-to-five-minute oral presentation or a short video titled "My Hometown" to introduce where your hometown is, how big the area is, what the population is, what the climate is like, if there are any important histories or cultures, if there are any famous scenic spots, and special diets and customs, etc.

Part II 短文: 四川省

I. Warm-up: Pre-reading Discussion

1. 你听说过四川省吗? 知道它在中国的哪里吗?
   Have you ever heard of Sichuan Province? Do you know where it is in China?
2. 你吃过火锅吗? 喜欢吗? 为什么?
   Have you ever tried hot pot? Do you like it? Why?
3. 你见过大熊猫吗? 在哪里见过? 你觉得我们应该保护大熊猫吗? 为什么?
   Have you ever seen a panda? Where did you see it? Do you think we should protect pandas? Why?

II. Interpretive Task: Listening Comprehension

Please listen to the text and choose True (T) or False (F) for each of the following audio recordings of the statements.

1. (错)   2. (对)   3. (错)   4. (对)   5. (错)

　　大家好,我是Melinda,今天给大家介绍我妈妈的老家: 四川。

　　四川省位于中国的西南部,由四川盆地和高原山地两大部分组成的。省会是成都市。四川气候复杂多样,春夏秋冬四季都有。最高平均温度是二十五到二十九摄氏度,最低平均温度是五到八摄氏度。全省面积四十八万四千一百多平方公里,是全国第五大的土地面积,人口有八千三百七十五万人,四川有很多方言,但是通用的方言是四川话。

　　四川风景优美,有名的景点包括九寨沟、峨眉山等等,还有很多好吃的菜。川菜是中国八大菜系之一,面食小吃和火锅都很有名。四川菜的口味以"辣"为主。

　　去四川一定得去看中国的国宝大熊猫。在大熊猫繁育中心,游客可以观赏可爱的大熊猫宝宝跟工作人员的互动情形,可是在卧龙大熊猫栖息地里,大熊猫并不是这样的,他们是喜欢独居的动物。工作人员为了不让大熊猫熟悉人的味道,进去都要穿着大熊猫的服装,还要把大熊猫的排泄物抹在衣服上。这样,大熊猫就闻不到人的味道了。工作人员花了很多心思在保护大熊猫上。

　　你想去四川旅游吗? 这是我的介绍,谢谢大家。

Sichuan Province

Hello, everyone, my name is Melinda. Today I will introduce my mother's hometown, Sichuan.

Sichuan Province is located in the southwest of China and consists of the Sichuan Basin and the plateau mountains. The provincial capital is Chengdu. The climate in Sichuan is complex and diverse, with four seasons in spring, summer, autumn, and winter. The highest average temperature is 25 to 29 degrees Celsius, and the lowest average temperature is 5 to 8 degrees Celsius. The province covers an area of more than 484,100 square kilometers, making it the fifth largest land area in the country, with a population of 83.75 million. There are many regional varieties of Chinese in Sichuan, but the commonly used one is the Sichuan dialect.

Sichuan has beautiful scenery, famous scenic spots, including Jiuzhaigou, Mount Emei, etc., and there are many delicious dishes. Sichuan cuisine is one of the eight major cuisines in China. Pasta and hot pot are very famous. Sichuan cuisine is mainly "spicy" in taste.

If you go to Sichuan, you must see the giant panda, the national treasure of China. In the Giant Panda Breeding Center, visitors can watch the cute baby pandas interact with the staff. However, in the Wolong Giant Panda Habitat, giant pandas are not like this. They like to live alone. In order to prevent giant pandas from being familiar with people, the staff must wear giant panda costumes and put giant pandas' poops on their clothes so that the giant pandas can't smell people. The staff put a lot of thought into protecting the pandas.

Do you want to travel to Sichuan? This is my introduction. Thank you all.

生词 Vocabulary

Students are required to recognize and pronounce all the vocabulary listed. For the characters/words in italics and bold, students are also expected to know how to write.

1.	位于	位於	wèiyú	v.	be located/situated
2.	部	部	bù	n.	part/section (usually a suffix of direction words such as 南部)
3.	盆地	盆地	péndì	n.	basin (geog.)
4.	高原	高原	gāoyuán	n.	plateau
5.	组成	組成	zǔchéng	v.	form/make up (into)
6.	**气候**	氣候	qìhòu	n.	climate
7.	复杂	複雜	fùzá	adj.	complicated; complex
8.	**四季**	四季	sìjì	n.	four seasons
9.	平均	平均	píngjūn	adj./adv.	average; equally
10.	温度	温度	wēndù	n.	temperature

11.	摄氏度	攝氏度	shèshìdù	n.	Celsius 华氏度 Fahrenheit
12.	面积	面積	miànjī	n.	surface area
13.	平方公里	平方公里	píngfānggōnglǐ	n.	square kilometer
14.	**风景**	風景	fēngjǐng	n.	scenery
15.	**景点**	景點	jǐngdiǎn	n.	scenic spots
16.	**面食小吃**	麵食小吃	miànshí xiǎochī	n.	cooked wheaten snacks
17.	火锅	火鍋	huǒguō	n.	hot pot
18.	口味	口味	kǒuwèi	n.	a person's taste
19.	辣	辣	là	adj.	spicy
20.	国宝	國寶	guóbǎo	n.	national treasure
21.	大熊猫	大熊猫	dàxióngmāo	n.	giant panda
22.	**游客**	遊客	yóukè	n.	tourist
23.	观赏	觀賞	guānshǎng	v.	enjoy sight of
24.	宝宝	寶寶	bǎobao	n.	baby
25.	互动	互動	hùdòng	v./n.	interact; interaction
26.	独居	獨居	dújū	v.	live alone
27.	熟悉	熟悉	shúxī	v.	know something/ someone well
28.	排泄物	排泄物	páixièwù	n.	excrement
29.	抹	抹	mǒ	v.	daub; rub
30.	闻	聞	wén	v.	smell
31.	**味道**	味道	wèidao	n.	taste; flavor; smell

Proper Names

1.	成都市	成都市	Chéngdū shì	City of Chengdu
2.	九寨沟	九寨溝	Jiǔzhàigōu	Jiuzhaigou
3.	峨眉山	峨眉山	Éméi shān	Mt. Emei
4.	大熊猫繁育中心	大熊猫繁育中心	Dàxióngmāo Fányù Zhōngxīn	Name of a place (Giant Panda Breeding Center)
5.	卧龙大熊猫栖息地	臥龍大熊貓棲息地	Wòlóng Dàxióngmāo Qīxīdì	Name of a place (Wolong Giant Panda Sanctuaries)

Sentence Patterns / Grammar

1. 位于 + place word is located in (place)

It is frequently used in written language.

四川省位于中国的西南部。
Sichuan Province is located in the southwestern part of China.

Examples:

1) 我的大学位于纽约市。
   My college is located in NY city.
2) 芝加哥位于美国的中西部。
   Chicago is located in the Midwest of the U.S.

1.1 Place words: direction + suffix

Direction	Suffix	English
上	头/边/面	above, 头 is used in spoken language more
下	头/边/面	down, 头 is used in spoken language more
前	头/边/面	front, 头 is used in spoken language more
后	头/边/面	back, 头 is used in spoken language more
左	边/面	left side
右	边/面	right side
里	头/边/面	inside, 头 is used in spoken language more
外	头/边/面	outside, 头 is used in spoken language more
东	部/边/面/方	eastern part/east side/ oriental
西	部/边/面/方	western part/west side/ western
南	部/边/面/方	southern part/south side/ the South
北	部/边/面/方	northern part/north side/the North
旁(páng)	边	next to

1) Direction + 部: included in the territory

Examples:

a. 广东在中国的南部。
   Guangdong is located in the southern part of China.
   (Here Guangdong is part of China.)

b.   加拿大在美国的北边。
Canada is north of America.
(Here Canada is not part of America.)

部 is more appropriate for a bigger place, not for a small area, such as school, town, or city.
For example:

"学校的东部" is awkward, and it is better to say "学校的东边".

2) Four directions ＋方: Meanings are different with different direction words.
东方、西方 mean East vs. West.
北方、南方 mean north part or south part of the territory.

2. S 由 …… 组成：S is composed of

由 is the import word in this pattern. What goes after 由 are the elements of the subject.

四川省由四川盆地和高原山地两大部分组成的。
Sichuan Province is composed of two geographic parts, Sichuan basin and plateau.

Examples:

1)   水是由氧(yǎng)和氢(qīng)组成的。
Water is composed of oxygen and hydrogen.
2)   这个大学是由四个学院组成的。
This university is composed of four colleges.

3. …… 之一: one of noun/number

This pattern is to express the idea of "one of something". The number after 之 can be fluid. For example, ⅔ is 三分之二.

川菜是中国八大菜系之一。
Sichuan food is one of the eight cuisines of Chinese food.

Examples:

1)   长城是世界最有名的景点之一。
The Great Wall is one of the most famous scenic spots in the world.
2)   他们班 (bān) 三分之一的学生是男生。
One third of the students in his class are male.

4. ⋯⋯ 等等: . . . and so on

Sometime is written in a single 等 instead. It is often used at the end of the sentence.

> 有名的景点包括九寨沟、峨眉山等等。
> Famous scenic spots include Jiǔzhàigōu and Mt. Emei and so on.

Examples:

1) 我们学校有很多外国人,有日本人、法国人、美国人等等。
   Our school has many foreigners, Japanese, French, American, and so on.
2) 我去过很多地方旅游(lǚyóu),中国、英国、希腊等等。
   I have traveled to many places, China, England, Greece, and so on.

III. Vocabulary and Grammar Exercise

1. Make at least five sentences with the characters provided. You can use the same character repeatedly as long as you use 15 different characters in total.

从	游	风	来	美
法	气	很	语	国
客	人	多	最	点
冷	韩	等	有	口
时	没	候	的	景

Example: 美国人很多。

1)
2)
3)
4)
5)

2. 选择填空 Fill in the blanks.

> 温度　等等　人口　西部　游客　景点　气候　省会

成都市是四川的＿＿1＿＿,位于四川盆地的＿＿2＿＿,那里的＿＿3＿＿很好,全年的平均＿＿4＿＿在15.2°C到16.6° C左右。成都的＿＿5＿＿有2000万左右。川菜很好吃,有火锅、面食小吃＿＿6＿＿。虽然成都好玩的＿＿7＿＿很多,但是＿＿8＿＿最喜欢去看大熊猫。

1)省会　2)西部　3)气候　4)温度

5)人口　6)等等　7)景点　8)游客

3. 读了课文以后, 你知道什么有关 (yǒuguān) 四川的事?

用拼音或汉字列出 (lièchū) 七个有关四川的事实 (shìshí)。

After reading this lesson, what do you know about Sichuan Province? Please list seven facts about Sichuan in Pinyin or characters.

1)
2)
3)
4)
5)
6)
7)

4. 小作文 Short essay :

请你写一篇最少300字的小作文介绍中国的一个省。请用所有的句型。作文要包括:

1) 位置 (wèizhì)
2) 面积
3) 气候
4) 人口
5) 有名景点和好吃的饭

Model our text and describe a Chinese province of no less than 300 characters with all the sentence patterns provided. In your essay, you need to include the following:

1) The location.
2) The surface area.
3) The climate.
4) The population.
5) Famous scenic spots and food.

句型 (patterns): 位于 + place word; ⋯⋯ 等等; 不但 ⋯⋯ 而且 ⋯⋯;另外; 虽然 ⋯⋯ 但是 ⋯⋯

IV. Post-reading Discussion

1. 你家在哪里? 那里的气候怎么样? 最高温度和最低温度是多少? 面积多大? 人口多少有什么有名的景点? 有什么好吃的东西和好玩的地方?
    Where is your home? What is the climate like there? What are the highest and lowest temperatures? How big is the area? What is the population? What are some famous scenic spots? What are the delicious foods and fun places?
2. 你知道中国的八大菜系包括哪些地方的菜吗? 你吃过哪些菜系的菜? 最喜欢哪个菜系的菜? 美国有菜系吗? 南方和北方的菜, 东部和西部的菜一样吗?

Do you know what the eight major cuisines in China include? What cuisines have you eaten? Which cuisine do you like best? Are there any cuisines in America? Is it the same as the food in the south and the food in the east and west?

3. 去四川可以在哪里看熊猫? 工作人员怎样保护大熊猫?

   Where can we see pandas when we go to Sichuan? How do workers there protect pandas?

4. 除了大熊猫以外, 你还知道中国有哪些濒危野生动物 (bīnwēi yěshēng dòngwù) 需要保护? 美国呢? 你认为我们应该怎么保护这些动物?

   Besides pandas, do you know other endangered wild animals that need to be protected in China? What about the U.S.? How do you think we should protect these animals?

V. Interpersonal Tasks

1. 请采访你的父母, 问问他们: (1) 说到老家, 他们会马上想到什么? 有什么感觉? 为什么? (2) 关于老家, 他们最喜欢的是什么? 最不喜欢的是什么? 为什么? (3) 他们的老家这些年有什么变化? 这些变化好吗? 为什么? (4) 什么是"落叶归根 (luòyè guīgēn)"? 为什么中国人老了的时候都希望落叶归根? (5) 他们希望以后在哪里养老? 为什么?

Please interview your parents and ask them, (1) What do they immediately think of when they talk about their hometown? How do they feel? Why? (2) What do they like the best about their hometown? What do they like the least? Why? (3) What changes have occurred in their hometown over the years, and whether they believe those changes are positive or negative and why? (4) What does the phrase "falling leaves back to the roots" mean to them, and why would Chinese people want to return to their hometown as they get older? (5) Where would they like to spend the rest of their life? Why?

VI. Presentational Tasks

2-3个同学一组, 从下面任选一个任务。
Work in a group of two to three students on one of the following tasks.

1. 中国野生动物保护

先从下面选择一个中国的濒危野生动物: 丹顶鹤 (dāndǐnghè)、金丝猴 (jīnsīhóu)、白暨豚(báijìtún)、华南虎 (huánánhǔ)、扬子鳄 (yángzǐ'è)、藏羚羊 (zànglíngyáng)。然后查阅(cháyuè) 相关资料, 做一个3-5分钟的公益广告 (gōngyì guǎnggào) 小视频, 介绍一下: (1) 这个野生动物主要生活在中国的哪里? (2) 它们的现状 (xiànzhuàng) 怎么样? (3) 中国政府已经采取 (cǎiqǔ) 了哪些措施 (cuòshī) 来保护它们? (4) 保护这种动物面临 (miànlín) 的挑战(tiǎozhàn) 是什么? (5) 你们觉得人们还可以做什么来保护这个野生动物?

Wildlife Conservation in China

First, please choose a wild animal from the following: red-crowned crane, golden monkey, Chinese river dolphin, South China tiger, Chinese alligator, and Tibetan antelope. Then look up relevant information and make a three-to-five-minute public service advertisement video to introduce the following: (1) Where does this wild animal mainly live in China? (2) What is their status quo? (3) What measures has the Chinese government taken to protect them? (4) What are the challenges in protecting this animal? (5) What else do you think people can do to protect this wild animal?

2. 美国野生动物保护

先上网查一下美国有哪些濒危野生动物, 选择一个, 然后查阅 (cháyuè) 相关资料, 做一个3-5分钟的公益广告 (gōngyì guǎnggào) 小视频, 介绍一下: (1) 这个野生动物主要生活在美国的哪里? (2) 它们的现状 (xiànzhuàng) 怎么样? (3)美国政府或组织 (zǔzhī) 已经采取 (cǎiqǔ) 了哪些措施 (cuòshī) 来保护它们? (4) 保护这种动物面临 (miànlín) 的挑战 (tiǎozhàn) 是什么? (5) 你们觉得人们还可以做什么来保护这个野生动物?

Wildlife Conservation in the United States

First, please find out what wild animals are endangered in the United States on the Internet. Choose one, then look up the relevant information, and make a short video of a public service advertisement for three to five minutes to introduce the following: (1) Where does this wild animal mainly live in the United States? (2) What is their current situation? (3) What measures has the U.S. government or organizations taken to protect them? (4) What is the challenge to protect this animal? (5) What else do you think people can do to protect this wild animal?

Unit Five
社区和社会

Lesson Nine 中国城

Learning Objectives

In this lesson, you will learn to do the folllowing:

1. Demonstrate knowledge of Chinese food cultures.
2. Narrate a story of dining in a restaurant.
3. Describe an ethnic community in details.
4. Create an advertisement for Chinatown.
5. Discuss the development of Chinatown.

I. Warm-up: Pre-reading Discussion

1. 你喜欢去中国城吗? 为什么? 你常常跟谁一起去? 去做什么?
   Do you like to go to Chinatown? Why? Who do you often go with? What do you do there?
2. 你觉得看中文菜单难不难? 你看过什么奇怪的菜名?
   Do you find it difficult to read the Chinese menu? What strange dish names have you seen?
3. 过年的时候, 你跟家人常常吃什么菜? 为什么吃? 有什么特别的意义吗?
   What food do you and your family often eat during the Spring Festival? Why? Is there any special meaning?

II. Interpretive Task: Listening Comprehension

Please listen to the lesson dialogue and choose True (T) or False (F) for each of the following audio recordings of the statements.

1. (错) 2. (错) 3. (错) 4. (对) 5. (对)

Main Text

Part I 对话： 奇怪的菜名

Joy: 中文学了几年了, 对菜单上的菜名还是有问题, 像 "蚂蚁上树"、"红烧狮子头"、"夫妻肺片"、"佛跳墙" 这些菜呀, 翻译成了英文以后, 把人吓昏了!

DOI: 10.4324/9781003352228-15

爸爸： 所以说呀，只看得懂汉字，还是不够的，文化和汉字是分不开的。
这些菜名都有故事。中国城餐馆的菜单还是比较传统的，原因大概是
来这里的客人多数是中国人吧。

Joy： 哎呀！我爱吃粉丝，所以常点蚂蚁上树。我的朋友要我翻译菜名，听
了以后都觉得很可怕，为什么我喜欢吃蚂蚁?!

爸爸： 你知道吗？汉字里面有很多字的发音一样或者很像，对中国人的生
活习惯也有影响。比如，过年的时候，人们常吃一些听起来很吉祥的
食物，像年糕，因为有"年年高"的意思。发菜听起来像"发财"，
还喜欢吃鱼，因为鱼的发音跟"余"一样。过年的时候，常说"年年
有余"，就是希望每年有好运气，越来越富裕。

Joy： 文化和汉字真的分不开。我看得懂这些字，但是不知道在特别的时
候，还有特别的意思呢！

妈妈： 哈哈！这种谐音字的学问可大了，有的时候还会影响到送礼物的习
惯呢！诶！你跟同学常来中国城吃饭吗？你以前好像不太喜欢来中国
城。

Joy： 我以前总觉得到中国城，除了吃饭以外，也就是买菜，像个工作一
样，没有意思。还有，周末的时候人总是很多，大家挤来挤去，很
不舒服。现在跟朋友来，还是吃饭、买东西，但是感觉不一样了，每
次都很开心。

妈妈： 是吗？开心就好。这家新开的餐馆，菜色挺多的，跟其他家不太一
样。

爸爸： 服务员都有广东口音，这家餐馆可能是广东人开的。我们还是快点
菜吧。服务员要过来了。我们点一个蚂蚁上树，还要叫什么呢？

Qíguài de càimíng

Joy： Zhōngwén xué le jǐnián le, duì càidān shàng de càimíng háishì yǒuwèntí, xiàng "Mǎyǐ shàngshù", "Hóngshāo shīzitóu", "Fūqī fèipiàn", "Fótiàoqiáng" zhèxiē cài ya, fānyì chéngle Yīngwén yǐhòu, bǎ rén xiàhūn le!

Bàba： Suǒyǐ shuō ya, zhǐ kàndedǒng hànzì, háishì bùgòu de, wénhuà hé hànzì shì fēnbukāi de. Zhèxiē càimíng dōuyǒu gùshì. Zhōngguóchéng cānguǎn de càidān háishì bǐjiào chuántǒng de, yuányīn dàgài shì lái zhèlǐ de kèrén duōshù shì Zhōngguórén ba.

Joy： Āiya! Wǒ ài chī fěnsī, suǒyǐ cháng diǎn Mǎyǐ shàngshù. Wǒ de péngyou yào wǒ fānyì cài míng, tīngle yǐhòu dōu juéde hěn kěpà, wèishéme wǒ xǐhuān chī mǎyǐ?!

Bàba： Nǐ zhīdào ma? Hànzì lǐmian yǒu hěnduō zì de fāyīn yīyàng huòzhě hěn xiàng, duì Zhōngguó rén de shēnghuó xíguàn yě yǒu yǐngxiǎng. Bǐrú, guònián de shíhòu, rénmen cháng chī yīxiē tīngqǐlái hěn jíxiáng de shíwù, xiàng niángāo, yīnwèi yǒu "nián nián gāo" de yìsi. Fàcài tīngqǐlái xiàng "fācái", hái xǐhuān chī yú, yīnwèi yú de fāyīn gēn "yú" yīyàng, guònián de

shíhòu, cháng shuō "niánnián yǒuyú", jiùshì xīwàng měinián yǒu hǎo
yùnqì, yuèláiyuè fùyù.

Joy: Wénhuà hé hànzì zhēnde fēnbùkāi. Wǒ kàndedǒng zhèxiē zì, dànshì bù
zhīdào zài tèbié de shíhòu, hái yǒu tèbié de yìsi ne!

Māma: Hāha! Zhè zhǒng xiéyīn zì de xuéwèn kě dà le, yǒude shíhòu hái huì
yǐngxiǎng dào sòng lǐwù de xíguàn ne! Éi! Nǐ gēn tóngxué cháng lái
Zhōngguóchéng chīfàn ma? Nǐ yǐqián hǎoxiàng bù tài xǐhuān lái
Zhōngguóchéng.

Joy. Wǒ yǐqián zǒng juédc dào Zhōngguóchéng, chúle chīfàn yǐwài, yě jiùshì
mǎi cài, xiàng ge gōngzuò yīyàng, méiyǒu yìsi. Háiyǒu, zhōumò de shíhòu
rén zǒngshì hěnduō, dàjiā jǐláijǐqù de, hěn bù shūfu. Xiànzài gēn péngyou
lái, háishì chīfàn, mǎi dōngxi, dànshì gǎnjué bù yīyàngle, měicì dōu hěn
kāixīn.

Māma: Shì ma? Kāixīn jiù hǎo. Zhè jiā xīnkāi de cānguǎn, càisè tǐngduō de, gēn
qítā jiā bù tài yīyàng.

Bàba: Fúwùyuán dōu yǒu Guǎngdōng kǒuyīn, zhè jiā cānguǎn kěnéng shì
Guǎngdōngrén kāi de. Wǒmen háishì kuài diǎncài ba, fúwùyuán yào
guòláile, wǒmen diǎn yīgè Mǎyǐ shàngshù, hái yào jiào shénme ne?

生词 Vocabulary

Students are required to recognize and pronounce all the vocabulary listed. For
the characters/words in italics and bold, students are also expected to know how
to write.

1.	菜名	菜名	cài míng	n.	dish name
2.	**翻译**	翻譯	fānyì	v./n.	translate; translation
3.	**中国城**	中國城	Zhōngguóchéng	n.	Chinatown
4.	**大概**	大概	dàgài	adv.	probably
5.	**客人**	客人	kèrén	n.	guest
6.	粉丝	粉絲	fěnsī	n.	vermicelli made from bean starch; fan
7.	**可怕**	可怕	kěpà	adj.	horrible
8.	蚂蚁	螞蟻	mǎyǐ	n.	ant
9.	**影响**	影響	yǐngxiǎng	n./v.	influence
10.	吉祥	吉祥	jíxiáng	adj.	auspicious
11.	年糕	年糕	niángāo	n.	rice cake

12.	发菜	髮菜	fàcài	n.	hair-like seaweed; fat choy
13.	发财	發財	fācái	v.o.	get rich
14.	运气	運氣	yùnqì	n.	luck
15.	富裕	富裕	fùyù	adj.	rich
16.	谐音字	諧音字	xiéyīn zì	n.	homophonic words
17.	学问	學問	xuéwèn	n.	knowledge
18.	周末	周末	zhōumò	n.	weekend
19.	挤来挤去	擠來擠去	jǐ lái jǐ qù	v.	squeeze around
20.	舒服	舒服	shūfu	adj.	comfortable
21.	点菜	點菜	diǎncài	v.o.	choose dishes from a menu; order dishes

Proper Names

1.	蚂蚁上树	螞蟻上樹	Mǎyǐ shàngshù	Sauteed vermicelli with minced pork
2.	红烧狮子头	紅燒獅子頭	Hóngshāo shīzitóu	Braised pork ball in brown sauce
3.	夫妻肺片	夫妻肺片	Fūqī fèipiàn	Sliced beef and ox tongue in chili sauce
4.	佛跳墙	佛跳墻	Fótiàoqiáng	Steamed abalone with shark's fin and fish maw

Sentence Patterns / Grammar

1. Verb 了 + quantity + 了: have done something for quantity up to now

The first 了 indicates the quantity of the action, and the second 了 indicates the action continues to now (so far).

我中文学了几年了，对菜单上的菜名还是有问题。
I have studied Chinese for several years now, but I still have problems with the names of dishes on the menu.

Examples:

1) 她已经看了三个小时的电视了。
   She has been watching TV for three hours.
2) 我今天喝了两杯咖啡了。
   I have drunk two cups of coffee so far.

1.1 S + quantity + 没有 + verb + 了. Have NOT done something for quantity.

Examples:

1) 她三天没有来上课了。
   She has not come to class for three days.
2) 我两年没回家了。
   I have not been back home for two years.

2. 可怕 vs. 害怕

可怕：awful; dreadful; fearful; frightful; scary; horrible; terrible. 可怕 is an adjective only. It is more commonly used in spoken Chinese.

Examples:

1) 这是一个可怕的故事。
   This is a terrible story.
2) 妈妈生气的样子太可怕了!
   Mom's angry look is terrible!

害怕：害怕 is similar to 怕 as a verb. It can be used alone or taken apart.

Examples:

1) 不要害怕考试, 每天复习就不觉得那么难了!
   Don't be afraid of exams; it won't be so difficult to review every day!
2) 我害怕大狗过来咬我!
   I'm afraid the big dog will come and bite me!

3. Verb 来 Verb 去：The structure literally means "back and forth", e.g., 走来走去, but metophorically, it means "over and over again".

中国城周末人总是很多, 在个小地方里挤来挤去的, 很不舒服。
There are always a lot of people in Chinatown on weekends. It's very uncomfortable to squeeze in a small place.

Examples:

1) 我想来想去, 还是决定不去朋友的生日会了。
   I thought about it over and over again and decided not to go to my friend's birthday party.
2) 小孩子在公园 (gōngyuán) 里跑来跑去, 开心极了!
   Children are running around in the park, and they are very happy.

吃来吃去 eat here and there
说来说去 talk again and again
走来走去 walk back and forth
讨论 (tǎolùn) 来讨论去 discuss again and again

4. 快 (点) + verb: quickly + verb

When using 快 (点) with verbs, it takes on a meaning similar to the phrase "do something quickly" in English.

我们还是快点菜吧。服务员要过来了。
Let's hurry up. The waiter is coming.

Examples:

1) 你快点走啊, 要不然就赶不上飞机了!
   Hurry up, or you will miss the plane!
2) 我真希望快点见到多年没见的奶奶。
   I wish I could see my grandmother soon, whom I haven't seen for many years.

5. Emphatic adverb "可": very

可 + adj. + 了
可 is generally used by northern speakers and is informal, generally only used in spoken Chinese. It is used to emphasize what follows 可.
这种谐音字的学问可大了, 有的时候还会影响到送礼物的习惯呢。
There is a lot of knowledge that goes into this kind of homophonic characters! Sometimes it will affect the customs of giving gifts.

Examples:

1) 我室友可聪明了。我带你去见见他。
   My roommate is so smart! I'll take you to meet him.
2) 我妈妈做的红烧肉可好吃了。你要不要吃一块?
   My mother's braised pork is very delicious! Would you like a piece?

III. Vocabulary and Grammar Exercise

1. Radical Recognition

Please identify the radicals of the following characters. Write down the radical and its meaning.

Examples: 好 → (女) <u>woman</u>

月 1) 肺 → (yuè) <u>moon</u>   小 2) 怕 → (xīn) <u>heart</u>

虫 3) 蚂 → (chóng) <u>insect</u>   见 4) 觉 → (jiàn) <u>see</u>

纟 5) 红 → (mì) <u>silk</u>   宀 6) 客 → (mián) <u>roof</u>

扌 7) 挤 → (shǒu) <u>hand</u>   讠 8) 译 → (yán) <u>speech</u>

米 9) 粉 → (mǐ) <u>rice</u>   亻 10) 佛 → (rén) <u>person</u>

永 11) 裕 → (yī) *clothing*　　　　貝 12) 财 → (bèi) *shell*

米 13) 糕 → (mǐ) *rice*　　　　讠14) 运 → (chuò) *go*

讠15) 详 → (yán) *speech*　　　　宀16) 富 → (mián) *root*

2. Word-building Exercises

For each of the characters in the next example, write three more words that include that character.

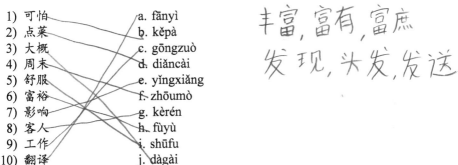

1)　员：服务员 _yuán gōng chéng mán huì yuán_　员工, 成员, 会员
2)　可：可怕 _kě yǐ kě ài kě néng_　可以, 可爱, 可能
3)　客：客人 _yóu kè kè qi fǎng kè_　游客, 客气, 访客
4)　粉：粉丝 _fěn sè fěn mò mǐ fěn_　粉色, 粉末, 米粉
5)　作：工作 _zuò yè zuò wéi dòng zuò_　作业, 作为, 动作
6)　糕：年糕 _mǐ gāo dàn gāo gāo diǎn_　米糕, 蛋糕, 糕点
7)　富：富裕 _fēng fù fù yǒu fù shù_　丰富, 富有, 富庶
8)　发：发财 _fā xiàn tóu fā fā sòng_　发现, 头发, 发送

3. Matching Exercise: Please match Pinyin and characters

1) 可怕　　　　a. fānyì
2) 点菜　　　　b. kěpà
3) 大概　　　　c. gōngzuò
4) 周末　　　　d. diǎncài
5) 舒服　　　　e. yǐngxiǎng
6) 富裕　　　　f. zhōumò
7) 影响　　　　g. kèrén
8) 客人　　　　h. fùyù
9) 工作　　　　i. shūfu
10) 翻译　　　　j. dàgài

4. Fill in the blanks with the appropriate words

菜名　夫妻　粉丝　点菜　粉丝　有余　年糕　菜单　发财　吉祥

中国菜非常多, 每个___1___都有不同的故事。很多外国人到中国餐厅___2___, 看到___3___上的菜名都被吓昏了! 比如蚂蚁上树, 其实是猪肉加上___4___, 非常好吃。还有夫妻肺片, 因为发明这道菜的人是一对___5___, 所以叫夫妻肺片。还有, 中国人喜欢吃听起来很___6___的食物, 比如发菜听起来像___7___; ___8___听起来像年年高; 吃鱼表示年年___9___。

1) 菜名　2) 点菜　3) 菜单　4) 粉丝　5) 夫妻
6) 吉祥　7) 发财　8) 年糕　9) 有余

5. Complete the following sentences with the given correlatives and words

1) 可怕 vs. 害怕

可怕
害怕

a. ___可怕___的飓风 (jùfēng; hurricane) 摧毁 (cuīhuǐ; destroy) 了整个村庄(cūnzhuāng; village)。
b. 我妈妈非常___害怕___打疫苗 (yìmiáo; vaccine)，她总是觉得疫苗不安全 (ānquán, safe)，很___可怕___。
c. Covid-19是一种___可怕___的病毒 (bìngdú; virus)。 可怕

可怕

2) **Verb 来 Verb 去**

> 讨论来讨论去 想来想去 挤来挤去 说来说去 走来走去 跑来跑去 吃来吃去

说来说去
想来想去
吃来吃去

a. 我室友整晚在房间里___走来走去___，我都睡不着觉。
b. 妈妈让我去中文学校，她___说来说去(shuō)___，我还是不同意。
c. 圣诞节快到了，我___想(xiǎng)___还是不知道买什么礼物送给妈妈。
d. 我___吃(chī)___还是觉得自己做的菜最好吃。
e. 好不容易上了车。但是车上人实在太多了，___挤来挤去___我差一点下不了车。
f. 在狗公园 (gōngyuán) 里，小狗们开心地___跑来跑去___。
g. 今天功课真难。大家一起___讨论(tǎo lùn)___还是讨论不出来。

讨论来讨论去

IV. Post-reading Discussion

1. 你吃过 "蚂蚁上树"、"红烧狮子头"、"夫妻肺片"、"佛跳墙" 吗? 你能介绍一下这几道菜吗? 比如，这几道菜分别是中国哪个地方的特色 (tèsè) 菜? 用什么做的? 味道怎么样?
   Have you tried "Mayi shangshu", "Hongshao Shizitou", "Fuqi feipian", and "Fotiaoqiang"? Can you introduce these dishes? For example, which part of China's specialties are these dishes? What is it made of? How does it taste?

2. 你家有没有什么拿手菜(náshǒucài)? 是哪道菜? 什么样的味道? 是怎么做的?
   Are there any special dishes in your family? Which dish? What kind of taste? How do you cook it?

3. 中国人过年吃 "年糕"、"发菜"、"鱼" 是因为谐音。你还知道哪些谐音字? 在中国人的生活习惯上有哪些影响?
   Chinese people eat "nian gao", "facai", and "fish" for Chinese New Year because of their homophonic sounds. What other homophonic characters do you know? What are the influences on the habits of Chinese people?

4. 你最喜欢的一家餐馆在哪儿? 为什么你最喜欢那儿? 请从不同的方面说说，比如: 菜色、价格、味道、服务、餐馆装潢 (zhuānghuáng) 等等。
   Where is your favorite restaurant? Why do you like it the most? Please talk about it from different aspects, such as food, price, taste, service, restaurant decoration (zhuānghuáng decoration), and so on.

5. 每个国家甚至 (shènzhì) 每个城市在吃的方面都有自己的特色 (tèsè)，比如，"深盘披萨" (shēnpánpīsa) 是芝加哥的特色。别的地方呢? 为什么会有这样的特色? 去那儿旅行，在哪儿可以吃到这样的特色食物 (shíwù)? 请跟同学分享。
   Every country and even every city has its own characteristics in terms of eating. For example, "deep dish pizza" is a characteristic of Chicago. What about

other places? Why is there such a feature? Where can I find such special food if traveling there? Please share with your classmates.

V. Interpersonal Tasks

1. 角色扮演 (juésè bànyǎn) Role-play

夏小京的生日快到了,她想跟Joy还有别的朋友一起出去吃饭。可是她刚来美国留学,还不知道哪儿有好餐馆。正好Joy回宿舍了,小京想问问Joy有什么建议(jiànyì)。

Xia Xiaojing's birthday is coming soon. She wants to go out to eat with Joy and other friends, but she just came to the United States to study and doesn't know where good restaurants are. It just so happened that Joy went back to the dormitory. Xiao Jing wants to ask Joy for suggestions.

2. 采访 (cǎifǎng) Interview

请去一家中国餐馆做一个采访。可以采访这家餐馆的老板(lǎobǎn)、服务员或者厨师(chúshī),问问 (1) 他们为什么决定来美国; (2) 在美国生活碰到什么困难吗; (3) 现在习惯了美国的生活吗; (4) 他们觉得在中国餐馆工作怎么样; (5) 他们的餐馆有哪些菜色;哪道菜最受欢迎(shòuhuānyíng);他们的餐馆有什么特点等等; (6) 你自己的问题。

Please go to a Chinese restaurant for an interview. You can interview the owner, waiter/waitress, or chef. Ask (1) why they decided to come to the United States; (2) if they faced any challenges while adjusting to life in the United States; (3) if they are used to life in the United States now; (4) how they feel about working in a Chinese restaurant; (5) what dishes their restaurant have, which dish is the most popular, what are the characteristics of their restaurants, etc.; (6) Additional questions of your choice.

Part II 短文: 波士顿的唐人街

I. Warm-up: Pre-reading Discussion

1. 请你说一说你去过的中国城是什么样子? 里面有什么?
   Please describe the Chinatown that you have been to in the past. What did you see there?
2. 你说到中国城,你第一个想到的是什么? 为什么?
   What do you think of first when you hear the word "Chinatown?" Why?
3. 你为什么去中国城?
   What are the reasons for you to go to Chinatown?

II. Interpretive Task: Listening Comprehension

Please listen to the text and choose True (T) or False (F) for each of the following audio recordings of the statements.

1. (对)   2. (错)   3. (错)   4. (对)   5. (对)

唐人街最早叫大唐街，也叫中国城、华埠和中华街。你去过吗？

波士顿的唐人街位于城市的中心。面积不大，长、宽占地大约六、七个街区。里面有三条大街，除了商店和餐馆以外，还有住户。唐人街的西边是波士顿公园 (Boston Common)，东边是火车站 (South Station)，南边是金融区，北边是最繁华的商业街。还有，离波士顿历史区很近，走路只要十多分钟。这里的华裔人口是麻州总人口的百分之二点二八，是波士顿人口最密集的地方之一。

1870年麻州北亚当斯 (North Adams) 的一家鞋厂雇用了75名从加州来的中国人。后来这些人一直住在火车站旁的一个巷子里，就成了今天的唐人街。最早来到这里的多数是广东人，所以广东话是这里最主要的语言。在这里，大部分的商铺都是广东人经营的。一个四川餐馆里面的人从服务员到老板可能都是广东人。想要在这里租房、开店和修建都得得到广东人的同意。

唐人街里的楼房破旧，道路又窄又脏，交通堵塞，跟市区简直是两个世界。为什么会这样？按照美国尊重少数族裔的政策，波士顿市政府的管理方式是以"华人社区自治"为主，不太干预唐人街的发展。

你住的城市有唐人街吗？是什么样子的？

Boston Chinatown

Tangrenjie was originally called Datangjie, and it also has several other names, such as Zhongguocheng, Huabu, or Zhonghuajie. Have you been to one?

Boston Chinatown is located in the center of the city, with a small area, covering about six or seven blocks in length and width. There are three main streets in Chinatown. In addition to shops and restaurants, there are residents there as well. To the west of the Chinatown is Boston Common, to the east is South station, to the south is the financial district, and to the north is a busy shopping area. Besides that, Boston Chinatown is very close to the Boston historical area, and it is only a ten-minute walk. The population of Chinese American in Chinatown is 2.8% of the total population of Massachusetts. It is one of the most populated areas in Boston.

In 1870, a shoe factory in North Adams, Massachusetts, hired 75 Chinese workers from California. They settled down in an alley near the train station, and later, it became the Chinatown today. The earliest immigrants of Chinatown were Cantonese, and therefore, Cantonese became the main spoken language in Boston Chinatown. Most shops are run by Cantonese. The owner and waiters of a Sichuanese food restaurant could very much be all Cantonese. Renting an apartment, opening a shop, or renovating a place in Boston Chinatown has to be approved by these Cantonese who are in charge of the Chinatown there.

Inside Chinatown, the buildings are old, the roads are narrow and dirty, and the traffic is always terrible. It is just like a different world from the whole city of Boston. Why is this? According to the U.S. policy of respecting ethnic minorities, minority self-governance, the Boston city government has adopted the idea of "Chinese community self-governance" and is not heavily involved in the development of Chinatown.

Do you have a Chinatown in your city? What is your Chinatown like?

生词 Vocabulary

Students are required to recognize and pronounce all the vocabulary listed. For the characters/words in italics and bold, students are also expected to know how to write.

1.	宽	寬	kuān	n./adj.	width; wide
2.	占地	占地	zhàndì	v.	land occupation
3.	大约	大約	dàyuē	adv.	about
4.	街区	街區	jiēqū	n.	block
5.	住户	住戶	zhùhù	n.	resident
6.	**公园**	公園	gōngyuán	n.	garden; park
7.	**火车站**	火車站	huǒchēzhàn	n.	train station
8.	金融	金融	jīnróng	n.	finance
9.	区	區	qū	n.	area; district
10.	繁华	繁華	fánhuá	adj.	bustling
11.	商业街	商業街	shāngyèjiē	n.	commercial street
12.	**百分之**	百分之	bǎifēnzhī	n.	percent
13.	密集	密集	mìjí	adj.	populated; crowded
14.	鞋厂	鞋廠	xiéchǎng	n.	shoe factory
15.	雇用	雇用	gùyòng	v.	hire; employ
16.	巷子	巷子	xiàngzi	n.	alley
17.	商铺	商鋪	shāngpù	n.	shop
18.	老板	老板	lǎobǎn	n.	boss
19.	**租房**	租房	zūfáng	v.o.	renting
20.	开店	開店	kāidiàn	v.o.	open a shop
21.	修建	修建	xiūjiàn	v.	build
22.	破旧	破舊	pòjiù	adj.	old and shabby
23.	道路	道路	dàolù	n.	road; path
24.	窄	窄	zhǎi	adj.	narrow
25.	交通	交通	jiāotōng	n.	transportation
26.	堵塞	堵塞	dǔsè	adj.	blocked
27.	市区	市區	shìqū	n.	urban area
28.	简直	簡直	jiǎnzhí	adv.	simply

29.	尊重	尊重	zūnzhòng	v.	respect
30.	*少数族裔*	少數族裔	shǎoshùzúyì	n.	ethnic minorities
31.	政策	政策	zhèngcè	n.	policy
32.	管理	管理	guǎnlǐ	v.	manage
33.	*方式*	方式	fāngshì	n.	way; manner; style
34.	社区	社區	shèqū	n.	community
35.	自治	自治	zìzhì	v.	enjoy autonomy
36.	干预	幹預	gānyù	v.	intervene

Proper Names

1.	华埠	華埠	Huábù	Chinatown
2.	*唐人街*	唐人街	Tángrénjiē	Chinatown
3.	大唐街	大唐街	Dàtángjiē	Chinatown
4.	波士顿	波士頓	Bōshìdùn	Boston
5.	麻州	麻州	Mázhōu	Massachusetts

Sentence Patterns / Grammar

1. 百分之 + number: this pattern is used to express percentage in Chinese. Different from English, you have to say 百分之 before numbers when talking about percentages in Chinese.

这里的华裔人口是麻州总人口的百分之二点二八。
The ethnic Chinese population here is 2.28% of the total population of Massachusetts.

Examples:

1) 根据2019年的人口统计 (tǒngjì) 报告, 华裔人口是亚裔总人口的百分之二十三。
   According to the 2019 demographic report, the Chinese population accounts for 23% of the total Asian population.
2) 据统计, 百分之四十五的亚裔住在美国西部。
   According to statistics, 45% of Asians live in the western United States.

2. 简直 simply; completely. As an adverb of mood, it is often used to modify adjectives or verbs to indicate "close to" with a tone of exaggeration or amazement on the part of the speaker. It is often used in the following structures:

1) **简直是 (+ measure word) + noun**

唐人街里的楼房破旧, 道路又窄又脏, 交通堵塞, 跟市区简直是两个世界。
The buildings in Chinatown are dilapidated, the roads are narrow and dirty, and the traffic is jammed, which is simply like a different world than the urban area.

过去的生活对她来说简直是一个梦(mèng)。
The life in the past was simply a dream for her.

2) **简直 (是) 太 + adj. + 了 or 简直 + adj. + 极了**

她简直太漂亮了。or 她简直漂亮极了。
She is so pretty.

北京的秋天简直太美了。or 北京的秋天简直美极了。
The autumn in Beijing is simply beautiful.

3) **简直是 + 在 verb**

妈妈说我不是在写汉字, 简直是在画汉字.
Mom said that I am not writing Chinese characters. I am simply drawing Chinese characters.

他走路走得非常快。对我来说, 他不是在走, 简直是在跑。
He walks very fast. For me, he is not walking, he is simply running.

4) **somebody / something + (verb +得) + 简直 + (就+) 是 / 像 / 跟 …… 一样**

这个留学生中文说得简直就跟中国人一样!
This international student speaks Chinese as well as a Chinese person!

我们的中文老师简直像我们的妈妈一样, 喜欢操心我们的生活和学习。
Our Chinese teacher is just like our mother and likes to worry about our life and study.

5) **somebody / something + verb + 得 + 简直 + 连 ……**

我的室友这几天又要准备考试又要找工作, 忙得简直连睡觉的时间都没有。
My roommate has to prepare for exams and find a job these days. He is so busy that he has no time to sleep.

我太想我的女朋友了, 想她想得简直连饭都不想吃, 觉也不想睡。
I miss my girlfriend so much that I don't even want to eat or sleep.

6) **Subject + 简直 + negation**

老师说话说得太快了。我简直听不懂他说的是什么。
The teacher spoke too fast. I simply cannot understand what he said.

上海变化太大了。我简直不敢相信自己的眼睛。
Shanghai has changed too much. I can't believe my eyes.

3. 按照 ……: "according to; in accordance with" is used only as a preposition to introduce a principle or formula according to which an action is carried out.

按照美国尊重少数族裔的政策, 波士顿市政府的管理方式是由 "华人社区自治" 为主, 不太干预唐人街的发展。

In accordance with the U.S. policy of respecting ethnic minorities, the Boston City government's management method is dominated by "Chinese community autonomy" and does not interfere with the development of Chinatown.

Examples:

1) 按照学校的规定 (guīdìng), 学生和老师在教室里都要戴口罩 (kǒuzhào)。
   According to school regulations, students and teachers must wear masks in the classroom.
2) 按照父母的期望 (qīwàng), 我毕业后成了一名医生。
   According to the expectations of my parents, I became a doctor after graduation.

* 按照 vs. 根据:

As explained previously, 按照 usually introduces a principle or formula according to which an action is carried out, whereas 根据 "on the basis of; basis" can be used as a preposition, a verb (e.g., 我们应该根据自己的兴趣来决定毕业后做什么工作。We should decide what job to do after graduation based on our own interests.), or a noun (e.g., 他说的话完全没有根据。What he said is totally groundless.) "根据" introduces the grounds on which some conclusion, decision, or judgment rests.

4. 尊重 vs. 尊敬

尊重: respect for people (peers and younger generations) or something (like somebody's decision 决定, rights 权利, freedom 自由, choice 选择, habits 习惯, etc.)
尊敬: respect for people, especially the elders or people who have higher social status.

Examples:

1) 政府应该尊重老百姓的权利。
   The government should respect the rights of the people.
2) 父母应该尊重孩子的选择吗?
   Should parents respect their children's choices?
3) 我不喜欢不尊重别人的人。
   I don't like people who don't respect others.
4) 子女要尊敬父母, 学生要尊敬老师。
   Children should respect their parents, and students should respect their teachers.

5. 以 ⋯⋯ 为主: "is dominated by . . .; mainly", often used to indicate "take something as the principal thing" or "give priority to".

波士顿市政府的管理方式是以 "华人社区自治" 为主。
The management style of the Boston City Government is mainly "Chinese Community Autonomy".

Examples:

1) 父母希望我在大学以学习为主, 不要做别的事。
   My parents hope that I will focus on studying at university and not do anything else.
2) 早期移民的工作以苦力为主。
   The work of early immigrants was mainly as a coolie.

[handwritten: 1) 唐人街 2) 位于 3) 住户 4) 经营 5) 租房 6) 破旧 7) 道路 8) 堵塞 9) 发展 10) 政策]

III. Vocabulary and Grammar Exercise

1. 选择填空 Fill in the blanks.

道路　发展　经营　政策　住户　租房　破旧　堵塞　唐人街　位于

　　中国城也叫＿＿＿1＿＿。美国最早的中国城＿＿2＿＿旧金山 (Jiùjīnshān, San Francisco)。中国城里除了商店和餐馆以外, 也有＿＿3＿＿, 他们大多都是广东人。如果你想在中国城＿＿4＿＿商铺或者＿＿5＿＿, 得先得到广东人的同意。中国城一般都离市区不太远, 但中国城里的房子比较＿＿6＿＿, ＿＿＿7＿＿＿又窄又脏, 也常常有交通＿＿8＿＿。这些都影响了中国城的＿＿＿9＿＿＿。希望政府以后有更多好的＿＿10＿＿来帮助中国城。

2. Complete the following sentences with given patterns or words.

1) 根据美国人口普查局 (rénkǒu pǔchájú, Census Bureau) 2019年的数据 (shùjù, data), 从2000年到2019年, 亚裔人口增长 (zēngzhǎng, increase) 了＿＿＿＿＿＿(95%)。现在亚裔人口占 (zhàn, constitute) 美国总人口的＿＿＿＿＿＿(7%)。华裔占美国亚裔总人口的＿＿＿ (23%)。

Please translate this paragraph into English:

2) 简直
   a. 我想像的美国和我看到的美国太不一样了, ＿＿＿＿＿。(两个国家)
   b. 你知道吗? 姚明身高2.26米, ＿＿＿＿＿＿＿! (高)
   c. 他想一夜之间就变成有钱人? ＿＿＿＿＿＿＿! (做梦zuòmèng, dream)
   d. 姐姐的这幅画画得＿＿＿＿＿＿＿＿。(真的)
   e. 这个问题太难了。我＿＿＿＿＿＿＿＿＿＿。(回答不了)
   f. 弟弟今天一个晚上只做完了两道数学题, 他＿＿＿＿＿＿。(慢)

3) 按照 vs. 根据

   a. *[handwritten: àn zhào]* 中国的传统, 过春节的时候要和家人团聚 (tuánjù, get together)。
   b. *[handwritten: gēn jù]* 政府的报告, 新冠疫情 (xīnguān yìqíng) 对国内的经济发展有很大的影响。
   c. 你怎么知道他说的不是假的? 你有什么 *[handwritten: gēn jù]*?

[handwritten: a) 按照 b) 根据 c) 根据]

(手写: a)尊敬   b)尊敬, 尊重)

4) 尊重 vs. 尊敬

    a. "尊老爱幼 (yòu, the young)" 的意思是: 我们要 *zūn jìng* 老人、爱护 (àihù, care for) 孩子。

    b. 孩子应该 *zūn jìng* 父母, 可是父母也要 *zūn zhòng* 孩子的选择, 让他们做自己喜欢的事情。

    c. 我的室友昨天跟她的男朋友分手了, 因为她觉得他男朋友不 *zūn zhòng* 她, 也不 *zūn jìng* 她的父母。

(手写: c)尊重, 尊敬)

5) 以 …… 为主

    a. 这所学校＿＿＿＿＿＿＿＿, 百分之九十五的学生都是白人。

    b. 很多华裔家庭的语言＿＿＿＿＿＿, 很少讲英文。

3. 小作文 Short essay:

写一篇最少350字左右的作文, 介绍一个美国的或者其他国家的中国城。请用下面的生词和句型。作文的内容可以包括:

1) 这个中国城在什么地方? 面积多大? 占地多少? 人口多少? 离市区近吗? 附近有什么?
2) 这个中国城里有什么店铺? 住户大多是从哪里来的?
3) 这个中国城有什么历史?
4) 这个中国城的现状 (xiànzhuàng) 怎么样?
5) 这个中国城和课文里介绍的波士顿的中国城一样吗? 有什么一样或者不一样的地方?

Write an essay of at least 350 words to introduce a Chinatown in the United States or in other countries. Please use the following words and sentence patterns. The content of the essay may include the following:

1) Where is this Chinatown? How big is the area? How much does it occupy? What is the population? Is it near downtown? What's nearby?
2) What shops are there in this Chinatown? Where do most residents come from?
3) What is the history of this Chinatown?
4) What is the status quo of this Chinatown?
5) Is this Chinatown the same as the Chinatown in Boston introduced in the text? What are the similarities or differences?

    生词(words): 位于、面积、占地、人口、市区、店铺、移民、尊重、简直

    句型(patterns): 百分之 + number; 又 …… 又 ……; 以 …… 为主; 按照 ……

IV. Post-reading Discussion

1. 你觉得中国城里什么代表了中国的传统和文化?

    What in Chinatown represents Chinese tradition and culture?

2. 你知道哪儿的中国城? 位于什么地方?
    Do you know a particular Chinatown? Where is it located?

3. 你去过别的移民社区吗? 比如小意大利、小东京、韩国城、跟中国城有什么不同?
    Have you been to other communities, such as Little Italy, Little Tokyo, Korea Town, and so on? What are the differences between these communities and Chinatown?

4. 你会不会想住在中国城里? 为什么?
    Would you want to live in Chinatown? Why?

5. 你认为唐人街应该怎么发展? 政府的角色是什么?
    What is your opinion on the development of Chinatown? What kind of role should the government play in Chinatown's development?

V. Presentational Tasks

请和同学查一查任何一个美国城市的唐人街, 比如历史、商铺、饭馆等等, 然后一起设计(shèjì, design)一个去这个唐人街旅游的半日游。

Please check the history of Chinatowns in any American city, such as history, shops, restaurants, and so on. With your group, design a half day tour for visiting this Chinatown.

Lesson Ten 中国城的未来

Learning Objectives

In this lesson, you will learn to do the following:

1. Identify the uniqueness of American Chinese restaurants.
2. State the significance of Chinatown to Chinese American communities.
3. Narrate a personal experience in Chinatown.
4. Discuss the challenges that a Chinatown faces.
5. Evaluate the impacts of Covid-19 pandemic on Chinatown around the world.

I. Warm-up: Pre-reading Discussion

1. 你住的城市有中国饭馆吗？他们做什么菜？有什么特点？你在中国饭馆常常点什么菜？
   Are there any Chinese restaurants in your city? What dishes do they cook? What are the characteristics of the dishes? What dishes do you usually order in Chinese restaurants?
2. 你对中国歌曲了解吗？请跟班上同学分享一首你知道的中国歌曲。
   Do you know anything about Chinese songs? Please share a Chinese song you know with your classmates.
3. 你看过 / 听过比较有意思的幸运饼干里的话有哪些？
   Have you come across any amusing words in fortune cookies?

II. Interpretive Task: Listening Comprehension

Please listen to the lesson dialogue and choose True (T) or False (F) for each of the following audio recordings of the statements.

1. (   ) 2. (   ) 3. (   ) 4. (   ) 5. (   )

Main Text

Part I 对话：过生日

今天是夏小京18岁的生日。Joy、Melinda、Eric和夏小京一起来中国城吃饭。

DOI: 10.4324/9781003352228-16

(在饭馆)

Joy:　小京, 这是你第一次来中国城, 感觉怎么样?

小京:　说实话, 中国城跟我想像的很不一样, 给我一种很破旧甚至很落后的感觉。拿超市来说吧, 中国的比我们刚去的那家现代多了。还有音乐, 中国城放的大多是八九十年代的港台歌曲, 太过时了。你们听, 现在饭馆放的是什么歌?

Eric:　我知道, 是《月亮代表我的心》, 我从小听到大, 是我妈妈最喜欢的一首歌。

小京:　哈哈, Eric, 你说对了。这应该是七十年代的歌吧, 很老了, 不过这样的老歌也给我一种很亲切的感觉。

Melinda:　嗯, 我是在中国城长大的, 这儿充满了我童年的回忆。很可惜, 受到疫情的影响, 我从小吃到大的那家蛋糕店关门了。

小京:　那Melinda, 对你来说, 中国城最有意义的一个地方是哪儿?

Melinda:　当然是小学啦! 我在那儿交到很多好朋友, 从小玩到大。

(吃完饭, 服务员拿来账单和幸运饼干。)

小京:　这是什么? 我从来没吃过。

Joy:　这是幸运饼干啊! 在美国, 买单的时候, 几乎每家中国饭馆都会给客人幸运饼干。中国没有吧? 这可以算是中国饭馆的"美国特色"了! 小京, 今天是你的生日, 快看看, 幸运饼干说了什么?

小京:　Don't worry about money. The best things in life are free.
別担心钱, 生活中最好的东西都是免费的! 真的吗? 那Joy, 今天你买单吧? 哈哈!

Joy:　哈哈, 没问题!

Melinda & Eric:　哈哈, 谢谢Joy!

Guò shēngrì

Jīntiān shì Xià Xiǎojīng shíbā suì de shēngrì. Joy, Melinda, Eric hé Xià Xiǎojīng yīqǐ lái Zhōngguóchéng chīfàn.

(Zài fànguǎn)

Joy:　Xiǎojīng, zhè shì nǐ dìyīcì lái Zhōngguóchéng, gǎnjué zěnmeyàng?

Xiǎojīng:　Shuō shíhuà, Zhōngguóchéng gēn wǒ xiǎngxiàng de hěn bù yīyàng, gěi wǒ yī zhǒng hěn pòjiù shènzhì hěn luòhòu de gǎnjué. Ná chāoshì lái shuō ba, Zhōngguó de bǐ wǒmen gāng qù de nà jiā xiàndài duō le. Háiyǒu yīnyuè, Zhōngguóchéng fàng de dàduō shì bājiǔshí niándài de Gǎng Tái gēqǔ, tài guòshí le. Nǐmen tīng, xiànzài fànguǎn fàng de shì shénme gē?

Eric:	Wǒ zhīdào, shì "Yuèliang dàibiǎo wǒ de xīn", wǒ cóngxiǎo tīng dào dà, shì wǒ māma zuì xǐhuān de yī shǒu gē.
Xiǎojīng:	Hāha, Eric, nǐ shuōduì le. Zhè yīnggāi shì qīshí niándài de gē ba, hěnlǎo le, bùguò zhèyàng de lǎogē yě gěi wǒ yīzhǒng hěn qīnqiè de gǎnjué.
Melinda:	Èn, wǒ shì zài Zhōngguóchéng zhǎngdà de, zhè'er chōngmǎn le wǒ tóngnián de huíyì. Hěn kěxī, shòudào yìqíng de yǐngxiǎng, wǒ cóngxiǎo chīdàodà de nàjiā dàngāodiàn guānménle.
Xiǎojīng:	Nà Melinda, duìnǐláishuō, Zhōngguóchéng zuì yǒuyìyi de yīgè dìfāng shì nǎ'er?
Melinda:	Dāngrán shì xiǎoxué la! Wǒ zài nà'er jiāodào hěnduō hǎopéngyou, cóngxiǎo wándàodà.

(Chī wán fàn, fúwùyuán nálái zhàngdān hé xìngyùn bǐnggān.)

Xiǎojīng:	Zhè shì shénme? Wǒ cónglái méi chīguò.
Joy:	Zhè shì xìngyùn bǐnggān a! Zài Měiguó, mǎidān de shíhòu, jīhū měijiā Zhōngguó fànguǎn dōuhuì gěi kèrén xìngyùn bǐnggān. Zhōngguó méiyǒu ba? Zhè kěyǐ suànshì Zhōngguó fànguǎn de "Měiguó tèsè" le! Xiǎojīng, jīntiān shì nǐde shēngrì, kuài kànkan, xìngyùn bǐnggān shuōle shénme?
Xiǎojīng:	Don't worry about money. The best things in life are free. Bié dānxīn qián, shēnghuó zhōng zuìhǎo de dōngxi dōu shì miǎnfèi de! Zhēnde ma? Nà Joy, jīntiān nǐ mǎidān ba? Hāha!
Joy:	Hāha, méi wèntí!
Melinda & Eric:	Hāha, xièxie Joy!

生词 Vocabulary

Students are required to recognize and pronounce all the vocabulary listed. For the characters/words in italics and bold, students are also expected to know how to write.

1.	说实话	說實話	shuōshíhuà	ph.	speak the truth; frankly
2.	想像	想像	xiǎngxiàng	v.	imagine; fancy
3.	**甚至**	甚至	shènzhì	adv./conj.	even
4.	落后	落後	luòhòu	v./adj.	fall behind; lag; retrogress
5.	**现代**	現代	xiàndài	adj./n.	modern; modern times
6.	音乐	音樂	yīnyuè	n.	music
7.	过时	過時	guòshí	adj.	old-fashioned; out of date

8.	知道	知道	zhīdào	v.	know; become aware of
9.	充满	充滿	chōngmǎn	v.	full of; brim; permeate
10.	童年	童年	tóngnián	n.	childhood
11.	回忆	回憶	huíyì	n./v.	memories; recall
12.	可惜	可惜	kěxī	adj.	unfortunate; it is a pity
13.	疫情	疫情	yìqíng	n.	pandemic
14.	蛋糕店	蛋糕店	dàngāodiàn	n.	bakery
15.	关门	關門	guānmén	v.o.	close a door; (a shop etc.) to close (for the night or permanently)
16.	有意义	有意義	yǒuyìyì	adj.	meaningful; significant
17.	交	交	jiāo	v.	make (friends); hand over; deliver; pay; intersect
18.	账单	帳單	zhàngdān	n.	bill
19.	幸运	幸運	xìngyùn	adj.	fortunate; lucky
20.	饼干	餅乾	bǐnggān	n.	biscuit; cracker; cookie
21.	买单	買單	mǎidān	v.o.	pay the restaurant bill
22.	几乎	幾乎	jīhū	adv.	almost; nearly; practically;
23.	特色	特色	tèsè	n.	characteristic; distinguishing feature or quality
24.	别	別	bié	adv.	do not
25.	免费	免費	miǎnfèi	adj.	free (of charge)

Proper Names

1.	港	港	Gǎng	harbor; port; here it is an abbreviation for 香港 (Xiānggǎng Hong Kong).
2.	台	台	Tái	platform; stage; classifier for machines, desk or table; here it is an abbreviation for 台湾 (Táiwān Taiwan)
3.	月亮代表我的心	月亮代表我的心	Yuèliang dàibiǎo wǒde xīn	The moon represents my heart; a famous Mandarin song sung by the Taiwanese singer Teresa Teng; 代表 (dàibiǎo, represent)

Sentence Patterns / Grammar

1. 给 someone 一种 ······ 的感觉: give someone a feeling of . . .

中国城跟我想象的很不一样, 给我一种很破旧甚至很落后的感觉。
Chinatown is very different from what I imagined, giving me a sense of being shabby or even backward.

Examples:

1) 这样的老歌也给我一种很亲切的感觉。
   Such old songs also give me a very cordial feeling.
2) 这里的装潢 (zhuānghuáng) 不美国也不中国, 给我一种很奇怪的感觉。
   The decoration here is neither American nor Chinese, giving me a very strange feeling.

2. 拿 ······ 来说 (吧): take . . . as an example . . .

中国城给我一种很破旧的感觉, 拿超市来说吧, 中国的比我们刚去的那家现代多了。
Chinatown gives me a very shabby feeling. Take the supermarket as an example, the ones in China are much more modern than the one we just went to.

Examples:

1) 移民美国有很多方式, 拿小京的父母来说吧, 他们想投资移民。
   There are many ways to immigrate to the United States. Take Xiaojing's parents as an example, they want to immigrate through investment.
2) 现在上大学不便宜, 拿学费来说吧, 一年几乎要6万美金。
   It's not cheap to go to college now. Take tuition for example, it costs almost $60,000 a year.

3. 从小 verb 到大: do something since childhood

The verb used in this pattern is often monosyllabic, as demonstrated in the following examples.

这首歌是《月亮代表我的心》, 我从小听到大, 是我妈妈最喜欢的一首歌。
This song is "The Moon Represents My Heart". I heard it from childhood, and it is my mother's favorite song.

Examples:

1) 我从小吃到大的那家蛋糕店关门了。
   The cake store that I constantly visited from childhood is permanently closed.
2) 我在那儿交到很多好朋友, 从小玩到大。
   I made many good friends there, and I grew up hanging out with them.

4. 受到 ⋯⋯ 的影响: be influenced by . . .

Sometimes you can also say "受 ⋯⋯ 的影响".

> 很可惜，受到疫情的影响，我从小吃到大的那家蛋糕店关门了。
> It's a pity that due to the impact of the pandemic, the cake shop that I constantly visited from childhood is permanently closed.

Examples:

1) 受到天气的影响，今天的航班飞不了了。
   Affected by the weather, today's flight will not be able to fly.
2) 我爸爸是一名工程师 (gōngchéngshī)，受到他的影响，我选了计算机专业。
   My dad is an engineer. Under his influence, I chose computer science as my major.

5. 几乎 vs. 差不多

> 几乎每家中国饭馆都会给客人幸运饼干。
> Almost every Chinese restaurant gives customers fortune cookies.

First, 几乎 is often used together with words that mean "all" such as 每 and 所有 to mean "almost all, being very close to all", indicating high degree. In this case, 几乎 is generally interchangeable with 差不多 (more or less; about; around); however, it is slightly more formal than 差不多, and the tone is stronger to emphasize "being very close to . . .". For example, it is fine to say 差不多每家中国饭馆都会给客人幸运饼干；however, the sentence is a bit less formal than the one with 几乎, and the tone is lighter.

Second, 差不多 can be put before a monosyllabic adjective while 几乎 cannot. In this case, "几乎一样" should be used. For example: 我跟她差不多高。= 我跟她几乎一样高。

Third, 差不多 can be put before quantity or time words. For example, 现在差不多三点。她差不多50岁。几乎 cannot be used in these sentences.

III. Vocabulary and Grammar Exercise

1. Character Writing

Please write at least three characters that contain the given radical.

Examples: 女 → 好 妈 她 奶

1) 讠 → 请 ___ ___ ___   2) 宀 → 家 ___ ___ ___
3) 扌 → 打 ___ ___ ___   4) 纟 → 纸 ___ ___ ___
5) 亻 → 他 ___ ___ ___   6) 日 → 时 ___ ___ ___
7) 口 → 吃 ___ ___ ___   8) 氵 → 清 ___ ___ ___
9) 艹 → 花 ___ ___ ___   10) 忄 → 忙 ___ ___ ___

11) 木→ 材 ___ ___ ___   12) 辶→ 逼 ___ ___ ___
13) 心→ 感 ___ ___ ___   14) 竹→ 筷 ___ ___ ___

2. Word-building Exercises

For each of the characters in the next example, write three more words that include that character.

1) 年: 今年 _____ _____ _____
2) 代: 时代 _____ _____ _____
3) 情: 疫情 _____ _____ _____
4) 费: 学费 _____ _____ _____
5) 运: 幸运 _____ _____ _____
6) 特: 特色 _____ _____ _____
7) 童: 童年 _____ _____ _____
8) 感: 感觉 _____ _____ _____

3. Matching Exercise: Please match Pinyin and characters

1) 想象   a. miǎnfèi
2) 破旧   b. huíyì
3) 甚至   c. yǐngxiǎng
4) 落后   d. xiǎngxiàng
5) 免费   e. zhàngdān
6) 充满   f. shènzhì
7) 回忆   g. tèsè
8) 影响   h. pòjiù
9) 账单   i. chōngmǎn
10) 特色   j. luòhòu

4. Fill in the blanks with the appropriate words

想象 破旧 现代 过时 买单 幸运 特色 有意义 交

　　今天夏小京跟朋友一起去中国城吃饭。不同的人对中国城有不同的感觉。小京觉得中国城跟她_____的很不一样,中国城给她一种很_____的感觉。比如,她觉得中国的超市比中国城的_____。另外,中国城放的音乐常常很_____。但中国城也有小京觉得好玩的东西,比如,_____的时候,饭馆会给客人_____饼干。Joy告诉她这是中国饭馆的"美国_____"。Melinda是在中国城长大的,中国城对她来说非常_____,她在中国城_____到很多好朋友,从小玩到大。

5. Complete the following sentences with the given words or patterns

1) 给 someone 一种 …… 的感觉

| 奇怪　亲切　落后 |

a. 我爸爸出生长大的城市很不发达,那儿房子都很破旧,给我一种 很_____的感觉。

b. 虽然这是我们第一次见面,但是她给我一种很_____的感觉,好像 我们已经认识很长时间了。

c. 她看见朋友从来不打招呼,给人一种很_____的感觉。

2) 拿 …… 来说 (吧)

a. 我们的宿舍跟我想象的不太一样,拿_____来说吧,_____。

b. 其实中国城很多地方都有"美国特色",拿饭馆来说吧,_____。

3) 从小 verb 到大

a. _____我从小听到大。(故事 / 歌曲)

b. _____我从小看到大。(电影 / 电视节目)

4) 受到 …… 的影响

a. 很多父母受到虎妈的影响,_____。

b. 我现在喜欢_____是受到_____的影响。

5) 几乎 vs. 差不多

a. 她今天喝了_____三杯咖啡。

b. _____每个人都听懂了老师说的话,可是我还是糊里糊涂。

c. 这儿的冬天跟芝加哥的_____冷。

IV. Post-reading Discussion

1. 你去过的中国城放的音乐过时吗? 有哪些歌? 美国的中国城是不是渐渐 地老年化 (lǎonián huà)? 请阅读一些中国城的英文资料, 比较中国城和其 他地方人口的平均年龄 (niánlíng)。

   Can you discuss the music played in the Chinatown you have visited? Are the songs outdated? Does Chinatown appear to be aging? Also, please research and compare the average age of the population in Chinatown to other areas by reading some English materials on the topic.

2. 对你来说, 中国城最有意义的一个地方是哪儿? (餐厅? 蛋糕店? 理发 店 lǐfà diàn?) 为什么?

   What is the most meaningful place to you in Chinatown? (Restaurant? bakery? barber shop?) Why?

3. 中国城的"中国特色"和"美国特色"分别有哪些?

   What are the "Chinese characteristics" and "American characteristics" of Chinatown?

4. 你喜欢吃幸运饼干吗? 你知道幸运饼干是谁发明的吗? 请上网查一下幸 运饼干的历史。

   Do you like eating fortune cookies? Do you know who invented the fortune cookie? Please check the history of fortune cookies online.

V. Interpersonal Tasks

1. 角色扮演 (juésè bànyǎn) Role-play

学期快结束了，你跟你的朋友计划去中国城吃饭。你的朋友第一次来这个城市的中国城。请你跟你的同学一起，从下面选至少8个词和3个语法完成一个讨论中国城的对话。

The semester is coming to an end. You and your friends plan to go to Chinatown for dinner. Your friends are coming to Chinatown for the first time. Please choose at least eight words and three patterns from the following to complete a dialogue about Chinatown.

生词(words)：破旧、落后、现代、过时、充满、回忆、疫情、影响、关门、可惜、账单、特色、几乎

句型(patterns)：给someone一种 …… 的感觉；拿 …… 来说(吧)；从小verb到大

2. 采访 (cǎifǎng) Interview

在中国文化里，老人和孩子住在一起是一种习惯 (xíguàn)，但在美国这并不常见。请采访一位住在中国城的老人，问问 (1) 他们为什么决定来美国；(2) 现在习惯了美国的生活吗? (3) 他们的子女多久来探望 (tànwàng, visit) 他们一次? (4) 他们喜欢住在中国城吗? 为什么? (5) 他们平日做什么活动? (6) 你自己的问题。

In Chinese culture, it is customary for the elderly to live with their children, but it is not common in America. Please interview a senior citizen living in Chinatown and ask (1) why they decided to come to America; (2) if they are used to American life now; (3) how often their children visits them; (4) if they like living in Chinatown and why; (5) what activities they do every day; (6) Additional questions of your choice.

Part II 短文：中国城的未来

I. Warm-up: Pre-reading Discussion

1. 中国城对华人来说重要吗? 为什么?
    Is Chinatown important to Chinese Americans? Why?
2. 中国城以后会消失吗? 为什么?
    Do you think Chinatown will eventually cease to exist and why?
3. 我们需要保护中国城吗? 为什么?
    Is it important to preserve Chinatown and why?

II. Interpretive Task: Listening Comprehension

Please listen to the text and choose True (T) or False (F) for each of the following audio recordings of the statements.

1. (   ) 2. (   ) 3. (   ) 4. (   ) 5. (   )

中国城顺发蛋糕店的老板名叫丁顺，"顺"是"顺利"的"顺"，可是丁顺的一生却不是很顺利。刚来美国的时候，因为语言不通，没有受过良好的教育，丁顺只能从事苦力工作，包括在中餐馆洗碗，去洗衣店打工等等。通过十年的努力，丁顺赚到了足够的钱，不但开了蛋糕店，而且在中国城买了一套一室一厅的公寓。虽然公寓不大，条件一般，家具简单，但是对丁顺来说，他在美国终于有一个家了。

我在中国城长大，从小到大一直亲切地称呼丁顺为"丁伯伯"。近几年，随着中国城的租金不断上涨，很多商店越来越不赚钱，丁伯伯的蛋糕店也是一样。丁伯伯想让儿子Kevin接手蛋糕店，但Kevin根本没有兴趣，大学毕业以后就搬出了中国城。2021年，疫情让蛋糕店的生意更糟糕。今年，丁伯伯决定把开了三十几年的店关了。

"中国城现在渐渐老年化，年轻人都走了，留下来的多数是像我这样的老年人。很快连我也要搬走了。地产商想把我住的那栋公寓楼改建成高档社区。楼里很多家庭买不起，也租不起，只好搬出中国城，去外面找更便宜的地方。"丁伯伯告诉我。

听到这个消息，我很难过。这里还是我熟悉的那个中国城吗？中国城未来还会是华人的文化、社交中心吗？中国城会渐渐消失吗？需要保护中国城吗？

The Future of Chinatown

The owner of Shunfa Bakery Shop in Chinatown is named Ding Shun. "Shun" is "smooth", but Ding Shun's life is not very smooth. When he first came to the United States, Ding Shun had to do coolie jobs, including washing dishes in Chinese restaurants and working in a laundry, because of language barriers and his poor education. After ten years of hard work, Ding Shun made enough money not only to open a bakery but also to buy a one-bedroom apartment in Chinatown. Although the apartment is small, the conditions are average, and the furniture is simple, for Ding Shun, he finally has a home in the United States.

Growing up in Chinatown, I have been affectionately calling Ding Shun "Uncle Ding" since my childhood. In recent years, with the rising rents in Chinatown, many shops have become less and less profitable, so is Uncle Ding's bakery. Uncle Ding wanted his son Kevin to take over the bakery, but Kevin had no interest at all and moved out of Chinatown after graduating from college. In 2021, the pandemic made the business of the bakery worse. This year, Uncle Ding decided to close the store that had been open for more than 30 years.

"Chinatown is getting old now, young people are gone, and most of those who stay are elderly people like me. Soon, I will also be moving away. The real estate developer wants to convert the apartment building that I live in into a high-end community. Many families in the building can't afford it or rent it, so they have to move out of Chinatown to find a cheaper place outside", Uncle Ding told me.

I am sad to hear this news. Is this still the Chinatown I am familiar with? Will Chinatown still be the cultural and social center of the Chinese in the future? Will Chinatown gradually disappear? Do we need to protect Chinatown?

生词 Vocabulary

Students are required to recognize and pronounce all the vocabulary listed. For the characters/words in italics and bold, students are also expected to know how to write.

1.	**未来**	未來	wèilái	n.	future
2.	顺利	順利	shùnlì	adj./adv.	smooth; successfully
3.	良好	良好	liánghǎo	adj.	good; often used in written language
4.	苦力	苦力	kǔlì	n.	laborer; coolie
5.	洗碗	洗碗	xǐwǎn	v.o.	wash dishes
6.	**打工**	打工	dǎgōng	v.o.	do a part-time job
7.	**努力**	努力	nǔlì	adv./adj.	diligent; diligently
8.	赚	賺	zhuàn	v.	make profit; gain
9.	足够	足夠	zúgòu	adj.	sufficient; enough
10.	套	套	tào	mw.	for sets; series; suites
11.	一室一厅	一室一廳	yīshìyītīng	ph.	one bedroom and one living room
12.	**公寓**	公寓	gōngyù	n.	apartment
13.	条件	條件	tiáojiàn	n.	condition; requirement
14.	家具	傢俱	jiājù	n.	furniture
15.	**终于**	終於	zhōngyú	adv.	finally; in the end
16.	称呼	稱呼	chēnghū	v./n.	address; form of address
17.	伯伯	伯伯	bóbo	n.	father's older brother, often used to address older male
18.	**随着**	隨著	suízhe	prep.	along with, in the wake of
19.	不断	不斷	bùduàn	adv.	continuously
20.	上涨	上漲	shàngzhǎng	v.	rise; go up
21.	**赚钱**	賺錢	zhuànqián	v.o.	make money
22.	接手	接手	jiēshǒu	v.o.	take over
23.	糟糕	糟糕	zāogāo	adj.	miserable; bad; terrible
24.	**关**	關	guān	v.	close; turn off; close down

25.	老年化	老年化	lǎoniánhuà	adj.	aging
26.	留	留	liú	v.	remain; keep; stay
27.	地产商	地產商	dìchǎnshāng	n.	real estate developer
28.	栋	棟	dòng	mw.	measure word for building
29.	改建	改建	gǎijiàn	v.	rebuild; reconstruct
30.	高档	高檔	gāodàng	adj.	high quality; high grade
31.	*消息*	消息	xiāoxi	n.	news; information
32.	*难过*	難過	nánguò	adj.	sad
33.	*社交*	社交	shèjiāo	n.	social contact
34.	消失	消失	xiāoshī	v.	disappear; vanish

Proper Names

1.	顺发蛋糕店	順發蛋糕店	Shùnfā dàngāodiàn	Shunfa Bakery
2.	丁顺	丁順	Dīng Shùn	Name of a person

Sentence Patterns / Grammar

1. 通过 ⋯⋯ 的努力: by means of/ through ... efforts

通过 means going through, so it implies a medium. The word modifies 努力 can be time duration or a person/ an organization.

通过十年的努力，丁顺赚到了足够的钱。
Through ten-year hard work, Ding Shun made enough money.

Examples:

1) 通过大家的努力，这个工程(gōngchéng)完成(wánchéng)了。
   Through everyone's efforts together, this project is finished.
2) 通过一年的努力，他终于考上最好的大学了。
   Through a year of hard work, he finally entered the best university.

2. 称呼A为B: address/call A as B

Instead of 叫, 称呼 is more a formal usage.

我称呼丁顺为"丁伯伯"。
I address him as "Uncle Ding".

Examples:

1) 我们称呼这个社区为中国城。
   We call this community Chinatown.

2) 称呼你的妻子 (qīzi) 为 "夫人" 是不对的。"夫人" 是用来称呼别人的妻子的。
   It is incorrect to address your wife as "Madame". This form of the address is only for other people's wives.

3. 随着 + sentence 1/a phrase, sentence 2: following situation 1, then situation 2 happens

In this pattern, sentence 1 and sentence 2 are closely related, and the second sentence is the focus of the whole structure. This structure is for describing a general situation, not for a personal situation. Another rule is that the meaning of sentence 1 should express changes; otherwise it is awkward to use it with this structure.

随着中国城的租金不断上涨, 很多商店也越来越不赚钱。
Following the rent increase continuously in Chinatown, many shops also make less and less profit.

Examples:

1) 随着生活水平的提高, 很多人都买得起房子了。
   Following the improvement of living standards, many people were able to buy houses.

2) 随着经济的发展, 人民的生活也越来越好了。
   Following the development of the economy, people's lives are getting better and better.

Frequent mistakes:

随着天气越来越热, 小王昨天去游泳(yóuyǒng, swim)了。(X)
随着天气越来越热, 游泳(yóuyǒng, swim)的人越来越多。(✓)

随着中文课, 我的中文越来越好了。(X)
每天上中文课, 我的中文越来越好了。(✓)

The sentences in the previous section are about personal experiences, so it is inappropriate to use 随着 in this situation.

4. V不起/V得起: can afford something/ cannot afford something

This is another potential complement that we previously have learned in other lessons. The word 起 means to be able to afford or not.

很多家庭买不起房子。
Many families cannot afford to buy houses.

Examples:

1) 这里的房租太贵了, 我住不起。
   The rent is too high here, and I cannot afford to live here.
2) 我没有足够的钱, 买不起车子。
   I don't have enough money, so I cannot afford to buy a car.

III. Vocabulary and Grammar Exercise

1. 用词写段落 Write a short and coherent paragraph with words provided. Use a connection word where necessary.

Example: 越来越、赚钱、努力→ 她努力赚钱, 所以她的生活也越来越好了。

1) 随着、提高、渐渐
2) 消息、终于、关
3) 条件、打工、买不起
4) 社区、未来、跟 …… 一样
5) 难过、越来越、把 + Object ……

2. 请用"随着"改写句子 Please rewrite the following sentences with 随着.

Example:

智能(zhìnéng smart)手机的出现
电脑和手机的功能(gōngnéng function)也越来越像了
→随着智能手机的出现, 电脑和手机的功能也越来越像了。

1) 公共 (gōnggòng) 交通工具 (gōngjù) 的发达

   开车进城的人也越来越少了

   _____

2) 中国的经济的发达

   想跟中国做生意的人也越来越多了

   _____

3. 选择填空 Fill in the blanks.

免费　难过　童年　熟悉　饼干　上涨　疫情　亲切　租不起　关

　　我从小就去丁伯伯的蛋糕店买_____, 他是一个非常_____的人, 要是他_____的客人来买东西, 有的时候会_____多给客人一点东西。有一天他说, 因为租金_____了很多, 还有_____以后, 蛋糕店越来越不赚钱, 他已经_____这个店了, 所以决定把蛋糕店_____了。我不知道怎么办, 觉得很_____, 这是我_____的时候最喜欢的地方。

4. 读了课文以后，你知道什么有关丁伯伯住的中国城的事？

After reading this lesson, what do you know about the Chinatown where uncle Ding lives?

用中文写下七个有关丁伯伯住的中国城的事。

Please list seven facts about the Chinatown where uncle Ding lives in Chinese.

1)
2)
3)
4)
5)
6)
7)

5. 小作文 Short essay:

请用所有的句型从丁顺的角度来写一篇最少350字的小短文。作文要包括：

1) 丁顺现在看到的问题；
2) 丁顺在这里开店的经验；
3) 丁顺的心情和看法；
4) 丁顺觉得最难过的事；
5) 丁顺的决定。

Write an essay no less than 350 characters long from Ding Shun's perspective and include **all** the sentence patterns provided. In your essay, you need to include the following:

1) What is happening now regarding Chinatown in Ding Shun's mind?
2) How did Ding Shun start his business in Chinatown?
3) How does Ding Shun feel?
4) What is the saddest thing in Ding Shun's mind?
5) What would Ding Shun do?

句型 (patterns): 位于＋ place word; ······ 等等; 不但 ······ 而且 ······; 随着; 虽然 ······ 但是 ······; 渐渐

IV. Post-reading Discussion

1. 你知道为什么蛋糕店叫"顺发蛋糕店"吗？
    Do you know why the bakery is called Shunfa bakery?
2. 丁顺在中国城的公寓怎么样？他以后还会住在那里吗？为什么？
    How is Ding Shun's apartment in Chinatown? Will he live there in the future? Why?

3. 哪些方面体现 (tǐxiàn) 了中国城渐渐老年化? 为什么中国城会老年化? 未来该怎么样吸引年轻人回到中国城工作、生活?
What aspects reflect the gradual aging of Chinatown? Why is Chinatown getting old? How to attract young people to work and live in Chinatown in the future?

4. 地产商在中国城建高档社区对中国城的发展有利 (yǒulì, beneficial) 吗? 为什么?
Will real estate developers building high-end communities in Chinatown benefit the development of Chinatown? Why?

5. 中国城还面临 (miànlín) 着哪些困境 (kùnjìng)?
What dilemmas are still facing Chinatown?

V. Interpersonal Tasks

小组讨论 (xiǎozǔtǎolùn): 2-3人一组, 讨论下面的题目 (tímù):

1. 回顾 (huígù, review) 一下你这学期了解到的移民故事, 跟你的同学分享一个你印象最深的故事, 说一说这个故事为什么让你印象深刻。

2. 你认为美国是一个大熔炉, 沙拉碗 (shālā wǎn) 还是马赛克 (mǎsàikè)? 为什么?

Group discussion: in groups of two to three, discuss the following topics.

1. Review the immigration stories you learned this semester, and then share with your classmates a story that impressed you the most. Please also explain why this story impressed you deeply.

2. What do you think the United States is, a melting pot, a salad bowl, or a mosaic? Why?

VI. Presentational Tasks

《新冠疫情下的中国城》 "Chinatown During the Covid-19 Pandemic"
2-3个同学一组, 选一个在美国或者其他国家的中国城, 查阅相关资料, 写一个研究报告, 介绍一下新冠疫情对这个中国城的影响。可以从下面几个方面来介绍:

1) 这个中国城的背景信息。比如: 位于哪里? 有什么历史? 有什么特色等等;
2) 新冠疫情之前这个中国城的情况。比如: 有什么商铺? 多少住户? 商铺的生意怎么样?住户的生活怎么样等等;
3) 2020年初新冠疫情爆发以来, 这个中国城有什么变化? 碰到了什么困难? 最大的困难是什么? 中国城的商户和住户的工作和生活受到了什么样的影响?
4) 当地政府采取 (cǎiqǔ) 了什么措施 (cuòshī) 或出台 (chūtái) 了什么政策来帮助中国城渡过难关 (dùguò nánguān)? 中国城的商户和住户对这些措施或者政策满意 (mǎnyì) 吗? 为什么?
5) 你们认为这个中国城未来的发展会怎样? 为什么? 对于这个中国城的未来发展, 你们有什么建议?

In groups of two to three students, choose one Chinatown in the United States or other countries, consult relevant materials, and write a research report to introduce the impact of Covid-19 pandemic on Chinatown. It can be introduced from the following aspects:

1) An overview of the chosen Chinatown, including its location, history, and unique characteristics.
2) The situation of this Chinatown before the Covid-19 outbreak. For example, What shops were there? How many households were there? How was the business? How was the life of the residents? etc.
3) What has changed in this Chinatown since the outbreak of Covid-19 in early 2020? What difficulties have they encountered? What was the biggest difficulty? What was the impact on the work and life of the merchants and residents in this Chinatown?
4) What measures or policies has the local government adopted to help Chinatown tide over the difficulties? Are the merchants and residents in Chinatown satisfied with these measures or policies? Why?
5) What do you think will be the future development of this Chinatown? Why? What suggestions do you have for the future development of this Chinatown?

Pinyin-English vocabulary

拼音 A	简体	繁體	词性	英文翻译	
àinǐkèsǐ	爱你克死	愛你克死		transliteration of Alex in Chinese; 死 sǐ means die	Lesson one
ānjiǎn	安检	安檢	n./v.	security check	Lesson two

拼音 B	简体	繁體	词性	英文翻译	
bǎifēnzhī	百分之	百分之	n.	percent	Lesson nine
bān	搬	搬	v.	move	Lesson one
bǎntú	版图	版圖	n.	domain, territory	Lesson eight
bāng	帮	幫	v.	help, assist	Lesson four
bǎobao	宝宝	寶寶	n.	baby	Lesson eight
bàogào	报告	報告	n.	report	Lesson one
bǎohù	保护	保護	n./v.	protect, protection, defend	Lesson eight
bāokuò	包括	包括	v.	include, comprise	Lesson four
bǎoliú	保留	保留	v.	keep, retain	Lesson two
bàozhǐ	报纸	報紙	n.	newspaper	Lesson six
bēi	杯	杯	mw.	cup, cupful, glassful	Lesson seven

(Continued)

(Continued)

拼音B	简体	繁體	词性	英文翻译	
běibian	北边	北邊	n.	north, north side, northern part, to the north of	Lesson eight
Běijīng	北京	北京		Beijing	Lesson one
bī	逼	逼	v.	to force, to compel	Lesson six
bǐjiào	比较	比較	adv./v.	relatively, compare	Lesson one
bǐrú	比如	比如	adv.	for example	Lesson one
bìyè	毕业	畢業	v.	graduate	Lesson four
bízi	鼻子	鼻子	n.	nose	Lesson five
biàn	变	變	v.	change, become	Lesson four
biānxiě	编写	編寫	v.	compile	Lesson four
biāozhǔn	标准	標准	n./adj.	standard	Lesson three
bié	别	別	adv.	do not	Lesson ten
bīng	冰	冰	n./adj.	ice; icy	Lesson seven
bǐnggān	饼干	餅乾	n.	biscuit, cracker, cookie	Lesson ten
bóbo	伯伯	伯伯	n.	father's older brother, often used to address older male	Lesson ten
bù	部	部	n.	part/section (usually a suffix of direction words such as 南部)	Lesson eight
bùduàn	不断	不斷	adv.	continuously	Lesson ten
bùguǎn	不管	不管	conj.	no matter, regardless of	Lesson two
bùfen	部分	部分	n.	part, share, section, piece	Lesson eight

拼音C	简体	繁體	词性	英文翻译	
càidān	菜单	菜單	n.	menu	Lesson six
càimíng	菜名	菜名	n.	dish name	Lesson nine
cānguǎn	餐馆	餐館	n.	restaurant	Lesson six
cānjiā	参加	參加	v.	join, attend, take part in	Lesson four
cāoxīn	操心	操心	adj./v.	concerned about, concern	Lesson five
chàbùduō	差不多	差不多	adv.	about, roughly	Lesson one
Chángchéng	长城	長城		Great Wall	Lesson eight
chángjiàn	常见	常見	adj.	common	Lesson one
Chángzhōu	常州	常州		Name of a city in Jiangsu province; it is about 185 km west of Shanghai	Lesson four
cháobài	朝拜	朝拜	v.	worship, pilgrimage	Lesson eight
cháodài	朝代	朝代	n.	dynasty	Lesson eight
chāoshì	超市	超市	n.	supermarket	Lesson seven
Chéngdū shì	成都市	成都市		City of Chengdu	Lesson eight
chēnghū	称呼	稱呼	v./n.	address, form of address	Lesson ten
chéngjì	成绩	成績	n.	score, grade	Lesson five
chōngmǎn	充满	充滿	v.	full of, brim, permeate	Lesson ten
chūshēng	出生	出生	v.	be born	Lesson one
chūxiàn	出现	出現	v.	appear, emerge	Lesson four
chuántǒng	传统	傳統	adj./n.	traditional, tradition	Lesson one

(Continued)

(Continued)

拼音 C	简体	繁體	词性	英文翻译	
chūnjié	春节	春節	n.	Spring Festival	Lesson three
cí	词	詞	n.	word	Lesson three
cíhuì	词汇	詞彙	n.	vocabulary	Lesson four
cōngming	聪明	聰明	adj.	intelligent, smart	Lesson six
cóngshì	从事	從事	v.	go in for, deal with (a profession)	Lesson six

拼音 D	简体	繁體	词性	英文翻译	
dǎ	打	打	v.	hit, break, fight, dial	Lesson two
dá'àn	答案	答案	n.	answer	Lesson two
dàduōshù	大多数	大多數	n.	the majority	Lesson six
dàgài	大概	大概	adv.	probably	Lesson nine
dǎgōng	打工	打工	v.o.	do a part time job	Lesson ten
dàxióngmāo	大熊猫	大熊猫	n.	giant panda	Lesson eight
Dàxióngmāo Fányù Zhōngxīn	大熊猫繁育中心	大熊猫繁育中心		Name of a place (Giant Panda Breeding Center)	Lesson eight
dàxué	大学	大學	n.	university	Lesson one
dàyuē	大约	大約	adv.	about	Lesson nine
dǎ zhāohu	打招呼	打招呼	v.o.	say hello	Lesson two
dǎzì	打字	打字	v.o.	type	Lesson four
dài	戴	戴	v.	to wear	Lesson five
dài	带	帶	v.	take along, bring, carry	Lesson five
dàitì	代替	代替	v.	take place of	Lesson four

拼音 D	简体	繁體	词性	英文翻译	
dàngāodiàn	蛋糕店	蛋糕店	n.	bakery	Lesson ten
dāngdì	当地	當地	adj.	local	Lesson six
dāngshí	当时	當時	adv.	at that time	Lesson one
dānmíng	单名	單名	n.	one-character name	Lesson one
dānxīn	担心	擔心	v.	worry	Lesson five
dàolù	道路	道路	n.	road, path	Lesson nine
dī	低	低	adj.	low	Lesson five
diǎncài	点菜	點菜	v.o.	choose dishes from a menu; order dishes	Lesson nine
diǎncān	点餐	點餐	v.o.	order food	Lesson seven
diànnǎo	电脑	電腦	n.	computer	Lesson four
diànshì	电视	電視	n.	television	Lesson four
diànyǐng	电影	電影	n.	movie	Lesson six
diào	掉	掉	adv./v.	drop; fall V + 掉; indicates that the position moves or disappears	Lesson three
dìchǎnshāng	地产商	地產商	n.	real estate developer	Lesson ten
Dì'èr cì shìjiè dàzhàn	第二次世界大战	第二次世界大戰		The World War II	Lesson six
dìfāng	地方	地方	n.	local; locality	Lesson three
Dīng Shùn	丁顺	丁順		Name of a person	Lesson ten
dīrényìděng	低人一等	低人一等	ph.	be inferior to others	Lesson six
dìzhèn	地震	地震	n.	earthquake	Lesson seven

(Continued)

(Continued)

拼音 D	简体	繁體	词性	英文翻译	
dǒng	懂	懂	v.	understand, know	Lesson three
dòng	栋	棟	mw.	measure word for building	Lesson ten
dōngtiān	冬天	冬天	n.	winter	Lesson three
dú	读	讀	v.	read	Lesson four
dújū	独居	獨居	v.	live alone	Lesson eight
dǔsè	堵塞	堵塞	adj.	blocked	Lesson nine

拼音 E	简体	繁體	词性	英文翻译	
édàn	鹅蛋	鵝蛋	n.	goose egg	Lesson five
Éméi shān	峨眉山	峨眉山		Mt. Emei	Lesson eight

拼音 F	简体	繁體	词性	英文翻译	
fācái	发财	發財	v.o.	get rich	Lesson nine
fàcài	发菜	髮菜	n.	hair-like seaweed, fat choy	Lesson nine
fādá	发达	發達	adj.	developed	Lesson six
fǎlù	法律	法律	n.	law	Lesson six
fāmíng	发明	發明	n./v.	invention, invent	Lesson four
fāngbiàn	方便	方便	adj./v.	convenient, make something convenient	Lesson three
fāngmiàn	方面	方面	n.	aspect	Lesson three
fāngyán	方言	方言	n.	Chinese topolects	Lesson three

拼音 F	简体	繁體	词性	英文翻译	
fāngshì	方式	方式	n.	way, manner, style	Lesson nine
fánhuá	繁华	繁華	adj.	bustling	Lesson nine
fānyì	翻译	翻譯	v./n.	translate, translation	Lesson nine
fāyīn	发音	發音	v.o./n.	pronounce, pronunciation	Lesson one
fāzhǎn	发展	發展	v./n.	develop, development	Lesson six
fēicháng	非常	非常	adv.	very	Lesson three
fēngjǐng	风景	風景	n.	scenery	Lesson eight
fěnsī	粉丝	粉絲	n.	vermicelli made from bean starch, fan	Lesson nine
Fótiàoqiáng	佛跳墙	佛跳墙		Steamed abalone with shark's fin and fish maw	Lesson nine
fù	副	副	mw.	pair	Lesson five
fù	付	付	v.	pay	Lesson five
fùdān	负担	負擔	n.	burden	Lesson five
fúhào	符号	符號	n.	symbol	Lesson one
fùnǚ	妇女	婦女	n.	women	Lesson six
Fūqī fèipiàn	夫妻肺片	夫妻肺片		Sliced beef and ox tongue in chili sauce	Lesson nine
fúwùyuán	服务员	服務員	n.	waiter, waitress	Lesson seven
fùyù	富裕	富裕	adj.	rich	Lesson nine
fùzá	复杂	複雜	adj.	complicated, complex	Lesson eight

拼音 G	简体	繁體	词性	英文翻译	
gǎijiàn	改建	改建	v.	rebuild, reconstruct	Lesson ten
gāng	刚	剛	adv.	just	Lesson one
Gǎng	港	港		harbor, port, here it is an abbreviation for 香港 (Xiānggǎng Hong Kong)	Lesson ten
gāngqín	钢琴	鋼琴	n.	piano	Lesson six
gǎnjǐn	赶紧	趕緊	adv.	hurriedly	Lesson two
gǎnjué	感觉	感覺	v./n.	feel, feeling	Lesson three
gānyù	干预	幹預	v.	intervene	Lesson nine
gāodàng	高档	高檔	adj.	high quality, high grade	Lesson ten
gàosu	告诉	告訴	v.	tell, inform	Lesson two
gāoyuán	高原	高原	n.	plateau	Lesson eight
gè	各	各	pron.	each	Lesson three
gēcí	歌词	歌詞	n.	song lyric	Lesson six
Gē Kūnhuà	戈鲲化	戈鯤化		Name of a person	Lesson six
gēnběn (bù/ méiyǒu)	根本 (不/ 没有)	根本 (不/ 沒有)	adv.	not at all, absolutely not	Lesson four
gēnjù	根据	根據	prep.	according to	Lesson one
gēqǔ	歌曲	歌曲	n.	song	Lesson six
gōngmín	公民	公民	n.	citizen	Lesson seven
gōngyù	公寓	公寓	n.	apartment	Lesson ten
gōngyuán	公园	公園	n.	garden, park	Lesson nine
gōngzuò	工作	工作	v./n.	work	Lesson five
guàibùdé	怪不得	怪不得	adv.	no wonder, so that's why, that explains why	Lesson three

拼音 G	简体	繁體	词性	英文翻译	
guān	关	關	v.	close, turn off, close down	Lesson ten
guānfāng	官方	官方	adj.	official	Lesson four
Guǎngdōng	广东	廣東		Guangdong province in south China	Lesson four
Guǎngxī	广西	廣西		Guangxi province in south China	Lesson eight
Guānhuà fāngyán	官话方言	官話方言		Guan (Mandarin) dialect (spoken primarily in northern and southwestern China)	Lesson four
guǎnlǐ	管理	管理	v.	manage	Lesson nine
guānmén	关门	關門	v.o.	close a door, (a shop etc.) to close (for the night or permanently)	Lesson ten
guānshǎng	观赏	觀賞	v.	enjoy sight of	Lesson eight
guānxi	关系	關係	n.	relation, relationship	Lesson six
guānxīn	关心	關心	v.	care for	Lesson three
guóbǎo	国宝	國寶	n.	national treasure	Lesson eight
guónèi	国内	國內	n./adj.	interior of country, domestic	Lesson two
guòshí	过时	過時	adj.	old-fashioned, out of date	Lesson ten

(*Continued*)

(Continued)

拼音 G	简体	繁體	词性	英文翻译	
guówáng	国王	國王	n.	king	Lesson eight
guòyè	过夜	過夜	v.	spend a night	Lesson five
gùshì	故事	故事	n.	story	Lesson one
gùyōng	雇用	雇用	v.	hire, employ	Lesson nine

拼音 H	简体	繁體	词性	英文翻译	
Hāfó dàxué	哈佛大学	哈佛大學		Harvard University	Lesson six
Hāfó shāngxué Yuàn	哈佛商学院	哈佛商學院		Harvard Business School	Lesson five
hànbǎo	汉堡	漢堡	n.	hamburger	Lesson seven
hángbān	航班	航班	n.	flight	Lesson two
Hánguó	韩国	韓國		Korea	Lesson two
hǎoxiào	好笑	好笑	adj.	laughable, funny	Lesson two
hē	喝	喝	v.	drink	Lesson seven
Hóngshāo shīzitóu	红烧狮子头	紅燒獅子頭		Braised pork ball in brown sauce	Lesson nine
hòulái	后来	後來	n.	later	Lesson two
huábù	华埠	華埠		Chinatown	Lesson nine
huàhuà	画画	畫畫	v.o.	draw a picture	Lesson six
huángdì	皇帝	皇帝	n.	emperor	Lesson eight
huā xīnsi	花心思	花心思	v.	put thought/ effort into	Lesson one
huáyì	华裔	華裔	n.	ethnic Chinese	Lesson one
hùdòng	互动	互動	v./n.	interact, interaction	Lesson eight

拼音 H	简体	繁體	词性	英文翻译	
huífù	回复	回覆	v.	reply	Lesson two
huíyì	回忆	回憶	n./v.	memories, recall	Lesson ten
hú li hútú	糊里糊涂	糊里糊塗	adj.	The mind is in a vague state, muddle-headed	Lesson three
hǔmā	虎妈	虎媽	n.	tiger mom	Lesson five
Hǔmā zhàngē	虎妈战歌	虎媽戰歌		Battle Hymn of the Tiger Mother	Lesson five
hùnxuè'ér	混血儿	混血兒	n.	multiracial children	Lesson two
huǒchēzhàn	火车站	火車站	n.	train station	Lesson nine
huǒguō	火锅	火鍋	n.	hot pot	Lesson eight
hùxiāng	互相	互相	adv.	each other, mutually, mutual	Lesson three
hùzhào	护照	護照	n.	passport	Lesson two

拼音 J	简体	繁體	词性	英文翻译	
jiā	家	家	mw.	individual measure for a family, individual measure for institutions and enterprises	Lesson seven
jiǎ	假	假	adj.	fake	Lesson seven
jiājù	家具	傢俱	n.	furniture	Lesson ten
jiǎndān	简单	簡單	adj.	simple	Lesson one
jiǎng	讲	講	v.	speak, be particular about	Lesson two

(*Continued*)

(Continued)

拼音 J	简体	繁體	词性	英文翻译	
jiānglái	将来	將來	n.	future	Lesson five
Jiànguó	建国	建國		boy's name, literary meaning of 'building country'	Lesson one
Jiāngsū	江苏	江蘇		Jiangsu province	Lesson four
jiànjiàn	渐渐	漸漸	adv.	gradually	Lesson eight
Jiànjūn	建军	建軍		boy's name, literary meaning of 'building army'	Lesson one
jiànlì	建立	建立	v.	establish, set up, found	Lesson eight
jiǎnzhí	简直	簡直	adv.	simply	Lesson nine
jiànzhù	建筑	建築	v./n.	build, building, architecture	Lesson six
jiāo	教	教	v.	teach	Lesson three
jiāo	交	交	v.	make (friends), hand over, deliver, pay, intersect	Lesson ten
jiàohuì	教会	教會	n.	church	Lesson four
jiāoliú	交流	交流	v.	communicate	Lesson one
jiàoshòu	教授	教授	n.	professor	Lesson five
jiāotōng	交通	交通	n.	transportation	Lesson nine
jiātíng	家庭	家庭	n.	family	Lesson one
jīchǎng	机场	機場	n.	airport	Lesson two
jìchéng	继承	繼承	v.	inherit	Lesson one
jīdàn	鸡蛋	雞蛋	n.	egg	Lesson two

拼音 J	简体	繁體	词性	英文翻译	
jìdé	记得	記得	v.	remember	Lesson three
jiéhūn	结婚	結婚	v.o.	marry, get married	Lesson one
jiémù	节目	節目	n.	program, show	Lesson four
jiēqū	街区	街區	n.	block	Lesson nine
jièshào	介绍	介紹	v.	introduce	Lesson five
jiēshǒu	接手	接手	v.o.	take over	Lesson ten
jīhū	几乎	幾乎	adv.	almost, nearly, practically	Lesson ten
jǐláijǐqù	挤来挤去	擠來擠去	v.	squeeze around	Lesson nine
jìmò	寂寞	寂寞	adj.	lonely	Lesson seven
jǐn	紧	緊	adj.	tight, strict	Lesson six
jǐngdiǎn	景点	景點	n.	scenic spots	Lesson eight
jīngguò	经过	經過	v.	pass, go through	Lesson eight
jīngjìxué	经济学	經濟學	n.	economics	Lesson four
jīngyíng	经营	經營	v.	manage, run	Lesson six
jīnróng	金融	金融	n.	finance	Lesson nine
jìnrù	进入	進入	v.	enter	Lesson six
jǐnzhāng	紧张	緊張	adj.	nervous, intense, tense	Lesson six
jìnzhǐ	禁止	禁止	v.	prohibit	Lesson six
jīpiào	机票	機票	n.	plane ticket	Lesson two
jíshǐ	即使	即使	conj.	even if	Lesson seven
jītóngyājiǎng	鸡同鸭讲	雞同鴨講	ph.	Individuals have difficulty communicating with each other, like a chicken talking to a duck.	Lesson four

(Continued)

(Continued)

拼音 J	简体	繁體	词性	英文翻译	
Jiǔzhàigōu	九寨沟	九寨溝		Jiuzhaigou	Lesson eight
jíxiáng	吉祥	吉祥	adj.	auspicious	Lesson nine
jù	句	句	mw.	measure word for sentences	Lesson one

拼音 K	简体	繁體	词性	英文翻译	
kāfēi	咖啡	咖啡	n.	coffee	Lesson seven
kāidiàn	开店	開店	v.o.	open a shop	Lesson nine
kāishǐ	开始	開始	v./n.	begin, beginning	Lesson three
kāixīn	开心	開心	adj.	happy	Lesson two
kǎolǜ	考虑	考慮	v./n.	consider, consideration	Lesson six
kǎoshàng	考上	考上	v.	pass entrance examination	Lesson four
kèběn	课本	課本	n.	textbook	Lesson eight
Kèjiāfāngyán	客家方言	客家方言		Hakka dialect (spoken primarily in south eastern China)	Lesson four
kěndìng	肯定	肯定	adv.	surely, certainly	Lesson six
kěpà	可怕	可怕	adj.	horrible	Lesson nine
kèrén	客人	客人	n.	guest	Lesson nine
kěxī	可惜	可惜	adj.	unfortunate, it is a pity	Lesson ten
kēxué	科学	科學	n.	science, scientific knowledge	Lesson six

拼音 K	简体	繁體	词性	英文翻译	
kèzhì	克制	克制	v.	restrain, control, self-control	Lesson one
kǒuwèi	口味	口味	n.	a person's taste	Lesson eight
kǒuyīn	口音	口音	n.	accent	Lesson three
kuàizi	筷子	筷子	n.	chopsticks	Lesson two
kuān	宽	寬	n./adj.	width, wide	Lesson nine
kǔlì	苦力	苦力	n.	laborer, coolie	Lesson ten
kuòdà	扩大	擴大	v.	expand, enlarge, broaden one's scope	Lesson eight

拼音 L	简体	繁體	词性	英文翻译	
lā	拉	拉	v.	pull	Lesson two
là	辣	辣	adj.	spicy	Lesson eight
Lābùlāduō quǎn	拉布拉多犬	拉布拉多犬		Labrador Retriever	Lesson one
Lādīngwén	拉丁文	拉丁文		Latin	Lesson six
Lādīng zìmǔ	拉丁字母	拉丁字母	n.	Latin alphabet	Lesson four
lǎobǎn	老板	老板	n.	boss	Lesson nine
lǎoniánhuà	老年化	老年化	adj.	aging	Lesson ten
liǎn	脸	臉	n.	face	Lesson five
liánghǎo	良好	良好	adj.	good, often used in written language	Lesson ten
Liǎnshū	脸书	臉書		Facebook	Lesson five

(Continued)

(Continued)

拼音 L	简体	繁體	词性	英文翻译	
liánxì	联系	聯繫	v.	contact; connect	Lesson five
lìngwài	另外	另外	conj.	additionally, in addition, besides	Lesson four
lìshǐ	历史	歷史	n.	history	Lesson six
lǐsuǒdāngrán	理所当然	理所當然	idm.	naturally; to be expected as a matter of course	Lesson five
liú	留	留	v.	remain, keep, stay	Lesson ten
liúlì	流利	流利	adj.	fluent	Lesson six
liúxuéshēng	留学生	留學生	n.	oversea student	Lesson one
lǐyóu	理由	理由	n.	reason, justification	Lesson six
luòhòu	落后	落後	v./adj.	fall behind, lag, retrogress	Lesson ten
lǚxíng	旅行	旅行	v./n.	travel, journey, trip	Lesson nine

拼音 M	简体	繁體	词性	英文翻译	
mài	卖	賣	v.	sell	Lesson seven
mǎidān	买单	買單	v.o.	pay the restaurant bill	Lesson ten
màipiàn	麦片	麥片	n.	cereal	Lesson seven
máng	忙	忙	adj.	busy	Lesson one
mǎnzú	满足	滿足	v.	satisfy	Lesson six
mǎyǐ	蚂蚁	螞蟻	n.	ant	Lesson nine
Mǎyǐ shàngshù	蚂蚁上树	螞蟻上樹		Sauteed vermicelli with minced pork	Lesson nine

拼音 M	简体	繁體	词性	英文翻译	
měi	每	每	pron.	every, each	Lesson one
Měnggǔ	蒙古	蒙古		Mongolia	Lesson eight
miǎnfèi	免费	免費	adj.	free (of charge)	Lesson ten
miànjī	面积	面積	n.	surface area	Lesson eight
miànshí xiǎochī	面食小吃	麵食小吃	n.	cooked wheaten snacks	Lesson eight
miáotiáo	苗条	苗條	adj.	slim	Lesson five
mìjí	密集	密集	adj.	populated; crowded	Lesson nine
Míngcháo	明朝	明朝		Ming dynasty (1368–1644)	Lesson eight
míng'é	名额	名額	n.	quota	Lesson seven
míngzi	名字	名字	n.	name	Lesson one
mǒ	抹	抹	v.	daub, rub	Lesson eight

拼音 N	简体	繁體	词性	英文翻译	
nánguài	难怪	難怪	adv.	no wonder	Lesson six
nánguò	难过	難過	adj.	sad	Lesson ten
nánxìng	男性	男性	n.	male	Lesson one
nào xiàohua	闹笑话	鬧笑話	v.o.	make a fool of oneself	Lesson four
nénggòu	能够	能夠	v.	to be able to, can	Lesson six
nénglì	能力	能力	n.	ability	Lesson four
niándài	年代	年代	n.	age, era, a decade of a century	Lesson one
niángāo	年糕	年糕	n.	rice cake	Lesson nine
niánjí	年级	年級	n.	grade	Lesson one

(*Continued*)

(Continued)

拼音 N	简体	繁體	词性	英文翻译	
niánxīn	年薪	年薪	n.	annual salary, yearly income	Lesson five
niúnǎi	牛奶	牛奶	n.	milk	Lesson seven
Niǔyuē	纽约	紐約		New York	Lesson one
nuǎnqì	暖气	暖氣	n.	heating	Lesson three
nǔlì	努力	努力	adj./adv.	diligent, diligently	Lesson six

拼音 P	简体	繁體	词性	英文翻译	
páiduì	排队	排隊	v.o.	stand in line	Lesson two
Páihuá fǎ'àn	排华法案	排華法案		The Chinese Exclusion Act	Lesson six
páixièwù	排泄物	排泄物	n.	excrement	Lesson eight
Pèiqí fǎ'àn	佩奇法案	佩奇法案		Page Act	Lesson six
péndì	盆地	盆地	n.	basin (geog.)	Lesson eight
pèng	碰	碰	v.	run into, bump into, touch	Lesson two
piányi	便宜	便宜	adj.	cheap, inexpensive	Lesson six
pífū	皮肤	皮膚	n.	skin	Lesson five
píngfāng gōnglǐ	平方公里	平方公里	n.	square kilometer	Lesson eight
píngjūn	平均	平均	adj./adv.	average, equally	Lesson eight
pīnyīn	拼音	拼音	n.	official Chinese alphabetic system	Lesson four
pòjiù	破旧	破舊	adj.	old and shabby	Lesson nine
pǔtōnghuà	普通话	普通話	n.	Putonghua, Mandarin	Lesson three

拼音 Q	简体	繁體	词性	英文翻译	
qián	钱	錢	n.	money	Lesson five
qiáng	墙	牆	n.	wall	Lesson six
qiángdà	强大	強大	adj.	powerful, strong	Lesson eight
qiàoshéyīn	翘舌音	翹舌音	n.	Retroflex; zh, chi, shi Some people say 卷舌音juǎn shé yīn.	Lesson three
qíguài	奇怪	奇怪	adj.	strange	Lesson two
qìhòu	气候	氣候	n.	climate	Lesson eight
Qīngcháo	清朝	清朝		Qing dynasty (1644–1911)	Lesson eight
qīngchǔ	清楚	清楚	adj./v.	clear, distinct, understand	Lesson two
qīnqiè	亲切	親切	adj.	dear, kind	Lesson three
Qín Shǐhuáng	秦始皇	秦始皇		the first emperor of a unified China	Lesson eight
qíshí	其实	其實	adv.	actually, in fact	Lesson two
qíshì	歧视	歧視	v./n.	discriminate; discrimina-tion	Lesson six
qìzhì	气质	氣質	n.	temperament, personality traits, manners	Lesson five
qízhōng	其中	其中	adv.	among	Lesson five
qū	区	區	n.	area, district	Lesson nine
quán	全	全	adv.	all	Lesson one
què	却	卻	adv./ conj.	yet, but, however	Lesson four
qún	群	群	mw.	group, herd	Lesson six
qùshì	去世	去世	v.	pass away	Lesson four

拼音 R	简体	繁體	词性	英文翻译	
rán'ér	然而	然而	conj.	but; however	Lesson six
ràng	让	讓	v.	allow, induce someone to do something	Lesson four
rènshi	认识	認識	v.	meet (a person), recognize	Lesson one
rènwéi	认为	認為	v.	think, believe	Lesson six
rényuán	人员	人員	n.	personnel	Lesson two
Rìběn	日本	日本		Japan	Lesson two
rìcháng	日常	日常	adj.	daily	Lesson four
rónglú	熔炉	熔爐	n.	melting pot	Lesson seven
róngrù	融入	融入	v.	adapt to; mingle with	Lesson seven
róngyì	容易	容易	adj.	easy	Lesson one
rùjìng	入境	入境	v.o.	enter a country	Lesson six

拼音 S	简体	繁體	词性	英文翻译	
sānmíngzhì	三明治	三明治	n.	sandwich	Lesson seven
sānshí érlì	三十而立	三十而立	idm.	age when a man should stand on his own feet	Lesson one
Shànghǎi huà	上海话	上海話	n.	Shanghai dialect	Lesson three
Shànghǎi rén	上海人	上海人		Shanghai-nese	Lesson three
shāngpù	商铺	商鋪	n.	shop	Lesson nine
shāngrén	商人	商人	n.	merchant	Lesson seven

拼音 S	简体	繁體	词性	英文翻译	
shāngyèjiē	商业街	商業街	n.	commercial street	Lesson nine
shàngzhǎng	上涨	上派	v.	rise, go up	Lesson ten
Shāng Zhōu	商周	商周		the earliest named Chinese dynasties	Lesson eight
shāohuǐ	烧毁	燒毀	v.	destroy by fire	Lesson seven
shǎoshùmínzú	少数民族	少數民族	n.	minority, ethnic group	Lesson eight
shǎoshùzúyì	少数族裔	少數族裔	n.	ethnic minorities	Lesson nine
shèjiāo	社交	社交	n.	social contact	Lesson ten
shēncái	身材	身材	n.	figure	Lesson five
shēnfèn	身份	身份	n.	identity	Lesson seven
shěng	省	省	n./v.	province, save	Lesson eight
shěngchījiǎnyòng	省吃俭用	省吃儉用	ph.	live frugally	Lesson five
shěnghuì	省会	省會	n.	provincial capital	Lesson eight
shēnghuó	生活	生活	n.	life	Lesson two
shēngqì	生气	生氣	v.o.	get angry	Lesson two
shēngyì	生意	生意	n.	business, trade	Lesson six
shēnqǐng	申请	申請	v.	apply	Lesson five
shěnwèn	审问	審問	n./v.	interrogation, interrogate	Lesson seven
shènzhì	甚至	甚至	adv./conj.	even	Lesson ten
shèqū	社区	社區	n.	community	Lesson nine
shètuán	社团	社團	n.	organization, group, club	Lesson five

(Continued)

(Continued)

拼音 S	简体	繁體	词性	英文翻译	
shèshìdù	摄氏度	攝氏度	n.	Celsius 华氏度 Fahrenheit	Lesson six
shídài	时代	時代	n.	age, era, epoch	Lesson eight
shìjiǎo	视角	視角	n.	viewpoint, perspective	Lesson six
shìpín liáotiān	视频聊天	視頻聊天	v.	video chat/ FaceTime	Lesson one
shíqī	时期	時期	n.	period (of time)	Lesson six
shìqū	市区	市區	n.	urban area	Lesson nine
shíxí	实习	實習	v./n.	intern, internship	Lesson five
shìyè	事业	事業	n.	career, un- dertaking	Lesson one
shìyǒu	室友	室友	n.	roommate	Lesson one
shìzhèngtīng	市政厅	市政廳	n.	city hall	Lesson seven
shòubùliǎo	受不了	受不了	v.	be unable to endure, cannot stand/bear	Lesson seven
shòudào	受到	受到	v.	be given, suffer the effects of	Lesson six
shǒudū	首都	首都	n.	capital	Lesson eight
shǒujī	手机	手機	n.	cell phone	Lesson four
shūfu	舒服	舒服	adj.	comfortable	Lesson nine
Shùnfā dàngāodiàn	顺发蛋糕店	順發蛋糕店		Shunfa Bakery	Lesson ten
shùnlì	顺利	順利	adj./ adv.	smooth, suc- cessfully	Lesson ten
shuōshíhuà	说实话	說實話	ph.	speak the truth, frankly	Lesson ten

拼音 S	简体	繁體	词性	英文翻译	
shúxī	熟悉	熟悉	v.	know something/ someone well	Lesson eight
Sìchuān	四川	四川		Sichuan province in southwest China	Lesson four
sǐ diào	死掉	死掉	v.	die, kick the bucket	Lesson three
sìjì	四季	四季	n.	four seasons	Lesson eight
suàn	算	算	v.	calculate, consider, count as	Lesson two
suì	岁	歲	n.	years old, year(of age)	Lesson one
suīrán	虽然	雖然	conj.	although	Lesson two
suízhe	随着	隨著	prep.	along with, in the wake of	Lesson ten
suǒyǒu de	所有的	所有的	adj.	all	Lesson six
sùshè	宿舍	宿舍	n.	dormitory	Lesson one

拼音 T	简体	繁體	词性	英文翻译	
Tái	台	台		platform; stage; classifier for machines, desk or table; here it is an abbreviation for 台湾 (Táiwān Taiwan)	Lesson ten

(Continued)

(Continued)

拼音 T	简体	繁體	词性	英文翻译	
Tángcháo	唐朝	唐朝		Tang dynasty (618–907)	Lesson eight
tán liàn'ài	谈恋爱	談戀愛	v.o.	be in a relationship	Lesson one
tào	套	套	mw.	for sets, series, suites	Lesson ten
tǎoyàn	讨厌	討厭	v./adj.	dislike, loathe, annoying, troublesome	Lesson six
tèbié	特别	特別	adj./ adv.	special, particularly	Lesson one
tèdiǎn	特点	特點	n.	character- istic, trait, feature	Lesson two
tèsè	特色	特色	n.	character- istic, dis- tinguishing feature or quality	Lesson ten
tiào	跳	跳	n./v.	jump, hop	Lesson four
tiáojiàn	条件	條件	n.	condition, requirement	Lesson ten
tiělù	铁路	鐵路	n.	railroad	Lesson six
tígāo	提高	提高	v.	raise, increase, improve	Lesson four
tīngdào	听到	聽到	v.	hear	Lesson three
tīngqǐlái	听起来	聽起來	v.	sound, 听 (聽): listen to, obey, comply	Lesson one
tōngguò	通过	通過	v.	pass, adopt	Lesson six
tóngnián	童年	童年	n.	childhood	Lesson ten
tóngshì	同事	同事	n.	colleague	Lesson four

拼音 T	简体	繁體	词性	英文翻译	
tóngxué	同学	同學	n.	classmate	Lesson two
tóngyì	同意	同意	v.	agree, approve	Lesson four
tǒngyī	统一	統一	n./adj.	unity, unified, unitary	Lesson eight
tóuzī	投资	投資	v./n.	invest, investment	Lesson seven
tǔdòubǐng	土豆饼	土豆餅	n.	hash brown	Lesson seven
tūrán	突然	突然	adv.	suddenly, abruptly	Lesson four

拼音 W	简体	繁體	词性	英文翻译	
wàigōng	外公	外公	n.	maternal grandfather	Lesson three
wàn	万	萬	num.	ten thousand	Lesson one
wǎncān	晚餐	晚餐	n.	dinner	Lesson seven
wàngnǚ chéngfèng	望女成凤	望女成鳳	idm.	have high expectations of one's daughter	Lesson five
wàngzǐ chénglóng	望子成龙	望子成龍	idm.	have high expectations of one's son	Lesson five
wánměi	完美	完美	adj.	perfect	Lesson one
wèidao	味道	味道	n.	taste, flavor, smell	Lesson eight
wèilái	未来	未來	n.	future	Lesson ten
wèiyú	位于	位於	v.	be located/ situated	Lesson eight
wén	闻	聞	v.	smell	Lesson eight
wēndù	温度	温度	n.	temperature	Lesson eight
wénhuà	文化	文化	n.	culture	Lesson one
wèntí	问题	問題	n.	question, problem	Lesson two

(Continued)

(Continued)

拼音 *W*	简体	繁體	词性	英文翻译	
wénzì gǎigé	文字改革	文字改革	n.	reform of writing system	Lesson four
wénzìxué	文字学	文字學	n.	philology	Lesson four
Wòlóng Dàxióng māo Qīxīdì	卧龙大熊猫栖息地	臥龍大熊貓棲息地		Name of a place (Wolong Giant Panda Sanctuaries)	Lesson eight
wǔcān	午餐	午餐	n.	lunch	Lesson seven
Wú fāngyán	吴方言	吳方言		Wu dialects (spoken primarily in Shanghai and surrounding areas)	Lesson four
wúliáo	无聊	無聊	adj.	bored, boring, silly	Lesson four

拼音 *X*	简体	繁體	词性	英文翻译	
xiàhūn	吓昏	嚇昏	v.	faint from fear, shell-shocked	Lesson six
xiàndài	现代	現代	adj./n.	modern, modern times	Lesson ten
xiàng	项	項	mw.	for rules, laws, projects	Lesson six
xiǎngxiàng	想像	想像	v.	imagine, fancy	Lesson ten
xiǎngyào	想要	想要	v.	intend, want	Lesson two
xiàngzi	巷子	巷子	n.	alley	Lesson nine
xiāoshī	消失	消失	v.	disappear, vanish	Lesson ten
xiǎoshíhou	小时候	小時候	n.	in one's childhood	Lesson two

拼音 X	简体	繁體	词性	英文翻译	
xiàoshùn	孝顺	孝順	v./adj.	show filial obedience, filial	Lesson five
xiāoxi	消息	消息	n.	news, information	Lesson ten
xiǎoyí	小姨	小姨	n.	mother's youngest sister	Lesson three
Xià Xiǎojīng	夏小京	夏小京		a person's name; 夏 (天) is summer	Lesson one
xiéchǎng	鞋厂	鞋廠	n.	shoe factory	Lesson nine
xiéyīn zì	谐音字	諧音字	n.	homophonic words	Lesson nine
xíguàn	习惯	習慣	n./v.	habit, be used to	Lesson two
xǐhuān	喜欢	喜歡	v.	like	Lesson one
Xīlàwén	希腊文	希臘文		Greek	Lesson six
xīn	新	新	adj.	new	Lesson one
xìnggé	性格	性格	n.	personality	Lesson five
xínglixiāng	行李箱	行李箱	n.	luggage, baggage	Lesson two
xìngyùn	幸运	幸運	adj.	fortunate, lucky	Lesson ten
xìnxī	信息	信息	n.	information	Lesson one
xīshēng	牺牲	犧牲	v./n.	sacrifice	Lesson five
xiūjiàn	修建	修建	v.	build	Lesson nine
xǐwǎn	洗碗	洗碗	v.o.	wash dishes	Lesson ten
xīwàng	希望	希望	v.	hope, wish	Lesson one
xǐyīdiàn	洗衣店	洗衣店	n.	laundromat	Lesson six
xīyǐnlì	吸引力	吸引力	n.	attractive-ness	Lesson six
xuǎn	选	選	v.	choose, pick, select	Lesson two

(Continued)

(Continued)

拼音 X	简体	繁體	词性	英文翻译	
xuéfèi	学费	學費	n.	tuition	Lesson five
xuéqī	学期	學期	n.	term, semester	Lesson two
xuéqū fáng	学区房	學區房	n.	house in a good school district	Lesson five
xuéwèn	学问	學問	n.	knowledge	Lesson nine
xuéxiào	学校	學校	n.	school	Lesson one

拼音 Y	简体	繁體	词性	英文翻译	
yālì	压力	壓力	n.	pressure	Lesson five
yángé	严格	嚴格	adj.	strict	Lesson five
yǎnjīng	眼睛	眼睛	n.	eyes	Lesson five
yánjiū	研究	研究	n./v.	research, study	Lesson six
yánjiūshēng	研究生	研究生	n.	graduate student	Lesson five
yánzhòng	严重	嚴重	adj.	serious, critical	Lesson six
yāoqiú	要求	要求	v./n.	request, require, requirement	Lesson five
yàoshi	钥匙	鑰匙	n.	key	Lesson three
yàyì	亚裔	亞裔	n.	of Asian descent	Lesson six
yàzhōu	亚洲	亞洲	n.	Asia	Lesson two
Yēlǔ dàxué	耶鲁大学	耶魯大學		Yale University	Lesson five
yībān	一般	一般	adj./adv.	ordinary, generally, in general	Lesson four
yīdìng de	一定的	一定的	adj.	certain, particular	Lesson one
yímín	移民	移民	v./n.	immigrate, immigrant	Lesson two

拼音 Y	简体	繁體	词性	英文翻译	
yímínjú	移民局	移民局	n.	Immigration Office	Lesson seven
yīncǐ	因此	因此	conj.	therefore, consequently	Lesson six
yīnggāi	应该	應該	v.	should, ought to, must	Lesson five
Yīng/Rì/Hán + yǔ	英/日/韩 +语	英/日/韓 +語		English/ Japanese/ Korean Language	Lesson two
yǐngxiǎng	影响	影響	n./v.	influence	Lesson nine
yínhángjiā	银行家	銀行家	n.	banker	Lesson four
yǐnshí	饮食	飲食	n.	diet	Lesson seven
yīnyuè	音乐	音樂	n.	music	Lesson ten
yǐqián	以前	以前	adv.	before	Lesson one
yìqíng	疫情	疫情	n.	pandemic	Lesson ten
yīshìyītīng	一室一厅	一室一廳	ph.	one bedroom and one living room	Lesson ten
yǐwéi	以为	以為	v.	think, believe, consider erroneously	Lesson two
yìyì	意义	意義	n.	meaning	Lesson one
yóu	由	由	prep.	by, from	Lesson eight
yǒudiǎnr	有点儿	有點兒	adv.	a little, somewhat, a bit	Lesson two
Yóuguǎn	油管	油管		YouTube	Lesson two
yóukè	游客	遊客	n.	tourist	Lesson eight
yǒumíng	有名	有名	adj.	famous	Lesson four
yóuxì	游戏	遊戲	n.	game	Lesson five

(Continued)

(Continued)

拼音 Y	简体	繁體	词性	英文翻译	
yǒuyìyì	有意义	有意義	adj.	meaningful, significant	Lesson ten
yóuyú	由于	由於	prep.	because of; owing to	Lesson six
yú	于	於	prep.	[indicating comparison] than, e.g., 低, [indicating beginning or source] from, e.g., 来自于	Lesson five
Yuáncháo	元朝	元朝		Yuan dynasty (1271–1368)	Lesson eight
yuánlái	原来	原來	adj./ adv.	original; originally 原来是这样 =I see	Lesson three
yuányīn	原因	原因	n.	reason	Lesson six
Yuè fāngyán	粤方言	粤方言		Yue dialect (spoken primarily in Guangdong, Guangxi, Hong Kong and Macau)	Lesson four
yuèláiyuè	越来越	越來越	adv.	more and more	Lesson six
Yuèliang dàibiǎo wǒde xīn	月亮代表 我的心	月亮代表 我的心		The moon represents my heart; a famous Mandarin song sung by the Taiwanese singer Teresa Teng; 代 表 dàibiǎo represent	Lesson ten

拼音 Y	简体	繁體	词性	英文翻译	
yǔfǎ	语法	語法	n.	grammar	Lesson four
yùnqì	运气	運氣	n.	luck	Lesson nine
yǔyán	语言	語言	n.	language	Lesson three
yǔyánxuéjiā	语言学家	語言學家	n.	linguist	Lesson four

拼音 Z	简体	繁體	词性	英文翻译	
zǎocān	早餐	早餐	n.	breakfast	Lesson seven
zāogāo	糟糕	糟糕	adj.	miserable, bad, terrible	Lesson ten
zhǎi	窄	窄	adj.	narrow	Lesson nine
zhàndì	占地	占地	v.	land occupation	Lesson nine
zhǎngbèi	长辈	長輩	n.	elders	Lesson one
zhǎngdà	长大	長大	v.	grow up	Lesson two
zhàngdān	账单	帳單	n.	bill	Lesson ten
zhànzhēng	战争	戰爭	n.	war, conflict	Lesson eight
zhǎo	找	找	v.	look for, seek	Lesson four
zhào...(de) shuōfǎ	照……(的)说法	照……(的)說法	ph.	according to	Lesson four
zhàogù	照顾	照顧	v.	take care of	Lesson three
zháohuǒ	着火	著火	v.	on fire, catch fire	Lesson seven
zhèngcè	政策	政策	n.	policy	Lesson nine
zhèngfǔ	政府	政府	n.	government	Lesson six
zhèngzhì	政治	政治	n.	politics	Lesson six
zhǐ	指	指	v.	point	Lesson three
zhǐ	纸	紙	n.	paper	Lesson seven
zhīdào	知道	知道	v.	know, become aware of	Lesson one
Zhījiāgē	芝加哥	芝加哥		Chicago	Lesson two

(Continued)

(Continued)

拼音 Z	简体	繁體	词性	英文翻译	
zhíjiē	直接	直接	adj./adv.	direct, directly	Lesson six
zhǒng	种	種	mw.	type, kind	Lesson three
Zhōngguó chéng	中国城	中國城	n.	Chinatown	Lesson nine
Zhōngguó shì	中国式	中國式	n.	Chinese style	Lesson five
zhòngshì	重视	重視	v.	value, attach importance to	Lesson six
zhòngyào	重要	重要	adj.	important, significant	Lesson four
zhōngyú	终于	終於	adv.	finally, in the end	Lesson ten
zhōu	州	州	n.	state (e.g. of the United States)	Lesson eight
zhōufǔ	州府	州府	n.	state capital	Lesson eight
zhōumò	周末	周末	n.	weekend	Lesson nine
Zhōu Yàopíng	周耀平	周耀平		a person's name	Lesson four
Zhōu Yǒuguāng	周有光	周有光		a person's name	Lesson four
zhuàn	赚	賺	v.	make profit, gain	Lesson ten
zhuànqián	赚钱	賺錢	v.o.	make money	Lesson ten
zhuānyè	专业	專業	n.	major	Lesson four
zhùhù	住户	住戶	n.	resident	Lesson nine
zhùsù fèi	住宿费	住宿費	n.	room and board cost	Lesson five
zhǔzhāng	主张	主張	v./n.	advocate, view	Lesson four
zǐnǚ	子女	子女	n.	children	Lesson one
zìzhì	自治	自治	v.	enjoy autonomy	Lesson nine

拼音 Z	简体	繁體	词性	英文翻译	
zōngsè	棕色	棕色	n.	brown	Lesson five
zǔchéng	组成	組成	v.	form/make up (into)	Lesson eight
zūfáng	租房	租房	v.o.	renting	Lesson nine
zúgòu	足够	足夠	adj.	sufficient, enough	Lesson ten
zuìjìn	最近	最近	adv.	recently, lately, in the near future	Lesson five
zūnzhòng	尊重	尊重	v.	respect	Lesson nine
zuòchuán	坐船	坐船	v.o.	by ship, take a boat	Lesson four